ELIZABETHAN
LYRIC POETRY AND
ITS MUSIC

Queen Elizabeth I playing a lute, by Nicholas Hilliard.

ELIZABETHAN LYRIC POETRY AND ITS MUSIC

WINIFRED MAYNARD

CLARENDON PRESS · OXFORD

1986

⊥

Oxford University Press, Walton Street, Oxford OX2 6DP
Oxford New York Toronto
Delhi Bombay Calcutta Madras Karachi
Kuala Lumpur Singapore Hong Kong Tokyo
Nairobi Dar es Salaam Cape Town
Melbourne Auckland

and associated companies in
Beirut Berlin Ibadan Mexico City Nicosia

Oxford is a trade mark of Oxford University Press

Published in the United States
by Oxford University Press, New York

British Library Cataloguing in Publication Data
Maynard, Winifred
Elizabethan lyric poetry and its music.
1. Songs, English—16th century—History and
criticism   2. Songs, English—17th century—
History and criticism
I. Title
784'.0942   ML1431.2
ISBN 0-19-812844-4

Library of Congress Cataloging-in-Publication Data
Maynard, Winifred.
Elizabethan lyric poetry and its music.
Bibliography: p.
Includes index.
1. Music and literature—16th century.   2. English
poetry—Early modern, 1500–1700—History and criticism.
3. Music—England—16th century—History and criticism.
I. Title.
ML79.M4 1986   784'.0942   86–2401
ISBN 0-19-812844-4

Set by Wyvern Typesetting Ltd, Bristol
Printed in Great Britain by
The Alden Press, Oxford

PREFACE

A lifelong interest in poetry and music and in the relations between them lies behind the writing of this book, in which I attempt to explore and illustrate in some depth the several ways in which lyric poetry and music interacted in Elizabethan England. The abundance of evidence of such interaction was shown by Professor Bruce Pattison—with whom I share a deep debt to the late Professor W. L. Renwick—in his early and valuable study, *Music and Poetry of the English Renaissance*, first published in 1948. The decades since then have been ones of intense musicological activity; far more is now known about early music, and far more of it has been made widely accessible, published from manuscript sources or reprinted from early publications in scholarly editions. The great *Musica Britannica* series was begun in 1951 and still continues—its next volume, scheduled for 1986, will be of English Lutenist Partsongs, edited by David Greer; and revision of the pioneering editions by E. H. Fellowes of lute-songs and madrigals, renamed *The English Lute-Songs* and *The English Madrigalists*, was begun by Thurston Dart in 1958 and has been carried on by Philip Brett and others. It is time now for the findings and insights of musical research of the last forty years to be brought to bear on the lyrics; and this is part of my aim.

In making a many-sided study of Elizabethan lyric poetry in relation to its various alliances with music and contexts in drama, I am of course indebted to the work of many scholars, especially those who have edited the lyrics: Edward Doughtie's *Lyrics from English Airs 1596–1622*, and the third edition of Fellowes's *English Madrigal Verse 1588–1632*, revised by F. W. Sternfeld and David Greer, are both invaluable. So are the editions of the poetic miscellanies made by H. E. Rollins in the 1920s and 1930s; further investigation of the links between the miscellanies and music has thrown fresh light on them, but his editions remain definitive.

I have pleasure in acknowledging permission to reproduce the following:

Queen Elizabeth playing a lute; miniature by Nicholas Hilliard. By permission of the Trustee of the Will of the 8th Earl of Berkeley deceased. Photograph: Courtauld Institute of Art.

Sir Henry Unton playing in a quartet of viols, with a boy singer; and the wedding masque at Wadley House, both from the Sir Henry Unton memorial portrait. By permission of the National Portrait Gallery, London.

Sir Henry Lee's tournament armour: from the Almain Armourer's Album. By permission of the Victoria and Albert Museum. Photograph: Crown Copyright Victoria and Albert Museum.

Music examples 5 and 6, from *The Mulliner Book*, ed. Denis Stevens. By permission of the Musica Britannica Trust, the Editor, and Stainer and Bell Ltd.

Music example 7, from *Consort Songs*, ed. Philip Brett. By permission of the Musica Britannica Trust, the Editor, and Stainer and Bell Ltd.

Music example 13, from *English Lute-Songs* 1st series, vol. 4/13. By permission of the Editors, Edmund Fellowes and Thurston Dart, and Stainer and Bell Ltd.; and Galaxy Music Corporation.

Music example 22, from *Four Hundred Songs and Dances from the Stuart Masque* (1978), ed. Andrew J. Sabol. By permission of the University Press of New England. Copyright 1978, 1982 by Brown University.

Music examples 9, 12, 15, 20, and 21, from printed books in the British Library, and music example 24, from BL Add. MS 4900. By permission of the British Library.

I am grateful to Oxford University Press for permission to reprint material from my article '*The Paradyse of daynty deuises* Revisited', which appeared in *RES* xxiv, 95, 1973.

The references to musical settings are given to direct readers to original sources and to one or more available modern editions; they are not intended to be exhaustive and works giving fuller listing of sources are cited in footnotes. For all books of English ayres and madrigals discussed, the volume number in *The English Lute-Songs* or *The English Madrigalists* series is given in the bibliography under the composer's name; for songs which are discussed in detail, or which a reader might not expect to find in these series, footnote reference is also given. For the lute-songs in their original form, with the accompaniments in tablature, see the facsimile edition published by the Scolar Press, *English Lute Songs 1597–1632*, general editor F. W. Sternfeld (9 vols.).

Original spelling and punctuation are retained for lyrics quoted from manuscripts and early editions, but for the songs of Shakespeare, Peter Alexander's text is used for the reader's ease of reference.

The breadth of scope of this book has kept it long a-growing, and some of my debts to institutions, librarians, colleagues, and friends are of long standing. I am grateful to the University of Edinburgh for periods of sabbatical leave, and to its Faculty of Arts Research Fund for grants. Amongst librarians I wish to express special thanks to Mr Michael Anderson, Librarian of the Reid Music Library of Edinburgh University: the library in his care is an excellent exemplar of the advantages of specialized collections, and his helpfulness, knowledge, and courtesy have been unfailing. Amongst colleagues my special thanks are due to Professor Peter Williams for his scrutiny of the whole book in typescript and his many pertinent comments; and to Dr Roger Savage and Professor Alastair Fowler for reading and commenting constructively on individual chapters.

To my family and friends, I offer thanks for their heroic suspension of disbelief.

W. M.

CONTENTS

ILLUSTRATIONS

Miniature of Queen Elizabeth I playing a lute (c.1580), by Nicholas Hilliard. By permission of the Trustee of the Will of the 8th Earl of Berkeley deceased. Photograph: Courtauld Institute of Art.   *Frontispiece*

ABBREVIATIONS

AM	*Annales Musicologiques*
BMQ	*British Museum Quarterly*
ELH	*English Literary History*
ELR	*English Literary Renaissance*
ELS	*English Lute-Songs*
EM	*English Madrigalists*
E&S	*Essays and Studies*
JAMS	*Journal of the American Musicological Society*
JCWI	*Journal of the Courtauld and Warburg Institutes*
LSJ	*Lute Society Journal*
MB	*Musica Britannica*
MD	*Musica Disciplina*
M&L	*Music and Letters*
MLN	*Modern Language Notes*
MLR	*Modern Language Review*
MQ	*Musical Quarterly*
MS	*Music Survey*
N&Q	*Notes and Queries*
PMLA	*Publications of the Modern Language Association of America*
PRMA	*Proceedings of the Royal Musical Association*
RES	*Review of English Studies*
RMA	*Royal Musical Association*
RN	*Renaissance News*
RQ	*Renaissance Quarterly*
SQ	*Shakespeare Quarterly*
SR	*Studies in the Renaissance*
SS	*Shakespeare Survey*

INTRODUCTION

L Y R I C S of earlier ages are coming to be regarded in much the same
way as minor buildings of some antiquity, which may be considered
worth preserving for their historical or architectural interest,
whether or not they are still used for their original purpose. Lyrics
are part of our literary heritage, and many are exquisitely made; so
they are preserved in anthologies and given a place in literary
histories, even if fewer and fewer people now enjoy reading or
hearing them. A major work such as *Paradise Lost* is more like a
cathedral: however one responds to its shape and its purpose, it has
an undeniable presence, and makes unmistakable affirmations; but
lyrics are slight in substance, and the resonances they once carried
may now be elusive.

If we are to repossess and enjoy Renaissance English lyrics as many
readers this century have learnt to repossess the great poems of the
period, we need to rediscover their nature. Rosemond Tuve
remarked of Elizabethan literary theorists:

Their ultimate critical questions are not 'What does the poem say?' and 'How
is it said?' but 'What is the poem for?' and 'How has that been
accomplished?'[1]

If we ask these questions about Elizabethan lyrics, it becomes clear
that for many of them, part of the answer to 'What is the poem for?' is
'It is for singing'; and that this part of the answer requires exploration. It raises the further question: for singing to what sort of music,
as what kind of song? A lyric may have been written to go to an
already existing tune used for a popular song or a courtly dance, as
the poems in *A Handefull of pleasant delites* were; it may have been
written to be made into a lute-song or madrigal; and, like some of the
lyrics of Jonson and Campion, Shakespeare and other dramatists, it
may have been made to be sung in a larger context, in a royal
entertainment or play or masque. Each kind of alliance, each kind of
context, affected lyrics designed for it in some way, and the ways are
different: the shapes and rhythms that characterize madrigals are

[1] *Elizabethan and Metaphysical Imagery* (Chicago, 1947; 1961 ed., p. 110).

different from those that characterize lute-songs, and a poet writing lyrics to be made into lute-songs would frame his verse and its rhythmic patterns accordingly. If we can recognize and distinguish such features, we can often answer the question 'What is the poem for?' not in the general terms of 'It is for singing' but in more specific terms: 'It is for making into a madrigal'; 'It is to go to a tune in galliard rhythm'; 'It has a special effect to make in a play'; and we can then consider the other question, of how its purpose has been accomplished.

In practice, the matter is more complex than that; not all Elizabethan lyrics were made for singing, and not all those that have some of the features characteristic of song were made with setting or singing in mind; patterns that proved effective in verse, whether rhyme-schemes deriving from madrigals, or the rhythmic figures of courtly dances, were absorbed into the general stock of resources of lyric verse, and might be used without conscious reference to their origins. But a reader who recognizes these origins is better placed to understand the provenance of a lyric's features and the sources of its appeal: the late Elizabethan miscellanies contain many lyrics by very minor writers that have a lightness and grace hard to account for in purely literary terms, but recognizable as qualities adopted or assimilated from various kinds of song. The madrigal especially, although its typical form did not lend itself easily to English use, affected English verse both for good and for ill, and the strands of its influence are worth unravelling.

For a reader today who wishes to experience the variety and observe the development of Elizabethan lyrics, the poetic miscellanies of the second half of the sixteenth century provide an unrivalled and unduly neglected approach. For most Elizabethans, these were the treasuries that gave them access to a wealth of verse, much of it written for unpublished circulation in court and literary circles, but gathered and published by astute printers. The most famous and popular of them, *Songes and Sonettes*, more generally known as *Tottel's Miscellany*, was published the year before Elizabeth's accession, and read throughout her reign. Its contents range over poems of several decades; and it presents a temptation to look back at least to the time of Wyatt, whose poems are drawn on more largely than those of any other author. Many of Wyatt's poems read as if they were meant for singing, and fifty or so of them can be sung to the tunes of songs in the manuscript collection known as

Henry VIII's Songbook;[2] a few of these partnerships show such close and apt fitting of the words to the music that it seems probable the poet had the existing part-song in mind. But this kind of connection is in the realm of probability or possibility, not of proof, and the findings of my investigation of Wyatt's songs are presented elsewhere;[3] in this book my concern is primarily with poems that are known to have been made for singing or setting, with the kinds of partnership to which they belong, and the purposes or contexts for which they were made.

The miscellanies provide a wide conspectus of kinds of lyric, written to be heard in several distinctive kinds of song and for varied contexts; there are the ballads of *A Handefull of pleasant delites*, part-songs and consort songs in *The Paradyse of daynty deuises*, ayres and madrigals and songs from royal entertainments in *The Phoenix Nest* and *Englands Helicon*. In the past thirty or forty years, much of the music associated with them has been identified, and the scholarly editing of songs of this period by Thurston Dart, Denis Stevens, Philip Brett, David Greer, and others has made most of it accessible in print. There is still much close detective work to do: the detailed exploratory work of John Ward in his article 'Music for *A Handefull of pleasant delites*'[4] has not been paralleled by comparable studies based on the other major miscellanies. But for each miscellany, the general lines of the picture of what kinds of song some of its lyrics were written to be, or were used as texts for, can now be drawn in, and the first two chapters attempt to present this picture, examining all the major and some of the minor Elizabethan printed poetic miscellanies and tracing their various links with music.[5]

Most of the verse in the miscellanies is the product of minor authors; but several notable poets also wrote lyrics framed as songs. Sidney's interest in exploring the possibilities and increasing the range of English lyric forms and patterns led him to make many kinds of experiment: his *Arcadia* alone in its original version contained more than seventy songs and lyrics with an unequalled range of shapes and kinds. Here, and in the songs in *Astrophil and Stella*, he

---

[2] BL Add. MS 31922; published as *Music at the Court of Henry VIII*, ed. John Stevens, *Musica Britannica*, vol. 18, rev. ed. 1969.

[3] 'The Lyrics of Wyatt: Poems or Songs?' in *RES* xvi (1965), 1–13 and 245–57.

[4] *JAMS* x (1957), 151–80.

[5] Complete listing of the miscellanies is attempted in A. E. Case's *Bibliography of English Miscellanies 1521–1750* (Oxford, 1935), and in Elizabeth W. Pomeroy's survey, *The Elizabethan Miscellanies* (Berkeley, 1973).

was writing verses that are presented as songs within the fiction and need have no musical substance in fact; but he wrote others to go to existing tunes, and still others inviting individual setting, and many composers found his verse attractive to set.

Campion, another fine poet, was his own composer: his lyrics were not only made to read like songs, like most of Sidney's; they were made for singing, and he set them himself. In his ayres for singing to the lute in a private, domestic setting, his words and music are most sensitively and delicately matched. He was also a writer and composer of masques, and for these he wrote songs in bolder style, fitted to make their impact in a sequence of dialogues, songs, and dances, and to be sung by several voices matched by consorts of instruments.

A more unified view of masque was held by Jonson: for him the poet's conception, or 'invention', was the factor shaping and inform-ing the whole, and the songs must be part of a sustained dramatic texture. In response, his musical partners evolved a style of setting well fitted to meet this requirement, Ferrabosco exploring the expressive and declamatory potential of the ayre, and Lanier devel-oping both the declamatory ayre and the musically less structured medium of recitative.

In his plays too Jonson made use of songs, as most contemporary dramatists did, Beaumont and Fletcher, Dekker, Heywood, and Middleton among them. Of them all, the playwright who exploited the dramatic potentialities of song most variously and most fully and functionally was Shakespeare; a study of the plays in which he uses songs shows his acute awareness of the different sorts of effect to be obtained by means of the several kinds, ballad and drinking-song, ayre and refrain-song. There is nothing random in the choices of kind that he makes, and nothing casual in his decisions to borrow an old song or write words for a new one: an old ballad sung in a moment of tragic foreboding can elicit immediate rapport and response from an audience; a new song tailor-made for its place in the plot can instigate the next move in the action.

Shakespeare's choice amongst kinds of song is unerring, his artistry in the framing of song-verse is virtuosic. The songs in his plays give a final focal point to this study as naturally as the miscellanies provide its starting-point. The miscellanies show the strands that went into the making of English verse, and reflect the rise and decline in popular or fashionable or musical appeal of many kinds of song. The work of the most notable poets and composers who practised these kinds, considered in the middle chapters, shows a wide diversity of aims and approaches, and high accomplishment in songs made in many forms and for various contexts. The songs in Shakespeare's plays are both summation and summit: the whole range of styles and resources is drawn on and displayed, and the songs of his own creation are the culmination and crown of lyric poetry of the age.

I

Early Song-books and Miscellanies

MANY of Wyatt's poems were first published in the book generally referred to as *Tottel's Miscellany*,[1] and for over 250 years they were known in the form in which they appeared there. It is hard now to estimate how much gratitude and how great a grudge is owed to Tottel; the success of his miscellany, published on 5 June 1557, necessitated two more editions by the end of July, and further editions followed in 1559, 1565, 1567, 1574, 1585, and 1587. It was not the first collection of the kind: *The Court of Venus*, containing some poems now known to be by Wyatt and others of uncertain authorship, had been printed about twenty years earlier, and it seems probable that another edition had brought it into notice again in 1549,[2] but it was Tottel's venture that started the vogue for publishing compilations of poems of several authors, known and unknown, which lasted until the end of the century and a little longer, providing both a model and an incentive to verse-writers. Without this incentive, there would probably have been no fewer Elizabethan poets, but there might well have been fewer of the Elizabethan poetasters of minimal talent whose products weigh heavily in succeeding collections.

Wyatt, as the texts of the best authenticated surviving manuscript, the Egerton MS, make clear, often wrote in what C. S. Lewis termed the pausing line, which had been much used in the previous century;[3] Tottel, or whoever was editing for him,[4] favoured a regular accentual

---

[1] *Songes and Sonettes*, written by the ryght honorable Lorde Henry Haward late Earle of Surrey, and other (1557). References are to H. E. Rollins's revised ed., *Tottel's Miscellany* (1557–1587), 2 vols. (Cambridge, Mass., 1965). There is a Scolar Press facsimile, 1966.

[2] See *The Court of Venus*, ed. Russell A. Fraser (Durham, NC, 1955), Intro., pp. 20–4, and C. A. Huttar, 'Wyatt and the Several Editions of *The Court of Venus*', *Studies in Bibliography* xix (1966), 181–95.

[3] 'The Fifteenth Century Heroic Line', *E&S* xxiv (1939), 28–41.

[4] For discussion of the editorship, see R. Hughey, 'The Harington Manuscript at Arundel Castle and Related Documents', *The Library*, xv (1935), 388–444, and Rollins, ed. cit. vol. ii, pp. 85–94 and 334–5.

iambic line and where necessary manipulated and flattened the material that came into his hands accordingly.[5] In the long term, the establishment of a metrical basis for English verse proved an enrichment, making possible the play of the varying patterns of speech rhythm against the steady background beat of metre, and the exploration of new ways of patterning poetic sound;[6] in the short term, the widespread currency Tottel gave to the new metre in its baldest form led to the dominance for several decades of verse that tramped with heavy metrical feet.

Succeeding collections were of varying kinds and quality: courtly, popular, for singing, for reading; they contained pastorals, madrigals, epigrams, sonnets; delightful lyrics and laboured tedium. Tottel's own book changed considerably in composition between the first and second editions: the first had forty poems by Surrey, ninety-seven by Wyatt, forty attributed to Grimald, and ninety-four to 'Uncertain Authors': in the second and subsequent editions thirty of those ascribed to Grimald were withdrawn and the number of unattributed poems was increased to 134.

Of the *Songes and Sonettes* as it first appeared, fifty are sonnets. How many are songs—lyrics made to be sung rather than spoken or read? 'My lute awake' is the only poem in the whole collection to refer to itself as song in a way that makes clear that the term is more than a synonym for poem, and it is noticeable how few of Wyatt's song-like poems appear: of about fifty that are apt for singing, only four are in Tottel. 'My lute awake', 'Perdy I sayd it not', and 'Maruell nomore' are, I think, songs, and perhaps 'Disdaine me not', despite its careful verbal patterning; but sonnets and epigrams predominate. Probably both preference and availability determined the choice: songs that had their life in an intimate social circle would not fall easily into a publisher's hands, and in any case the newer, more literary forms would be more highly esteemed.

The poems by Surrey include a dozen sonnets, several reflective and sententious pieces, and one courtly song, 'O Happy dames, that may embrace'—the only known poem of his to appear in the Devonshire MS—for which music by Shepherd has survived in Thomas Mulliner's book.[7] Here is a different kind of partnership

[5] See D. W. Harding, 'The Rhythmical Intention of Wyatt's Poetry', *Scrutiny*, xiv (1946), 90–102.

[6] See John Stevens's Inaugural Lecture *The Old Sound and the New* (Cambridge, 1982).

[7] Printed in *The Mulliner Book*, ed. Denis Stevens (*Musica Britannica* vol. i, rev. ed.

from that which seems probable in the case of Wyatt's lyrics.[8] It is a part-song for four voices; the composer has taken his lead from the text, but he develops a wholly musical response: thus, the opening phrase gives him the rhythm

Ex. 1

but the musical phrase embodying it is used to bring in the voices in sequence. Some, but not excessive, repetition of words and phrases is called for. The Mulliner book also contains a setting of a similar kind, with more extensive use of imitation between the voices, of Surrey's paraphrase of Martial, 'Martiall, the thinges that do attayn'.[9] Music has survived in three early sources for a long piece in poulter's measure which is a species of *chanson a personnages*, the narrator encountering a man who complains of unrequited love, 'In winters iust returne, when Boreas gan his raigne'.[10] It was registered in 1557–8 as 'A ballett, in wynters Juste Retorne', and at least one other poem was written to the tune.[11] Since the music has to be repeated for every couplet of Surrey's poem, and there are forty-one couplets, the singer would presumably make a selection.

1954), no. 111. Also ed. by Stevens for four voices (Novello, 1955). See also *The Mulliner Book, a Commentary*, by D. Stevens (1952). This musical commonplace-book, BL Add. MS 30513, compiled in the middle decades of the sixteenth century, is of unique value and interest; as Dr Stevens says, it 'runs the whole gamut of sixteenth-century music: Latin motets, English anthems, arrangements of part-songs, transcriptions of consort music, plainsong fantasias for organ, dance-music for clavichord or virginals, music for cittern and gittern' (ed. cit., Intro., p. vii).

[8] For a discussion of changes in musical style in part-songs towards the end of the reign of Henry VIII, see D. Stevens, 'Tudor Part-Songs', *Musical Times*, 96 (1955), 360–2.

[9] Ed. cit., no. 70. Also ed. by Stevens for four voices (Novello, 1955), entitled 'The happy life'.

[10] BL MS Royal Appendix 58, Folger Shak. Lib. MS V.a.159, and the commonplace-book owned by James M. Osborn. See John Ward, *JAMS* x (1957), 179, and 'The Lute Music of MS Royal Appendix 58', *JAMS* xiii (1960), 117–25, and I. L. Mumford, 'Musical Settings to the Poems of Henry Howard Earl of Surrey', *English Miscellany* 8 (1957), 9–20. (Miss Mumford suggests that this music is also by Shepherd, like that for 'O Happy dames', in view of Gascoigne's admonition in the Preface to *Posies* (1575): 'Laugh not at this, lusty younkers, since the pleasant ditty of the noble Earl of Surrey beginning thus: 'In winter's just return' was also constructed to be made indeed by a Shepherd'. But Gascoigne's allusion is sufficiently explained by the fact that the narrator in Surrey's poem is a shepherd.)

[11] By Thomas Howell: 'In vttringe his plaint, he declareth the vncertainty of fained frendship. To the tune of winters iust returne', in his *Newe Sonets, and pretie Pamphlets* (c.1568). Noted by Rollins, ed. cit. vol ii, p. 144.

Two other of Surrey's pieces became known as ballads. 'When ragyng loue with extreme payne', which is in octosyllabic six-line stanzas, with a monotonous degree of coincidence of rhythm and metre, was registered as a ballad in 1557–8, 1560–1, and 1561–2; a presumed moralization, an imitation, and a parody were also registered, and a ballad in the next song-book to appear, *A Handefull of pleasant delites*, was written to its tune. The music however is elusive: the only known surviving version, in a commonplace-book, is for playing on a gittern and from its nature Ward infers that it may give the harmonies only.[12] The tune of 'If care do cause men cry, why do not I complaine?' on the other hand is found in several manuscripts and in one seventeenth-century printed collection.[13] One of the manuscripts[14] contains statutes of the reigns of Henry V and Henry VI, with music in lute tablature written in on blank leaves at the beginning and end; the folio on which this song appears is headed

The xviij[th] daie of maye the same writtin by one Ralphe Bowle to learne to play on the lutte in anno 1558.

In 1557–8 'yf Care may Cause men crye' was registered as a ballad, and an imitation, perhaps a pious one, 'Care Causethe men to Crye newly altered', followed in 1562–3. The partnership between words and tune is straightforward, each repetition of the melody taking one couplet.

Among the rest of Surrey's poems in Tottel are a few which may have been sung: 'Geue place ye louers, here before', for instance, has the same structure as 'When ragyng loue' and could go to the same tune; for the most part, however, I think these were poems for reading, so far as their maker was concerned. He speaks once of 'this carefull song' and elsewhere says 'I wepe and syng': two references only, and of the kind that mean nothing; perhaps it is significant that his catalogue of pleasures once enjoyed in Windsor makes no mention of songs. It seems unlikely that he cared much about them.

There is scarcely room even for doubt with regard to Nicholas Grimald. His choice of metres makes plain that he is no song-writer; eighteen of the forty poems ascribed to him are in iambic verse

[12] *JAMS* x, 165–6.
[13] For details see Ward, ibid., p. 179. Bruce Pattison, *Music and Poetry of the English Renaissance* (2nd ed. 1970), p. 165, prints the tune from John Forbes's *Songs and Fancies* (Aberdeen, 1662, 1666, 1682).
[14] BL MS Stowe 389.

rhyming in couplets, and there are three sonnets, two pieces in blank verse, and a fifteen-line iambic poem with alternate rhyme, the initial letters of the lines spelling out the lady's name—an essentially visual play which not even the quickest wits could take in by ear. There are also nine pieces in fourteeners and seven in poulter's measure; lines in both these metres can be split up and set if desired, but none of Grimald's contributions were registered as ballads, no tunes are mentioned in association with any, and only the most conventional references to song occur, and in only three poems. A singer would find little to tempt him here.

The poems by 'Vncertain auctours' offer more scope, but chiefly to a ballad-singer. Six or seven were registered as ballads;[15] five of them are in poulter's measure (used either at full length or formed into quatrains) or in fourteeners, and quite probably several others of the two dozen pieces in these measures were also sung. Our knowledge that a poem was sung as a ballad is dependent on such pieces of evidence as a revealing reference in a play or elsewhere, or the survival of a tune in association with it. The opening words of 'Thestilis a sely man, when loue did him forsake', which was not registered as a ballad, appear with lute tablature in a manuscript containing sixteenth-century music.[16] Tunes have survived for only two of the poems that were registered, and the same manuscript provides a setting for one of these, Lord Vaux's lyric, unattributed in Tottel, 'I lothe that I did loue', which furnished Shakespeare with his gravedigger's song in *Hamlet*; another tune for it was recorded by G. F. Nott.[17] The other registered ballad for which tunes are now known

15 Nos. 180, 181, 199, 211, 212, and 251 in Rollins's edition, and as he suggests no. 172 may be the ballad registered in 1568–9 as 'Pygmalyn'. Not all ballads would be sung, but it was very common practice to fit a poem published in broadside form to a suitable tune.

16 BL Add. MS 4900 (f.58). Probably written early in the seventeenth century. It contains the accompaniment for this song; the vocal part is missing.

17 Nott found tunes for eleven poems in the miscellany written in the margins of a 1557 copy now lost: he included them in his 1814 edition, which was almost wholly destroyed by fire, but not in his 1815 edition. The copy found by Professor Hughey at Arundel Castle contains the tunes. The date when they were written in against the 1557 text is not known. Ward (*JAMS* x. 169) mentions these 'curious musical snippets' in connection with other pieces of recitation-like style which he considers may be formulae used for poems not associated with known tunes. (See below, p. 14.) A poem in *A gorgious Gallery, of gallant Inuentions*, 1578, is to go 'to the tune of I lothe that I did loue'. Both settings are given, and discussed, by F. W. Sternfeld, *Music in Shakespearean Tragedy* (1963), pp. 151–5. The setting found in BL Add. MS 4900 is given in Ex. 24 below, pp. 168–9.

seems never to have had its own: 'Who loues to liue in peace, and marketh euery change' was described as

A dittie most excelent for euerie man to reade that dothe intend for to amende and to repent with speede to the tune of a rich marchant man or John come kiss me now.[18]

The absence of known tunes for songs such as 'Geue place you Ladies and be gon' and 'Phylida was a fayer mayde'[19] sharpens the realization of our dependence upon the chances of survival of laboriously made music copies; music printing was still expensive and rare in this country. Only two songs from *Tottel* are known to have reached music print within even a hundred years or so of the miscellany's publication, Surrey's 'If care do cause men cry', and the anonymous 'Lyke as the lark within the marlians foote'; they were printed in Forbes's *Songs and Fancies*.[20] Since the sonnet form of 'Lyke as the lark' does not lend itself to strophic setting, in Melvill's book the last couplet is dispensed with and in Forbes's book the poem is expanded into five quatrains. The repeated opening note of the melody and its restricted range, except for one higher-ranging melodic phrase, show some care to fit the mood of the poem: the intention to express in music the emotion and meaning of the words, which in the late decades of the sixteenth century was to be so much cultivated, is perceptible here. Ex. 2 gives the first stanza with Forbes's version of the tune (transferred to treble clef).

One of the finest anonymous lyrics, 'Vaine is the fleting welth', was added in the second edition (also of 1557); the bass part of a

---

[18] For the tune of 'John, come kiss me now', and a tune for 'The rich merchant man' which may be the original one, and discussion of sources, see C. M. Simpson, *The British Broadside Ballad and its Music* (New Brunswick, New Jersey, 1966), pp. 396–8 and 602–4.

[19] Two tunes, or formulae, for 'Phylida was a fayer mayd' were recorded by Nott. Professor Hughey ('The Harington Manuscript') notes that a 1557 copy now in the library of Carl Pforzheimer associates a tune with this poem, and also assigns tunes to five others for which no tunes were in the lost copy seen by Nott; but the tunes are not written in.

[20] 'Lyke as the lark' must have been popular for at least a century; it is found in manuscript sources from c.1570 on: for voices in Thomas Wode's part-books and several later Scottish manuscript collections, including David Melvill's *Ane Buik off roundells*, 1612 (which also contains 'If care do cause men cry'), and as a keyboard piece in the Dublin Virginal Manuscript, c.1570. (See John Ward's edition of this last (Wellesley, Mass., 2nd ed. 1964), p. 54, for details of sources.) Hall's *Court of Vertue* (1565) includes a devotional parody to a different setting.

Ex. 2

Like as the Lark with in the Mar - leons foot, with pi - teous

voice doth chirk her yeel - ding lay; Even so do I, since

is no o - ther boot, Ren-dring my Song un-to — — your will o - bey.

setting by W. Parsons survives.[21] The five stanzas are through-set, perhaps in deference to the defiant rhythm used for the opening phrase of the first, fourth, and fifth stanzas, which runs counter to the metrical pattern.

A few courtly songs, and a handful of ballads; it looks as if the compiler of the manuscript or manuscripts Tottel was drawing on was primarily interested in making a collection of verse, not in assembling a song-book.[22] More than we recognize may on occasion have been sung, for a man in quest of singable verse could always find something to his purpose in a collection which by its second edition included over seventy pieces in poulter's measure and fourteeners, and nearly as many in quatrain-patterns:[23] but probably the compiler's, and certainly the printer's, main aim was to gather what had been 'wel written in verse'.

The miscellany was soon to be followed by an avowed song-book; its musical links give some truth to its title-page claims:

A Handefull of pleasant delites, Containing sundrie new Sonets and delectable Histories, in diuers kindes of Meeter. Newly deuised to the newest tunes that are now in vse, to be sung: euerie Sonet orderly pointed to his

---

[21] In a part-book in the Public Record Office, State Papers I, vol. 246. It contains basses also for Surrey's 'O Happy dames' and his paraphrase of Martial, here beginning 'My friends'. See D. Stevens, 'A Part-Book in the Public Record Office', *MS* ii (1950), 161–70. William Parsons lived c.1515–c.1563.

[22] Rollins considers that Tottel had probably acquired a manuscript, or manuscripts, that had been compiled for the owner's private pleasure, and had decided, most of the authors being by this time dead, to print its contents and other poems, especially by Surrey and Wyatt, that he managed to obtain. See ed. cit. vol. ii, pp. 92–3.

[23] For a table of the verse-patterns, see J. Thompson, *The Founding of English Metre* (1961), Appendix A. Rollins also describes them, ed. cit. vol. ii, pp. 102–4.

proper Tune. With new additions of certain Songs, to verie late deuised Notes, not commonly knowen, nor vsed heretofore, By Clement Robinson and diuers others.

The stress on newness was a bold pretence; what Richard Jones, the printer, had gathered to offer his readers—'You that in Musicke do delight your minds for to solace . . .'—was a collection of ballads, all of which had appeared in broadsheet form before the book came out in 1584. Most had been printed before 1566, when a licence was granted to Jones 'for prynting of a boke intituled of *very pleasaunte Sonettes and storyes in myter* by clament Robynson', which was almost certainly the first edition of the same book.[24] Hence it is not an early successor of Tottel's enterprise; rather it initiates another kind of enterprise, the making of 'garlands' of ballads for the pleasure of the people, to give them a 'handful' of songs to sing. But the market for such collections was probably due to the spreading of the taste of late Tudor court circles for singing to the lute; as Ward pointed out,[25] few pre-Elizabethan ballad tunes survive, and there is little indication that the practice of fitting lyrics to existing tunes, used since the fifteenth century in Italy and Spain, was yet widespread in England. Before it became so, it is possible that a ballad-singer had a repertoire of musical formulae to accommodate the common verse-patterns.[26] That 'Though wisdom wold I should refrain' in *A Handefull* was to go to 'Raging loue', the tune for Surrey's poem, supports the supposition that the setting and singing of courtly lyrics such as Wyatt's and Surrey's led to the more popular vogue.

These are cheerier wooings and tauntings than Tottel's; they do not suggest that their makers are dying for love, but that they have a mind to make a song. And what could be easier? They had only to let a familiar or a newly fashionable tune run in their minds, and invent a set of verses to it. For twenty-six of the thirty-two pieces, tunes are

[24] See *A Handful of Pleasant Delights*, 1584, by Clement Robinson and Divers Others, ed. H. E. Rollins (Cambridge, Mass., 1924), Intro., pp. x–xv and Notes, *passim*; and H. E. Rollins, 'A Handful of Pleasant Delights', *MLN* xli (1926), 327. There is a Scolar Press facsimile, 1973.

[25] *JAMS* x. 177–80. Ward here identifies and discusses sixteen of *A Handefull*'s tunes (he gives further findings in 'Apropos *The British Broadside Ballad and Its Music*', *JAMS* xx (1967), 28–86).

[26] The nature and degree of relationship between such tunes and psalm tunes, and the possible links of both with courtly song, need further investigation. See Nicholas Temperley, *The Music of the English Parish Church*, 2 vols. (Cambridge, 1979), vol. i, pp. 34–6.

named,[27] and another is to go 'To anie pleasant tune'; of the rest, all but one are known to have been sung. Some were to go, as the title-page says, 'to verie late deuised Notes, not commonly knowen', and these tunes would be likely to take their names from this first partnership; for 'Attend thee, go play thee', for instance, no tune is named, but a later collection has verse written to a tune called 'Attend thee, go play thee'.[28] The poem beginning 'The life that erst thou ledst my friend' was no doubt sung, for it is a reply to a lost one quoted by Petruchio:

> 'Where is the life that late I led?
> Where are those—'[29]

Since he *sings* this, it was presumably a song, even though Pistol quotes it in speech (and implies that the second line ended '. . . pleasant days'),[30] for his poetic stock probably consisted of ballads he had heard sung. The intention that *A Handefull*'s contents should all be sung is emphasized by the direction for 'I smile to see how you deuise': it is simply 'To anie pleasant tune'.[31] A lyric need not have been made to a tune to serve as a ballad; for quatrains especially it is easy to find musical partners, if compatible structure, regardless of sentiment, will suffice, and many alliances here are of this rule-of-thumb kind.

The writers of some of these ballads, however, wrote with particular tunes in mind, and so an influence on verse-forms more far-reaching than we can ever with certainty trace is suggested: for precisely to the extent that the writers were leaning on music, basing verse-form and metre on musical structure, the tunes that they wrote to were stamping their patterns on lyric verse. William Webbe, writing two years after *A Handefull* appeared in its later form, was in no doubt of this: he set out to describe the metres of English verse,

---

[27] The tenth song probably also had its tune ('King Solomon') named, but the leaf is missing from the only extant copy.

[28] 'Not light of loue lady', in *A gorgious Gallery, of gallant Inuentions* (1578). (The tune could not be that now known as 'Light o' Love', which has no musical parallel to the very short line in these verses.)

[29] *Taming of the Shrew*, iv. i. 124–5.   [30] *2 Henry IV*, v. iii. 139–40.

[31] Through Thomas Mulliner's commonplace-book we know that these verses were associated with music that accommodated two quatrains, to good effect; the sixth quatrain, for instance, embarks on the contrasting rhythmical movement of the second musical strain with the words 'So thou in change doth take delight', and the accentuation is apt throughout. This part-song for four voices was probably expressly made for the words. (Ed. cit., no. 88. Also ed. by Stevens for four voices (Novello, 1955).)

but made no attempt to be exhaustive for the variations were so many:

> neither is there anie tune or stroke which may be sung or plaide on instruments, which hath not some poetical ditties framed according to the numbers thereof, some to Rogero, some to Trenchmore, to downe right Squire, to Galliardes, to Pauines, to Iygges, to Brawles, to all manner of tunes which euerie Fidler knowes better then my selfe . . .[32]

All these are dances, and so are many of the tunes named in *A Handefull*: the 'New Rogero', the 'New Almaine', 'Kypascie', 'Quarter Braules', 'Cicilia Pavin', 'Downe right Squier', 'Blacke Almaine', and others. Initially some of these dances would themselves have been based upon song-tunes: half a century earlier, Sir Thomas Elyot, discussing dancing in ancient times, wrote that the names of dances

> were taken as they be nowe, either of the names of the firste inuentors, or of the measure and nombre that they do containe, or of the firste wordes of the dittie, whiche the songe comprehendeth whereof the daunse was made.[33]

The name of the tune 'Down right squire' (or in the Folger version, 'The upright esquier') suggests that it would be an example of the last. By Elizabethan times many dance-tunes of Continental origin were also in vogue. More and more sets of verses were written to favourite tunes, which thus, by their patterns and rhythms, continued to influence English verse, some of them for centuries.

Of the tunes named in this song-book, 'Greensleeves' must surely have had the most lasting and far-reaching effect. From the month that Richard Jones entered in the Stationers' Register 'A newe northen Dittye of ye Ladye Greene Sleves' in September 1580, 'Greensleeves' has gone singing down English verse for generation after generation.[34] 'Ye Ladie Greene Sleves answere to Donkyn hir frende' was registered the same day; within the month came 'Greene Sleves moralised to the Scripture Declaringe the manifold benefits and blessings of God bestowed on sinfull manne' and 'Greene Sleves and Countenaunce in Countenaunce is Greene Sleves', and within

---

[32] *A Discourse of English Poetry* (1586), reprinted in *Elizabethan Critical Essays*, ed. G. Gregory Smith (1904), vol. i, pp. 226–302.

[33] *The Gouernour* (1531), xx; Everyman ed. (1907), p. 93.

[34] And dancing: it entered Playford's *The Dancing Master* in the 7th edition, 1686, and appeared in other country dance books, and its modal version continues in use as a morris tune. See Simpson, *The British Broadside Ballad*, pp. 268–78.

the year 'a merry newe Northen songe of Greenesleves begynninge the boniest lasse in all the land', 'A Reprehension againste Greene Sleves by William Elderton', and 'Greene Sleeves is worne awaie, Yellowe Sleeves Comme to decaie, Blacke Sleeves I holde in despite, But White Sleeves is my delighte'. It was made to serve in many causes: to admonish traitors, in 1588; to support the Cavaliers—at least fourteen songs against the Rump Parliament were written to it; and to provide 'A Caroll for New-yeares day'.

It is not surprising that 'Greensleeves' alone of the collection is still widely known as a song today; both words and music have a grace of movement fully shared by no others. For the most part the verses, many of them based on octosyllabic lines or combining fourteeners and poulter's measure, have a jog-trot movement, with rhythm reinforcing metre, and some of the surviving tunes are less than delightful. There are however one or two near rivals to 'Greensleeves'. One is 'Faine would I haue a pretie thing'; both refrain and verses have alternate eight- and seven-syllabled lines, the latter produced by feminine endings. This replaces the plod of fourteeners with a light, lilting movement that would soon pall in reading, but enables this slyly improper 'proper Song' to run well to the rhythms of 'lustie Gallant'.[35]

Ex. 3

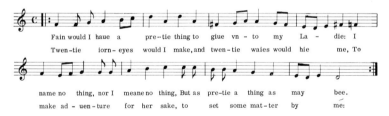

Fain would I haue a pre-tie thing to giue vn-to my La - die: I
Twen-tie iorn-eyes would I make, and twen-tie waies would hie me, To

name no thing, nor I meane no thing, But as pre-tie a thing as may bee.
make ad-uen-ture for her sake, to set some mat-ter by me:

Equally successful is 'When as I view your comly grace'. This 'Sonet of a Louer in the praise of his lady' is full of Petrarchan

[35] The song seems to have been popular enough to change the name of the tune (unless the words had acquired a new tune of their own), for a ballad on Troilus and Cressida registered in 1565–6 was to go 'To the tune of Fayne woold I fynde sum pretty thynge to geeve unto my lady'. Two moralizations modelled on the words were licensed the following year. The music is found in Wm. Ballet's lute book, Trinity College, Dublin, MS D.1.21 (p. 83), and, untitled, in a lute book in Archbishop Marsh's Library, Dublin, MS Z.3.2.13 (p. 61). Ex. 3 sets the words to Ballet's version of the tune.

epithets, and when the lines are read, as they are printed, in stanzas each of three octosyllabic couplets, the conceits and rhymes combine to produce glibness; but the melody clothes the lines with grace, separating them with the refrain 'Calen o Custure me'. The words are well-framed for singing, with many long open vowels, and recurring phrase-rhythms; four or five couplets make an attractive song. Pistol's garbling of the refrain in answer to the captured French soldier,

Fr. sol Je pense que vous êtes le gentilhomme de bonne qualité.
Pistol. Cality! Calen o custure me! Art thou a gentleman? . . .[36]

is probably only a mimicry of sound, but may carry a suggestion of effeminacy by association with the English words of the ballad.[37] Ex. 4 gives Byrd's statement of the tune from the Fitzwilliam Virginal Book.

Ex. 4

A tune that makes a strong impress on verse written to it is 'Row wel ye Marriners', which kept its place in *The Dancing Master* right down to the 1725 edition.[38] Its shape is reflected in the lover's plea 'As

[36] *Henry V*, iv. iv. 2–4.
[37] Pistol would not understand the refrain phrase itself. Suggested Irish phrases underlying it give various meanings including 'The girl from beside the [river] Suir' and 'Young girl, O treasure'. (See, e.g., Simpson, *The British Broadside Ballad*, p. 79.)
[38] As Ward notes, *JAMS* x. 158. He suggests it may have been used for a jig or a round dance. Several moralizations were made to it.

one without refuge', especially in the two four-syllabled lines of each stanza, but some of these short lines are not only gauche when read, they are awkwardly stressed when sung—a cavil, perhaps, to make of this kind of alliance, but there are insufficient compensations here. The next song in *A Handefull* must have palled even in its own day: in 'The Historie of Diana and Acteon. To the Quarter Braules', ungainly verse is aligned with monotonous music, and after the first eight lines, the lengthy stanzas fall into considerable disarray. They are reshaped more simply in seventeenth-century broadside copies, in one of which, of 1624, they are to be sung to another of the tunes Webbe names, 'Rogero'.[39]

The interest of *A Handefull* today for most readers lies less in intrinsic poetic merit than in its preservation of 'Greensleeves', its indication of a widespread taste for singing ballads to existing tunes, and the pointers it provides towards recognizing the influence of this practice on verse forms. Of all the song-books it is least fitted, because not at all intended, to be merely read; it is still more enjoyable to sing the songs for which the tunes have been found than simply to read the texts. One which has lost its own tune almost compels a reader to improvise one for its alternating refrains and galvanic rhythms:

> Mayde will ye loue me yea or no?
> tell me the trothe, and let me goe

and many are saved by the presence of music in the writers' minds from the heaviness of much of the consciously literary verse in other collections. In tone and subject-matter too, while it avoids the more lurid events and nine days' wonders often celebrated in the broadside ballads,[40] it has a lightness and spirit that are rare in the more self-conscious and pretentious miscellanies that followed it.

---

[39] The tune originated as a descant on the popular Italian ground bass which became known as 'Ruggiero' from its association with Canto 44, stanza 61, of Ariosto's *Orlando Furioso*.

[40] It provides the complaint of a spurned lover for the tune 'the nine Muses', for example: the collection of Daniel (*An Elizabethan Garland*; being a Descriptive Catalogue of Seventy Black-Letter Ballads, printed between the years 1559 and 1597. In the possession of George Daniel, of Canonbury, London, 1856) has for this tune a ballad 'Of the horrible and woful Destruction of Sodome and Gomorra'. This collection also includes a partnership of 'Down right Squire' with a more plebeian tale by far than Danea's welcoming home her lord from the war: 'A merie newe Ballad intituled the pinnyng of the Basket', which tells of a 'Joyner's man, of a chandler, and his shrewish wife'. Two of the ballads go to 'The Blacke Almaine', one written in 1570

Between the appearance of the first version of this song-book in 1566 and its publication as *A Handefull of pleasant delites* in 1584 there came out several collections that clearly address themselves to more courtly circles, and their musical links are with courtly kinds. The first was not an anthology of poems by several authors, although it presented itself as such, but a collection of verse, and some prose narrative and commentary, by one court writer. *A Hundreth sundrie Flowres*, of 1573, so closely concerned the affairs of the author or of noble acquaintances that its publication was enmeshed in elaborate pretences concerning both circumstances and authorship.[41] When it was reprinted in revised form two years later it was as *The Posies of George Gascoigne Esquire* and Gascoigne accepted sole authorship. There is mention of several of the songs being sung. In the prose that links the poems in 'A discourse of the aduentures *passed by Master F.I.*' a lengthy piece in poulter's measure, 'In prime of lustie yeares, when Cupid caught me in', is introduced with these words:

If it please you to followe (quod he) you shall see that I can iest without ioye, and laugh without lust, and calling the musitions, caused them softly to sound the *Tyntarnell*, when he clearing his voyce did *Alla Napolitana* applie these verses following, vnto the measure.

The poem apparently

aunswered very aptly to the note which the musike sounded, as the skilfull reader by due triall may approue.

This is the only poem described as being sung to a ready-made tune, a dance-tune the musicians could be expected to know. A piece in eleven-lined stanzas with the two penultimate lines very short, beginning 'Dame Cinthia hir selfe (that shines so bright,' is followed by the comment

This Ballade, or howsoeuer I shall terme it, percase you will not like, and yet in my iudgement it hath great good store of deepe inuention, and for the order of the verse, it is not common, I haue not heard many of like proporcion, some will accompt it but a dyddeldome: but who so had heard *F.I.* sing it to the lute, by a note of his owne deuise, I suppose he would esteme

---

'against Rebellious and false Rumours'; and to 'Labandala Shot' it has, not the pathetic adieu of George Mannyngton as he awaited his death in 1576, but the 'brief sonet' of ten years later 'declaring the lamentation of Beckles, a Market Towne in Suffolke which was in the great winde upon S. Andrewes eve pitifully burned with fire'.

[41] See the Introduction to C. T. Prouty's edition (Columbia, 1942), which dissolves the arguments for multiple authorship. There is a Scolar Press facsimile (1970).

it to bee a pleasaunt dyddeldome, and for my part, if I were not parciall, I would saye more in commendacion of it than nowe I meane to do . . .

The partiality is natural, for F. I. and the commentator G. T. were mask and mouthpiece for George Gascoigne, and in his desire to present his poem to best advantage he lets this fact virtually appear. He draws attention to the existence of a setting so that those who are interested can seek it out; the tone of his reference suggests that singing to the lute was by now a familiar practice, and one that was found to enhance the attraction of suitable verse. One of his acknow-ledged poems, '*De profundis*', has the same stanzaic pattern[42] and this too was sung, as he points out in a note in which his keenness for the poems to be heard as songs is declared: it follows 'Gascoignes good morow' and 'Gascoignes good nyghte':

These good Morowe and good nyght, together with his Passion, his Libell of diuorce, his Lullabye, his Recantation, his De profundis, and his farewell, haue verie sweete notes adapted vnto them: the which I would you should also enioy as well as my selfe. For I knowe you will delight to heare them. As also other verie good notes whyche I haue for dyuers other Ditties of other mens deuyse whiche I haue before rehersed.

(In fact these 'other Ditties' too were almost certainly of his devising.)

It sounds as if Gascoigne would have been glad to see the music for his songs in print; after all, Thomas Whythorne had just had his songs printed. But Whythorne's *Songes* of 1571 was only the second book of English secular songs to be published in London, after a gap of over forty years since the first,[43] and no more appeared until the late 1580s.

In 1576 another collection of poems by many writers was published: *The Paradyse of daynty deuises*. It was compiled as a manuscript miscellany by Richard Edwards, and printed ten years after his death by a publisher into whose hands it had come. It contains a dozen or more poems each by Edwards himself, William Hunnis, and Lord Vaux, and several each by Francis Kinwelmarsh, Jasper Heywood, and the Earl of Oxford. The contents varied from edition to edition; in all 125 poems by nearly thirty poets appeared in

---

[42] So (with a slight change of rhyme-scheme) has 'O Curteous Care whom others (cruell) call', in 'Dan Bartholmew of Bathe'; it could be sung to the same tune, or tunes, as the other two.

[43] *XX Songes* (1530), by various composers. (The printer was not Wynkyn de Worde, as formerly thought.)

it. Few of them are love-lyrics; moral poems predominate and many use acrostics or other forms of word-play clearly meant for the attentive eye: the ear would not collect the summarizing moral provided by the opening words of the lines in this poem by Hunnis,[44] for instance, if it were to be sung:

Behold the blast which blowes, the blossomes from the tree,
The end whereof consumes and comes, to nought we see,
Ere thou therefore be blowen, from life that may not last,
Begin for grace, to call for time mispent and past.

Haue mind on brittle life, whose pleasures are but vayne,
On death likewyse bethinke, how thou maist not remaine.
And feare thy Lord to greeue, which sought thy soule to saue,
To synne no more be bent, but mercie aske and haue.

For death who dooth not spare, the kinges on earth to kill,
Shall reape also from thee, thy pleasure, life, and will.
That lyfe which yet remaynes, and in thy brest appeares,
Hath sowne in thee sutch seedes, you ought to weede with teares.

And life that shall succeede, when death is worne and past,
Shall spring for euer then, in ioy or paine to last.
Where death on life hath power ye see, that life also,
Hath mowen the fruites of death, which neuer more shall growe.

Similarly in Lord Vaux's poem 'What greeues my bones, and makes my body faint?' the shifting placing in successive verses of 'tosse', 'turne', 'change', 'stretche' is a device that presupposes a reader rather than a listener.

Some of the moral pieces may have been sung as ballads, since several, including three by Edwards, were registered for publication in broadside form,[45] and there are also several love-lyrics and

---

[44] The first edition only attributes it to 'D. S.'; subsequent editions assign it to Wm. Hunnis.

[45] Nos. 7, 52, 53, possibly 98, 103, 116, and 117 in Rollins's edition, *The Paradise of Dainty Devices* (1576–1606) (Cambridge, Mass., 1927). No. 7, 'In youthfull yeeres when fyrst my young desyres began', by Edwards, was registered in 1563–4 and again in 1565–6; a tune for it, with lute accompaniment, survives in the Dallis lute book, Trinity College, Dublin, MS D.3. 30/1, ascribed to 'Mr Parsons', and, with different lute-setting and unascribed, in BL Add. MS 15117. David Greer transcribes it from the latter, in *Songs from Manuscript Sources*, 1 (1979). BL Add. MS 15117 also contains a setting for voice and lute of no. 108, Hunnis's poem 'Alacke when I looke backe, vpon my youth thatz paste'. No. 53 was registered in 1568–9—after Edwards's death but before the printed appearance of his miscellany; no. 103 was registered by Disle the same year that he published *The Paradyse*; the others were registered for broadside printing after appearing in the collection.

dialogues with refrains that ask to be sung to a suitable tune, such as Lord Oxford's 'The Liuely Larke did stretche her wyng' with its refrain

Laradon tan tan, Tedriton teight.

But the book has other, enlightening, links with music: with courtly songs of two kinds. The publication of Thomas Mulliner's musical commonplace-book in 1951 showed that several of the poems were made into four-part songs in the late Tudor style; the publication in 1967 of a collection of consort songs[46] including seven from *The Paradyse* shows it to contain some of the earliest known songs designed for a mode of performance that was increasing in favour. In this light the long popularity of *The Paradyse* becomes more comprehensible. It seemed strange that a collection consisting mainly of sententious verse, much of it advocating a prudential approach to life, should have had more appeal for the Elizabethans than any comparable volume—there were at least eight editions over the next thirty years; now we can see that it catered for many interests and moods, offering not only serious poems for reading alone and ballads to recite or sing, but also poems that composers had made into part-songs, and others that had just been set for the now favoured combination of voice and consort of viols.[47]

Here was a perfect book of words for many an occasion of domestic music-making such as 'Claudius Hollybande' had just described in one of the dialogues of his instruction book *The French Schoolemayster*.[48] His picture of English life has the element of oddity and excess characteristic of phrase-books in their ardour to supply every verbal need, but basically it rings true. When the family, and all the guests who have been invited or have called in for Sunday dinner—fifteen or sixteen in all—have worked their way through a vast range of dishes, and reach the cheese and fruit, the father suggests that they sing:

[46] *Consort Songs*, ed. Philip Brett (*Musica Britannica*, vol. 22, 1967).
[47] The work of musical scholars, notably Brett and Denis Stevens, has opened the way to a far fuller understanding of the musical associations of poetic miscellanies than was possible when Rollins was making his fine editions. His statement 'Although no tunes are named in *The Paradyse*, most of the poems were written with definite tunes in mind' (Intro., p. lxviii) needs modification: some of the poems would be made in this way, but probably more were written with the expectation that settings would be made for individual poems. Others again would be chosen by composers in search of texts, irrespective of whether the poets had designed them with setting in mind.
[48] Published 1573: the author's real name was Claude de Sainliens.

Roland, shal we haue a songe?

Sir: where be your bookes of musicke? for they bee the best corrected.

They bee in my chest. Katherin, take the key of my closet, you shal finde them in a litle till at the left hand: beholde, there be faire songes at foure partes. Who shall singe with mee?

You shal haue company enough: Dauid shal make the base: John, the tenor: and James the treble.

Begin: James, take your tune: go to: for what do you tarry?

I haue but a rest.

Roland, drinke afore you begin, you will singe with a better courage.

There is more talk of drink, roast chestnuts are called for, and then a song is sung. A guest then says to the father:

There is a good songe: I do maruell who hath made it.

It is the maister of the children of the Queenes chappell.

What is his name?

Maister Edward.[49] Is he aliue? I heard say that hee was dead.

It is already a good while a go: it is at the least fiue yeares and a halfe.

Truely it is pitie: he was a man of a good wit, and a good poet: and a great player of playes.[50]

Yes; and a good judge of the making of a miscellany too.

How many of *The Paradyse*'s poems were set as part-songs we do not know, because all too few of the part-books that must have been carefully copied out by hand and treasured in so many families have survived four centuries, and in the absence of printed song-books our knowledge depends largely upon the few that remain. Thomas Mulliner may have arranged all the songs he could find or he may have selected. At any rate, he has preserved five, and provided part of a sixth one set by himself: this is written in on the first leaf of his book and initialled TM, and is for the two lines of a poem probably by Hunnis, 'The higher that the Ceder tree'.[51] It alone is given in song form: Mulliner was making a collection of music for keyboard use, to play on a small organ, or virginals, and arranging music of many kinds, both sacred and secular, to serve his purpose. So the songs appear as keyboard pieces without words, but the titles or opening

---

[49] That is, Richard Edwards. He was Master of the Children of the Chapel Royal from 1561 until his death in 1566, and in this capacity wrote and produced plays for the Children; only his *Damon and Pithias* survives.

[50] 1598 edition, pp. 56–9.

[51] Reproduced by Stevens in his *Commentary*, p. 55. He refers to the poem as by Vaux, but only the first edition ascribes it to him, subsequent editions assigning it to Hunnis, whom Rollins considers to be the author.

phrases that head them point to the texts, and where these can be traced it has proved possible, with the aid of other manuscript sources, to reconstitute the songs in four parts, which can be seen to be the form in which Mulliner knew them.[52] Ex. 5 gives Tallis's setting of Hunnis's poem 'Like as the dolefull Doue'[53] with the words set out to the music. The fact that they need be written out only once to serve as a guide for all four voices draws attention to the straightforward, harmonic style; the parts keep together in mostly simple rhythmic phrases. But the restraint is eloquent and the plaintiveness well matches the words. This homophonic style is also used in a setting, assumed to be by Edwards, of his lyric 'Where gripyng grief the hart would wound'.[54] Its opening lines are still familiar because in *Romeo and Juliet*, Peter sings them and catechizes the musicians on them in the scene after Juliet's supposed death.[55]

The other three pieces from *The Paradyse* are more contrapuntal in style. In the anonymous setting for Jasper Heywood's lyric 'The bitter sweate that straines my yelded harte' (which reappeared in *A gorgious Gallery*), the parts move in shapely phrasing;[56] both the others, like the settings of poems by Surrey referred to earlier,[57] use points of imitation between the voices. The setting of Kinwelmarsh's poem 'By painted woordes, the silly simple man'[58] is by Edwards, and probably he also set his own best-known poem, 'In goyng to my naked bedde, as one that would haue slept'. The setting for this takes the octave fourteener stanzas without repeating strains, and its style is a happy blend of contrapuntal and harmonic; imitative entries between voices at the beginning of the first, fourth, sixth, seventh, and last lines give musical interest, but for much of the time the voices are together so the words are not obscured. Ex. 6 gives Mulliner's version, with the words of the first stanza added above the treble.[59]

---

[52] Denis Stevens has made several reconstructions: see following footnotes.

[53] *Mulliner Book*, no. 115. Also reconstructed by Stevens (Stainer & Bell).

[54] *Mulliner Book*, no. 113. Also edited by Stevens for four voices (Novello, 1955). A version for solo voice and accompaniment, with the words of the first verse, is given by F. W. Sternfeld, *Music in Shakespearean Tragedy*, pp. 120–1, based on a lute-music source, Brogyntyn MS 27.

[55] IV. v. 122–39.

[56] *Mulliner Book*, no. 114. Also reconstructed by Stevens (Stainer & Bell).

[57] pp. 8–9 above.

[58] *Mulliner Book*, no. 79.

[59] Ibid., no. 81. A reconstruction for four voices, based on the Mulliner MS and on BL Add. MS 36526, is given in *The English Madrigalists* (ed. Fellowes; rev. Dart *et al.*, 37 vols. so far, 1958–), vol. 36. (Series hereafter referred to as *EM*.)

Ex. 5

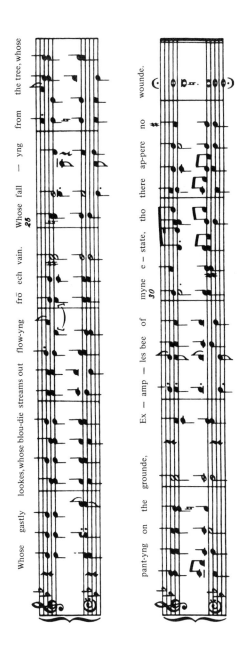

But *The Paradyse* is linked also with a newer fashion in courtly song, and this connection has long gone unrecognized.[60] The clue is present in the dedicatory letter of the publisher, Henry Disle, to Lord Compton. After commending the authors, he proceeds:

Furthermore, the ditties both pithy and pleasant, as well for the inuention as meter, and wyll yeelde a farre greater delight, being as they are so aptly made to be set to any song in .5. partes, or song to instrument.[61]

Why does Disle specify *five* parts? The early Tudor court-songs were mostly in three parts, their successors, such as those in the Mulliner book, were in four. If we knew of no kind of song that answered the question, we might take his remark as a publisher's hopeful puff; but the lucky survival of even a small number of part-books and manuscripts containing such songs, some of them actually from *The Paradyse*, shows that it described current practice. A set of part-books written by Robert Dow at Oxford in the 1580s and preserved at Christ Church,[62] an early seventeenth-century set in the British Library,[63] and a number of other sources[64] prove to contain songs written in five parts, to be sung by one voice to a consort of viols. Music for viols was winning increasing favour, and these consort songs combined the attraction of song with that of their instrumental texture. They were as adaptable as Disle's description implies: all parts could be taken by voices, or voices and viols could be used together in a number of acceptable combinations.

Dow's part-books contain consort settings for six of *The Paradyse*'s poems; other manuscript sources provide two,[65] and there are printed settings of particular interest for two more. Among those in Dow's books are one for Edwards's poem 'When MAY is in his prime'[66] and one for Hunnis's 'In terrours trapp with thraldome thrust',[67] and Brett suggests that the settings may be by the authors: both were Gentlemen of the Chapel Royal, and successively Master

[60] I first drew attention to it in '*The Paradyse of daynty deuises* Revisited', *RES* xxiv (1973).

[61] 'Instruements', in the edition of *c.*1590.

[62] Music MSS 984–8.   [63] BL Add. MSS 17786–91.

[64] See Brett's List of Sources, *Consort Songs*. See also his article, 'The English Consort Song, 1570–1625', *PRMA* 88 (1961–2), 73–88.

[65] See Brett, *Consort Songs*, for details of manuscript sources.

[66] *Consort Songs*, no. 23. (There is another setting in Forbes's *Songs and Fancies*.)

[67] Ibid., no. 18. (Words ascribed to 'T. M.' in the first edition but to Hunnis in later ones.)

of the Children of the Chapel Royal, Hunnis following Edwards in the post. There is an anonymous setting for Hill's 'The sainct I serue, and haue besought full oft',[68] and one by Strogers of 'Mistrust not troth, that truely meanes',[69] which is a hortatory piece by D. S. 'song before the Queenes Maiestie at Bristowe', its heading in *The Paradyse* states: the visit to Bristol was in April 1574. Robert Parsons, a Gentleman of the Chapel Royal who had died in 1570, set 'Enforst by loue and feare, to please and not offende'.[70] The remaining settings in Dow, composers unknown, are for poems by Vaux: 'The day delay'd of that I most do wish',[71] and 'How can the tree but wast, and wither awaie'.[72] The latter (Ex. 7) is uncompromisingly homophonic—there would be no difficulty in fitting the words to the other parts—and, so far as notation alone can serve as guide, it suggests that the song's effect in performance would be hauntingly sombre.

A setting for another piece by Vaux, 'Mistrust misdemes amisse, whereby displeasure growes',[73] survives in three manuscript sources. The setting by Strogers of 'O Heauenly God, O Father dere'[74] is preserved in two part-books and is also found arranged for voice and lute accompaniment. The lyric is assigned to F. K. in early editions of *The Paradyse* but has also been ascribed to the first Earl of Essex because it is recorded that the night before he died he requested his musician to play on the virginals and sing:

plaie (said he) my songe Willm Hewes, and I will singe it my self, so he did most ioyfullie not as the howling *Swanne* wch still loking downe whileth her end but as a sweete. *Larcke*. . . .

---

[68] Ibid., no. 20.   [69] Ibid., no. 21.

[70] Ibid., no. 5. The Dallis book setting of 'In youthfull yeeres' is ascribed to Parsons, and Mary Joiner suggests consort song origin ('British Museum Add. MS 15117: A Commentary, Index and Bibliography, *RMA Research Chronicle* No. 7, 1969, pp. 59–60).

[71] Brett includes this in the Appendix of Doubtful and Spurious Songs to vol. 15 of *The Collected Works of William Byrd*, but does not attribute it to Byrd. It occurs also in a lute book of about 1600, which contains many of Byrd's songs, BL Add. MS 31992.

[72] *Consort Songs*, no. 17. It made a deep impression; surviving manuscript sources include arrangements for voice and lute, and for cittern, and Barley printed it for voice and bandora in *A new Booke of Tabliture* (1596). Barley's version is reprinted in *Twenty Songs from Printed Sources*, ed. D. Greer (*The English Lute-Songs*, ed. Fellowes, rev. Dart et al. (1959–; series hereafter referred to as *ELS*), 2nd series, vol. 21).

[73] *Consort Songs*, no. 19.   [74] Ibid., no. 22.

Ex. 6

In go-yng to my na-ked bedde, as one that would haue slept, I

heard a wife syng to her child, that long be-fore had wept; She sighed sore and sung full sore, to bryng the babe to

rest, That would not rest but cri-ed still, in suck-yng at her brest. She was full wearie of her watche, and gre-ued

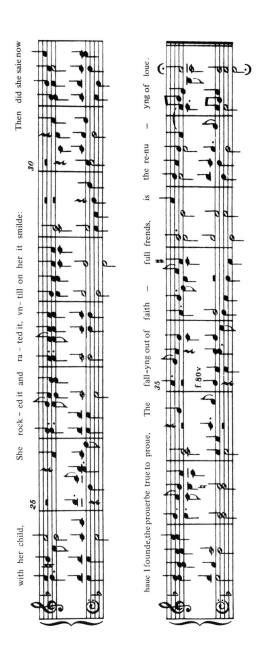

Ex. 7

2. What foodless beast can live long in good plight?
   Or is it life, where senses there be none?
   Or what availeth eyes without their light?
   Or else a tongue to him that is alone?
   Is this a life? nay death you may it call,
   That feels each pain, and knows no joy at all.

3. Whereto serve ears if that there be no sound?
   Or such a head, where no device doth grow?
   But all of plaints, since sorrow is the ground,
   Whereby the heart doth pine in deadly woe.
   Is this a life? nay death you may it call,
   That feels each pain, and knows no joy at all.

1. A consort song: Sir Henry Unton playing in a quartet of viols, accompanying a boy singer.

and the account is followed by the words of this song, headed

The Songe of his Hono^r songe the nighte before he died.[75]

Rollins points out that the song was already in print in *The Paradyse* before Essex's death later in 1576: it may have been a favourite of his, rather than of his own composition. This devotional piece must have long kept its appeal; two other settings besides that of Strogers survive, one in the Dallis lute book, which was compiled from 1583 on, the other in Myriell's manuscript anthology of 1616; and it seems to have been sung in a more popular manner too, for in the only known copy of the 1596 edition of *The Paradyse* an early hand has written in 'To the Tune of Rogero'.

Kinwelmarsh's authorship of 'From Virgins wombe, this day dyd spring' is unquestioned, and Byrd's setting of it was printed in his *Songs of sundrie natures* (1589). The other printed song not known in manuscript is later, but made while *The Paradyse* itself was still being reissued: it is Richard Alison's setting of the first two verses of 'The sturdy Rocke, for all his strength', by M. T. (Master [John] Thorn), in *An Howres Recreation in Musicke* (1606). Fellowes included both these song-books in his great series *The English Madrigal School*;[76] now it is recognized that these collections contain songs quite different in approach from the Italianate madrigal style, and the term 'madrigal' is reserved for vocal compositions that are essentially polyphonic, all parts having equal importance, and that make much use of pictorial illustration of the words, and of points of free imitation between the voices. The range of Byrd's collection is wide, as its title-page shows:

Songs of sundrie natures, some of gravitie, and others of myrth, fit for all companies and voyces. Lately made and composed into Musicke of 3.4.5. and 6. parts: . . .

He set Kinwelmarsh's carol in two sections (printing them apart as nos. 24 and 35), the chorus for four voices and the verses for solo voice and four viols: it is thus a consort song, with a choral refrain.[77]

---

[75] BL MS Harl. 293, ff. 115–20.   [76] Vols. 15 (Byrd) and 33 (Alison); rev. ed. Dart.

[77] The form of Kinwelmarsh's poem 'For Whitsunday' seems designed for singing, and is awkward to read:

> Come holy ghost eternall God, and ease the wofull greefe:
> That thorough the heapes of heauy sinne, can no where find releefe.
> > Doo thou O God redresse
> > The great distresse
> > Of sinfull heauinesse.

But I know of no setting.

The contrast between the flowing polyphony and rhythmic variety of Byrd's part-writing, and the four-square harmonic setting of 'How can the tree but wast' reveals the wide range of musical texture to be found in songs of this kind. Alison described his songs as 'apt for Instrumentes and Voyces', some being in four parts, some in five; the two verses of 'The sturdy Rocke, for all his strength' are separately set, in five parts, as nos. 15 and 16. The first section uses imitation between the parts in a basically simple, note-for-word style of setting that shows that in 1606 the style of the consort song was still as much alive as the verse of *The Paradyse*; the second section's use of musical illustration, in the onomatopoeic repetition for 'yelping' hounds and the roulade for 'the swiftest bird that flies about', shows that the madrigal style was taking effect.

Such facts suggest that it is well worth noting the elements of continuity in native secular song. The finer distinctions that can now be made between different kinds and styles are valuable helps towards understanding; but links and overlaps that provide clues to a continuous tradition should not be lost sight of. The four-part songs found in the Mulliner book are primarily for unaccompanied voices; the five-part consort songs are designed to exploit the interplay between voice and instruments: but both kinds provide verse with mainly strophic settings[78] and allow the words to be closely fitted and clearly heard. So do the ayres of the lutenist composers; and consort songs are often found in collections of lute-music, arranged for voice and lute.[79] Composers themselves often framed their songs for performance in more than one way: Byrd said in the preface to his earlier collection, *Psalmes, Sonets, & songs of sadnes and pietie made into Musicke of five parts* (1588):

heere are divers songs, which being originally made for Instruments to expresse the harmonie, and one voyce to pronounce the ditty, are now framed in all parts for voyces to sing the same.

They were originally, that is to say, consort songs.[80] The title-page of his 1611 volume shows expectation of varied performance:

[78] Except consort songs in the context of drama: the laments which were a feature of the choirboy plays were usually through-composed; they also used rhetorical repetition of words and phrases.

[79] For example, Brett's List of Sources shows that eight of the songs in *Consort Songs* appear in Brogyntyn MS 27 (National Library of Wales), arranged for voice and lute accompaniment.

[80] Many of Byrd's songs survive in this form in a set of part-books now at Harvard. See below, pp. 92–3.

Psalmes, Songs, and Sonnets: some solemne, others ioyfull, framed to the life of the Words: Fit for Voyces or Viols of 3.4.5. and 6. Parts.

Campion said he designed most of the songs in his *Two Bookes of Ayres* (?1613) for solo voice with lute or viol but preferred to provide extra vocal lines rather than have singers improvising in order to join in; and there are indications that many of the serious and more musically intricate ayres of the lutenists originated as songs for solo voice and several instruments.[81]

In view of such flexibility then, it is clear that over-rigid definitions now will produce an unduly fragmented impression: there are similarities, persistences, and recurrences of musical habit that testify to an indigenous tradition resilient enough to ride even the tidal wave of the madrigal, assimilating what could be of benefit in the strophic setting of English verse and continuing on its way both through and after the surge of Italian influence. But it is the differences that point to the key to the long success of *The Paradyse*: it offered songs old and new and exhilaratingly different—ballads, court-songs of the later four-part style, and verses 'aptly made to be set' to give the extra delight of a voice combined with the blending viols.

If the public who acclaimed that miscellany hoped to find a similar range of attractions in the next one to appear, *A gorgious Gallery, of gallant Inuentions*, which came out two years later, in 1578, they were disappointed, and their disappointment may be reflected in the failure of this anthology, so far as is known, to reach even a second edition. Its compiler, Thomas Proctor, offered nothing new: only the same types of poem as had appeared in *Tottel's Miscellany* and the early version of what was to reappear as *A Handefull*, and even several of the same individual poems. From Tottel, or from sources similar to Tottel's such as broadside ballad versions, he took two poems there printed among those of 'Vncertain auctours';[82] he also has a poem, 'Passe forth in doulfull dumpes my verse', which not only is to go 'To the tune, when Cupid scaled first the Fort', but uses some lines of the poem by Vaux to which it alludes; and another poem, 'You graues of grisly ghosts' is to go 'to the Tune of I lothe that I did loue'. *A Handefull*, in its early form, was an obvious model and source for a compiler wanting a sprinkling of ballads: lines and

---

[81] See David Greer, 'The Part-Songs of the English Lutenists', *PRMA* 94 (1967–8), 97–110.

[82] 'My ioyful dayes bee past' and 'Eche thing must haue a time, and tyme doth try mens troth'.

passages are borrowed from it and there are ballads written to several of the tunes it names or refers to—to 'Attend thee go play thee', 'Where is the life that late I led', and 'lusty Gallant'. Broadside ballads not in other anthologies are also drawn on, and there is a willow-song.[83] *The Paradyse* is plundered for three poems, one being Jasper Heywood's 'The bitter sweete, that straynes my yeelded harte',[84] which the Mulliner book shows to have been set as a part-song.

One borrowed part-song,[85] no consort songs, and a bunch of ballads: this may well be an incomplete musical tally,[86] but unless it is disproportionately so it suggests one reason for *A gorgious Gallery*'s lack of impact. It did not sufficiently cater for musical interest: there is no mention of music on the title-page or in the preliminaries, Anthony Munday's commendatory poem and Owen Roydon's address to critics. It was not a thoroughgoing book of singable ballads, like *A Handefull*—there were too few to leaven the lump of long-winded lamenting and moralization—nor had it the appeal to more musically accomplished circles that *The Paradyse* had. It was probably at least partly in consequence of its poverty of musical appeal that the Elizabethans showed little interest in it. While *The Paradyse* went from edition to edition, and *A Handefull* made a fresh appearance in 1584, the derivative and backward-looking *A gorgious Gallery* sank from sight almost without trace.

[83] Not the one Desdemona sings, but it has the same rhythmic movement and both could go to the same tune. Willow-refrains were popular in sixteenth- and seventeenth-century songs; see Sternfeld, *Music in Shakespearean Tragedy* pp. 30–1.

[84] The others are 'I would I were Acteon, whom Diana did disguise' and 'To seeme for to reuenge, eche wrong in hastie wise'.

[85] Alison did not draw his text of 'O heauy hart whose harmes be hid', for *An Howres Recreation in Musicke*, from *A gorgious Gallery*, which by 1606 would be almost forgotten. He set five verses as a group of five songs (nos. 3–7): the anthology has only three.

[86] Composers would be unlikely to turn to an unpopular collection when looking for texts, but there are twenty or so more poems that it would otherwise not be surprising to find in alliance with music. Nearly all of these are in the first part of the book, preceding 'Pretie Pamphlets, by T. Proctor'; if Rollins is right in inferring that this part was put together by Owen Roydon, Roydon shows markedly more interest in providing songs than Proctor. (See *A Gorgeous Gallery of Gallant Inventions* (1578), ed. H. E. Rollins (Cambridge, Mass., 1926), Intro., p. xx.)

2

The Later Song-books and Miscellanies

THE song-books so far considered have all been books of poems printed without music; and whilst a song-book without music may please a mere reader, it is dry fare for singers, although better than no text at all. But music printing was late and slow to develop in England; it was expensive, and not lightly to be ventured upon for secular songs. Service-books and metrical psalms with music had a more assured sale; of about two hundred items of music printing known for the period up to and including the year 1600, seventy-eight are printings of Sternhold's *Psalms*, and several others are of other sets of psalms.[1] Hall's *The Court of Vertue*, with its improving parodies, was published about 1565; otherwise, the only successors to the book of twenty songs printed in 1530 had been a book of chansons by Orlando di Lasso in 1570, and the next year, Thomas Whythorne's *Songes, for three, fower and fiue voyces*, words and music of his own composing, printed in a self-confessed bid to advance himself as a teacher of music.[2]

In 1575, Thomas Tallis and William Byrd, both Gentlemen of her Majesty's Chapel, were granted a privilege for twenty-one years to be sole printers and sellers of music-books and ruled music-paper. (This did not include the metrical psalms with music, for which John Day held the licence.) They made little use of their monopoly; they were fully engaged in composing and performing, and their printer, Vautrollier, who owned the fount of music type, was involved in printing work of other, including more controversial, kinds. Their *Cantiones Sacrae* were printed the year the patent was granted, but nothing followed in the next twelve years. In 1588 however, three years after Tallis's death, Byrd assigned his patent to Thomas East,

---

[1] See Robert Steele, *The Earliest English Music Printing* (1903; photographic reprint with corrections, 1965), and D. W. Krummel, *English Music Printing 1553–1700* (1975).

[2] See his *Autobiography* (Oxford, 1961, modern spelling version 1962). When he followed his part-songs, nearly twenty years later, with *Duos*, 1590, this was the first English collection of songs for two voices.

who had just inherited a music fount from Vautrollier, and East began to publish with vigour. That year there appeared two most notable collections: Byrd's own *Psalmes, Sonets, & songs of sadnes and pietie*, and Nicholas Yonge's compilation, *Mvsica Transalpina*.

The printing of two song-books in one year was in itself an event, a double godsend to singers starved for interesting music to sing. It is difficult to estimate how much singers had at this time to draw on; many songs by Byrd survive in manuscript and were not printed in his lifetime, and some by other composers too, and no doubt far more were written than have survived.[3]

Players and singers borrowed manuscript copies and compiled their own part-books, not only of English songs but also of any they could get from abroad, French chansons or Italian madrigals.[4] But the first half of Elizabeth's reign may not have been rich in composed secular song; the new generation of composers was just being born. Tallis indeed spanned most of the century, living from 1505 to 1585, and he composed some secular songs as well as all kinds of church music, and Byrd had been born in 1543; but Morley was born in or about 1557, Dowland and Campion in the sixties, Wilbye and Weelkes in the seventies.

Certainly Nicholas Yonge gives evidence, in the Dedication of his volume to Gilbert, Lord Talbot, of a keen desire for more songs to sing. Yonge himself was a singing-man at St Paul's Cathedral, and his friends, 'Gentlemen and Merchants of good accompt', gathered daily in his house to sing; there he was able to provide books of music

yeerely sent me out of Italy and other places, which beeing for the most part Italian Songs, are for sweetness of Aire, verie well liked of all, but most in account with them that vnderstand that language. As for the rest, they doe either not sing them at all, or at the least with little delight. And albeit there be some English songs lately set forth by a great Maister of Musicke, which for skill and sweetness may content the most curious: yet because they are not many in number, men delighted with varietie, haue wished more of the same sort. For whose cause chiefly I endeuoured to get into my hands all such

---

[3] Some songs, by Whythorne and others, were collected by P. Heseltine, *Elizabethan Songs* (1926). See also *The Collected Works of William Byrd*, ed. Fellowes, rev. Dart and Brett, vols. 12–15; *The Byrd Edition*, ed. Brett, vol. 16; *Musica Britannica*, vols. 15 and 22; and *Songs from Manuscript Sources*, 1 and 2, ed. Greer, 1979.

[4] There is a set of such part-books, dated 1564, containing French chansons and Italian madrigals of twenty years earlier, in the Fellows' Library of Winchester College.

English Songs as were praise worthie, and amongst others, I had the hap to find in the hands of some of my good friends, certaine Italian Madrigales translated most of them fiue yeeres agoe by a Gentleman for his priuate delight . . .[5]

The great master is clearly Byrd, whose book of songs had just appeared and found a ready welcome. It is worth noticing that Yonge and his friends were looking for more songs like his, not seeking Italian songs for novelty's sake: a fact which suggests that the subsequent vogue of the madrigal was at least partly an accident of demand and supply. If there had been enough songs like 'Though Amaryllis dance in green', English singers would probably have been well content and less effort would have been made to collect and translate Italian madrigals. But as Yonge indicates, the most delightful songs pall if there are only a handful and singers meet nightly; and so, before Byrd's second set of songs came out the next year, Yonge published his gathering of fifty-seven madrigals by Ferrabosco, Marenzio, Palestrina, Orlando di Lasso, and lesser composers, with the English translations.[6]

In printing the translations, Yonge was doing a service to English singers, but going against the expressed wishes of the gentleman, who had given him permission to collect and sing them, but refused repeated requests for permission to print them. It is only fair to the translator to record this, and to remember his aims. He did not mean his renderings to be read on their own as verse: they were made for the madrigals they translated, and for the pleasure of private groups of English singers, who liked to know what they were singing about. They were no poetic match for the original poems, which were by Petrarch, Ariosto, Tasso, and Bembo amongst others, but they served their purpose and were well liked and commended, not only by the singers, according to Yonge,

but of many skilfull Gentlemen and other great Musiciens, who affirmed the accent of the words to be well mainteined, the descant not hindred, (though some fewe notes altred) and in euerie place the due decorum kept.

The translator was rightly receiving approval for modelling the

---

[5] *Mvsica Transalpina*, 1588; facs. ed. and intro. Denis Stevens (Farnborough, 1972).

[6] The inclusion of madrigals for four voices, no longer favoured in Italy, and of madrigals that had appeared in collections printed at Antwerp by Pierre Phalèse, and other features, indicate that the Netherlands were among the 'other places', besides Italy, from which Yonge had obtained music that he drew on for his collection.

accentuation of his English words on that of the Italian verses, so that it accorded well with the music, for preserving the patterning of the vocal lines, and for rendering the originals fitly. He was in all respects making the words to the music's mould. So with the naturalization of a large collection of Italian madrigals in England came the introduction of a reversal of the roles of words and music which had a lasting effect on English madrigal verse and stunted its stature. For this is a mirror-image of the original madrigal method. Historically and practically, words had the precedence and pre-eminence in the Italian madrigal. It had developed in a literary context, fostered by Pietro Bembo and others, who consciously encouraged the growth of a kind of music more dignified than the frottola to partner the poetry of Petrarch and his followers. The music wove its subtle web of interweaving voices in response to the words, enhancing them by interpretation. The humanist ethos and aesthetic, with its high concern for the supremacy of words, underlies Italian madrigals and in part explains the depth, even sublimity, of many of them.[7] The Italian madrigalist composer's art was at the service of the finest Italian poetry; the English madrigalist composer made practical use of a text, but did not hold it in comparable esteem, and rarely set verse of high poetic worth; he had no feeling of engaging in a lofty artistic endeavour. In consequence, English madrigalists never attain such power as Marenzio, Gesualdo, Monteverdi: English madrigals are often delightful, but rarely profound; they enchant with beauty and prettiness, but they do not ravish with splendour.

   This difference in conception of the madrigal's scope and intent is traceable largely to the impact of Yonge's book, and the successors to it; for the music reached English hearers in all its beauty: the words came changed and dimmed. Translation of any kind tends to dim a poem's lustre, but this was translation that had to be matched to music that had itself been made to fit features of Italian language and verse. One feature will serve here as example: most Italian words have vocalic endings, so disyllabic rhymes predominate in Italian verse. The madrigal embodies them in its musical rhythms; if a translation is to match the melodic phrasing, it must therefore adopt

---

   [7] The authoritative study of Italian madrigals is Alfred Einstein's *The Italian Madrigal*, 3 vols. (Princeton, 1949). For discussion of English madrigals in relation to Italian ones, see J. Kerman, *The Elizabethan Madrigal* (New York, 1962). Alfredo Obertello gives the Italian originals as well as the English versions used in the madrigal books of Yonge, Watson, and Morley in his *Madrigali italiani in Inghilterra* (Milan, 1949). I cite their texts from his book.

these rhythms too. But they do not run so naturally in English, and feminine rhymes are in shorter supply. Yonge's translator is ingenious and often deft, and avails himself fully of accented past participles:

> The faire Diana neuer more reuiued,
> hir louer's hart that spied hir in the fountaine,
> while she hir naked lyms in water dyued,
> then me the country wench set by the mountayne,
> washing a vaile to cloth the lockes refyned,
> that on faire Laura's head the gold resemble,
> which made me quake, although the sunne then shined,
> and euery ioynt with louing frost to tremble.

He is translating Petrarch:

> Non al suo amante piu Diana piacque,
> Quando per tal ventura tutt'ignuda,
> La vid'in mezo de la gelid'acque
> Ch'a me la pastorella alpestre'e cruda
> Post'a bagnar un leggiadretto velo
> Ch'a Laur'il vago e biondo capel chiuda
> Tal che mi fece hor quand'egl'ard'il Cielo
> Tutto tremar d'un amoroso gielo.

Word-order, phrase-order, and syntax all show the strain, but it would be difficult to better the verse whilst keeping in step with di Macque's music: this translator encompassed an exacting task in accepting the original verse form and framing the original content in it.

Thomas Watson, although not unadventurous as poet or translator, contented himself with less.[8] The success of Yonge's volume, and the growing vogue for madrigals, led to Watson's similar but not identical enterprise. He compiled, and published in 1590, *The first sett, Of Italian Madrigalls Englished, Not to the sense of the originall dittie, but after the affection of the Noate*. His chief concern was to provide English words that matched the characteristic quality—the 'affection'—of the music. The 'sense of the originall dittie' (that is, the verse) is sometimes retained, with greater or lesser freedom, but

---

[8] His *Hecatompathia, or Passionate Centurie of Loue*, 1582, was the first published English sequence of what he regarded as sonnets—eighteen-line stanzas made up of three quatrains each followed by a couplet. The previous year he had published his Latin translation of Sophocles' *Antigone*, with some poems in Latin metres.

sometimes departed from altogether. The sonnet of Tasso's which provides the text for two madrigals by Marenzio is a love poem and describes Amazons jousting: Watson does not 'English' it at all, but writes an elegy for Sir Francis Walsingham, who had died that year, describing the soul of Meliboeus being greeted in heaven by Astrophil.[9] Another stanza that parts company with the original names Sidney directly: madrigal XIX no longer carries the love-message a young goatherd sends with a nosegay to his beloved, but voices a consolation on the death of Sidney:

> How long with vaine complayning,
> How long with dryry teares, & ioyes refrayning,
> Shall we renewe his dying,
> Whose happy soull is flying,
> Not in a place of sadnes,
> But of eternall gladnes,
> Sweet Sydney liues in heau'n, therefore let our weeping,
> Be turnd to hymns & songs of plesant greeting.

Even with freedom to devise new content, the effort to conform to the pattern of the verse and the musical setting has fettered the writer. In *Mvsica Transalpina* and *Italian Madrigalls Englished* alike the gulf is great between the original poems and the newly made verse. An Italian reading the sonnet of Petrarch beginning

> Zefiro torna e'l bel tempo rimena
> E i fiori e l'herbe sua dolce famiglia

was in the presence of poetry: an Englishman singing from *Mvsica Transalpina*

> Zephirus brings the time that sweetly senteth,
> With flowres and herbes, and winters frost exileth

or from Watson's more fanciful rendering

---

[9] He may have taken one feature from Tasso: both poems describe salutes between friends of the same sex—but with different degrees of seriousness. His verse for madrigal XXVII also commemorates Walsingham; and includes his most desperate bid for double rhyme:

> The fates, alas, too cruell,
> Haue slaine before his day, Dianaes cheefest iewel;
> But worthie Meliboeus, euen in a moment,
> With Astrophill was plac't aboue the firmament,
> O they liue both in pleasure,
> Where ioys excel all measure.

Zephyrus breathing, now calls nimfs from out their bowres,
To play & wanton, in roobes of sundry flow'rs

was not. But, for the first time, he had at hand a wealth of splendid music to sing; some madrigals had been circulating in England already, but not in such profusion, not easily available, and not with the riches of many composers gathered together and provided with English words.

For English composers, these volumes served as spur and as model; by the time that further Italian anthologies followed, Yonge's second volume in 1597, Morley's choice of Italian canzonets the same year, and of Italian madrigals the next, English composers were already producing their own. Morley himself was first in the field with his set of canzonets for three voices in 1593, then madrigals for four voices, canzonets for two, balletts for five voices (these last two closely indebted to Italian originals), and in 1597, canzonets for five and six voices;[10] he was never surpassed as an English composer in the lighter Italian madrigal and related kinds. 1597 was a kind of leap year in music publishing; Byrd's monopoly had expired the previous year and it was not until the following one that Morley obtained it: meanwhile, music printing was open to anyone. Thomas East, who had been printing as assignee of Byrd, published books of madrigals by Weelkes and Kirbye, as well as Yonge's second volume of *Mvsica Transalpina*; the printer Peter Short branched out with a variety of items, including Dowland's *First Booke of Songes*, and Morley's canzonets and his famous text-book, *A Plaine and easie introduction to practicall musicke*.

Morley treats madrigal composing in detail. He presents his treatise as, if not child's play, at least students' relaxation, in the form of a dialogue between a master and two pupils who come to him to learn about music whilst home for the vacation. It is thus not written for those intending to become professional musicians, but for young gentlemen wishing to acquire some musical accomplishment. The pupils are put through a thorough course of instruction and made to work practical examples before learning how to make 'the Madrigal, or louer's music'. This is expounded in the third part of the book, 'Treating of Composing or Setting of Songs'.[11] The pupils are

---

[10] Canzonets and balletts are described below, pp. 61–2.

[11] A modern reader who is not a musicologist might well begin with this part. Otherwise, once past the opening dialogue of the first part, he must face the intricacies

instructed in the art of descant,[12] in handling the compass of parts, syncopation, and imitation; they are taught that points of imitation (short musical phrases passed from voice to voice at different melodic levels, sometimes in inversion) should be handled lightly, not lengthily pursued, that one voice and then another should come into play while others rest, and so on. Then come the 'Rules to be observed in dittying', often quoted but worth quoting from again because of the important implications and consequences for the English madrigal and its verse of this very practical approach to the setting of words:

Now having discoursed unto you the composition of three, four, five, and six parts with these few ways of canons and catches, it followeth to show you how to dispose your music according to the nature of the words which you are therein to express, as whatsoever matter it be which you have in hand such a kind of music must you frame to it. You must therefore, if you have a grave matter, apply a grave kind of music to it; if a merry subject you must make your music also merry, for it will be a great absurdity to use a sad harmony to a merry matter or a merry harmony to a sad, lamentable, or tragical ditty.

You must then when you would express any word signifying hardness, cruelty, bitterness, and other such like make the harmony like unto it, that is somewhat harsh and hard, but yet so that it offend not. Likewise when any of your words shall express complaint, dolour, repentance, sighs, tears, and such like let your harmony be sad and doleful. So that if you would have your music signify hardness, cruelty, or other such affects you must cause the parts proceed in their motions without the half note, that is, you must cause them proceed by whole notes, sharp thirds, sharp sixths, and such like . . . you may also use cadences bound with the fourth or seventh which, being in long notes, will exasperate the harmony. But when you would express a lamentable passion then must you use motions proceeding by half notes, flat thirds, and flat sixths, which of their nature are sweet, specially being taken in the true tune and natural air with discretion and judgement. . . .

Also if the subject be light you must cause your music go in motions which carry with them a celerity or quickness of time, as minims, crotchets, and quavers; if it be lamentable the notes must go in slow and heavy motions as semibreves, breves, and such like; and of all this you shall find examples everywhere in the works of the good musicians.

of the Great and Less Moods Perfect and Imperfect, the More Prolation, the Less Prolation, the Prolation Imperfect in the Perfect Time, and other arcane matters already obsolescent in Morley's day. My quotations are from R. A. Harman's modernized edition (1952), *A Plain and Easy Introduction to Practical Music*.

[12] That is 'singing a part extempore upon a plainsong' (ed. cit., p. 140), either using the plainsong as bass and making a treble descant, or taking the plainsong as treble and extemporizing a bass.

Moreover you must have a care that when your matter signifieth 'ascending,' 'high,' 'heaven,' and such like you make your music ascend; and by the contrary where your ditty speaketh of 'descending,' 'lowness,' 'depth,' 'hell,' and others such you must make your music descend; for as it will be thought a great absurdity to talk of heaven and point downwards to the earth, so will it be counted great incongruity if a musician upon the words 'he ascended into heaven' should cause his music descend, or by the contrary upon the descension should cause his music to ascend.

We must also have a care so to apply the notes to the words as in singing there be no barbarism committed; that is that we cause no syllable which is by nature short be expressed by many notes or one long note, nor no long syllables be expressed with a short note. . . .

Lastly you must not make a close (especially a full close) till the full sense of the words be perfect. So that keeping these rules you shall have a perfect agreement and, as it were, an harmonical consent betwixt the matter and the music, and likewise you shall be perfectly understood of the auditor what you sing, which is one of the highest degrees of praise which a musician in dittying can attain unto or wish for.[13]

These precepts clearly apply to the setting of both sacred and secular words, in the motet and its profane counterpart, the madrigal. The latter is described as

a kind of music made upon songs and sonnets such as Petrarch and many poets of our time have excelled in. This kind of music were not so much disallowable if the poets who compose the ditties would abstain from some obscenities which all honest ears abhor, and sometime from blasphemies such as this 'ch'altro di te iddio non voglio,' which no man (at least who hath any hope of salvation) can sing without trembling. As for the music it is, next unto the Motet, the most artificial and, to men of understanding, most delightful. If therefore you will compose in this kind you must possess yourself with an amorous humour (for in no composition shall you prove admirable except you put on and possess yourself wholly with that vein wherein you compose), so that you must in your music be wavering like the wind, sometime wanton, sometime drooping, sometime grave and staid, otherwhile effeminate; you may maintain points and revert them, use Triplas, and show the very uttermost of your variety, and the more variety you show the better shall you please.[14]

It is noticeable that to the setting of words in madrigals, Morley brings observation, study, experiment, and thought; but the words as poetry, even their metrical aspect as verse, seem not to concern him at all. They exist to give rise to delightful music. The composer is to take

[13] *Plain and Easy Introduction*, ed. cit., pp. 290–2.
[14] Ibid., p. 294.

up their mood, and use pitch and interval and length to express it; negatively, he is to refrain from doing them violence by accenting them falsely or breaking them up or unduly drawing them out. But Morley (if the Master may be taken to speak or keep silence for him) could as well be speaking of prose as of verse: poetic structure and quality are not taken into account. Nor does he say where the madrigalist is to look for his texts; just that they are the sort that Petrarch and others have excelled in.

His readers must have been left with many questions in mind. If they were to try their hands at the madrigal too, were they to turn to Italian poetry for texts? If so, should they set the original words, or look for or make translations? Byrd had set a stanza from *Orlando Furioso*, 'La virginella è simil' alla rosa' and published it in Italian in his own song-book; but when Yonge included this and Byrd's setting of the next stanza in *Mvsica Transalpina* the same year, the words were 'brought to speake English with the rest'. Where did Morley himself get his texts? Were any English writers trying their hands at this kind of verse?

These were some of the musical currents of interest flowing in the 1590s, when at last there appeared some new miscellanies of verse. No new ones had come out in the 1580s, although some of the old ones still held their appeal. *Tottel's Miscellany* went into further editions, and so did *The Paradyse*, while the edition of *A Handefull of pleasant delites* of 1584 kept these ballads in circulation for the pleasure of readers and singers of less sophistication. In the 1590s, only one notable new collection appeared, *The Phoenix Nest* of 1593. The other miscellanies of the decade were further ventures by the printer of *A Handefull* and *A gorgious Gallery*, Richard Jones. The appearance of the name or initials of a well-known writer on the title-page of a book of verse was likely to benefit its sale, and Jones picked upon Nicholas Breton as suitable. In 1575 he had printed *A Smale Handfull of Fragrant Flowers* with the initials N.B. on title-page and dedicatory letter, although Breton was not the author of this poem in praise of the flowers of constancy, modesty, and other virtues, with a concluding prayer for gentlewomen and others to use. Sixteen years later he issued *Brittons Bowre of Delights*, 'Contayning Many, most delectable and fine deuices, of rare Epitaphes, pleasant Poems, Pastorals and Sonets by N. B. Gent.'. Breton denounced the printer for using his name on the title-page of this collection, but Jones was undeterred from associating him with a further miscellancy—as his preface admits it to be—*The Arbor of amorous Deuises*, in 1594 and 1597.[15]

Both these collections contained poems by Breton along with poems by many other writers, all the authors apparently being unaware of Jones's activity until his compilations appeared. The verse in *Brittons Bowre* would be meant by its makers for the private enjoyment of a courtly and mutually acquainted society: several of Queen Elizabeth's maids of honour are complimented in stiltedly ingenious verse that names its addressees in acrostics, spelling out the names of Penelope Rich and others. This would guarantee some interest in Jones's offering, and the inclusion of six poems on Sir Philip Sidney, whose memory was still deeply revered, would add more serious interest. Few of these lyrics are known as songs: 'If women would be faire, and yet not fond', which in a manuscript is attributed to the Earl of Oxford, Edward de Vere,[16] had already appeared, with some textual differences, in Byrd's 1588 song-book. That great favourite, 'Like to an Hermit poore in place obscure', now generally considered to be by Ralegh, appeared in the first edition of *Brittons Bowre* but was dropped in 1597; by then it had been included in *The Phoenix Nest*. It was set by the younger Ferrabosco in his *Ayres*, 1609;[17] and in the mid-seventeenth century by Nicholas Lanier, and also by an unknown composer.[18] One piece was written to go to a specified tune, 'A Sonet to the tune of a hone a hone', beginning 'Come solemne Muse and helpe me sing';[19] and a version of 'On a hill there growes a flower' was later printed in broadside ballad form to go to the tune of the Frog Galliard.[20] From Jones's

---

[15] H. E. Rollins has edited facsimiles of both: *Brittons Bowre of Delights 1591* (Cambridge, Mass., 1933), and *The Arbor of Amorous Devices* (Cambridge, Mass., 1936). Jones registered '*The Arbour of Amorus delightes*. by N. B. gent.' in 1594: no book corresponding to this entry is known, but the 1597 book is presumably a second edition of it.

[16] Bod. MS Rawl. Poet. 85. The authorship of poems in *Brittons Bowre* is hard to establish; one or two are attributable to Oxford and one or two to Ralegh.

[17] See below, p. 52, for comment on the setting.

[18] Another piece from *Brittons Bowre*, 'Her face, her tongue, her wit', which has been associated with Ralegh but may not be his, was printed in Barley's *A new Booke of Tabliture*, 1596, but without music. His address 'To the Reader' is followed by three poems without settings, including this one. See below, p. 53, for discussion of his book.

[19] Pattison (*Music and Poetry of the English Renaissance*, p. 172) conjecturally fits it to part of 'The Irish Ho-hone' tune of the Fitzwilliam Virginal Book, but it was probably written to an earlier tune of lament.

[20] Rollins dates the ballad as about 1620 (ed. cit., p. 82). The verses were reprinted both in *The Arbor of amorous Deuises* and in *Englands Helicon*.

later gathering *the Arbor of Amorous Deuises*, Byrd probably drew the text of his song for voice and viols, 'Come pretty babe'; 'Clime not too high, for feare thou catch a fall' was made into a consort song by Nathaniel Pattrick, and 'Come *Caron* come with speede' was set by an unknown composer for two voices and viols;[21] but his books were little drawn on as sources for song-texts.

Jones's miscellanies were eclipsed in both poetic worth and textual value by one that appeared between them, *The Phoenix Nest*, 1593. He did not hide his discontent that it deprived him of some projected plunderings: he says in his preface to *The Arbor*,

had not the Phoenix preuented me of some the best stuffe she furnisht her nest with of late: this *Arbor* had bin somewhat the more handsomer trimmed vp . . .

But almost certainly the Phoenix had the better claim to its twigs: as Rollins suggested, from the high textual quality of this collection it seems likely that the editor obtained his copies direct from the authors, whom he probably knew.[22] This unknown editor was as reticent as Jones was rash, concerning his own and his authors' identities. He signed himself simply 'R. S.' and gave initials, and indications of rank, for about a third of the poems, but no names in full; the writers may have given consent for publication but not wished to make parade of these slight pieces. R. S. held both contents and authors in esteem: *The Phoenix Nest* was

Built vp with the most rare and refined workes of Noble men, woorthy Knights, gallant Gentlemen, Masters of Arts, and braue Schollers. Full of varietie, excellent inuention, and singular delight.

Its variety extends to kind and quality, metre, subject, and source. Some very diverse pieces precede the 'Excellent Ditties' or lyrics that make up its second half. The first half comprises a prose defence of the late Earl of Leicester, and a prose dialogue between Constancy and Inconstancy from an entertainment presented to the Queen; two 'Dreames', allegorical poems on a garden plot and on the game of

---

[21] Brett edits Byrd's song from the only known musical source, a set of part-books of c.1600–20 (now New York Pub. Lib. Drexel MSS 4180–5), with further stanzas from *The Arbor*, in Byrd's *Collected Works*, vol. 15, *Consort Songs for Voice and Viols*. The other two songs are in *Musica Britannica* vol. 22, *Consort Songs*, ed. Brett, nos. 32 and 31; Brett notes that the latter may be the earliest setting of a 'Charon-dialogue', of which there are several other examples.

[22] See his edition, *The Phoenix Nest*, 1593 (Cambridge, Mass., 1931), Intro., pp. xxxi–ii. There is also a Scolar Press facsimile (1973).

chess, and an elegy and two epitaphs, one of them by Ralegh, on Sidney. A conceit made explicit in the elegy underlies the miscellany's shaping idea and glosses its title: the phoenix left her native Arabia and built her nest and pyre in a cedar here; at Sidney's death it took fire, and the ashes were blown abroad. Hence there will never be such another, although some lesser offspring may arise from the cinders. By implication, both those whose poems appear in this volume, and Sidney, are honoured: they are of truly poetic birth, he remains without peer.

Detective work by Rollins and others has traced many of the poems to their authors, who include Ralegh and Lodge, the ubiquitous Breton, and Peele. Many of the lyrics translate or are modelled on poems of Petrarch, Desportes, and Ronsard; the range of verse-forms used is wide, a few pieces harking back to poulter's measure and fourteeners, with a predominance of six-line decasyllabic verses of various patterns, and a fair number of quatrains and sonnets. In Rollins's view, 'T. L. (the initials of Thomas Lodge) is, whatever the basis of judging, the most important contributor, with sixteen poems to his credit'.[23] With this assessment I find it hard to agree; reading the miscellany without tracing its authors, I found a dozen or so poems to stand out in poetic individuality and worth. Five of these prove to be firmly attributable to Ralegh, and five others conjecturally so; only one is by Lodge. Many of Lodge's contributions are too perceptibly factitious; a neat conceit or a device such as a string of antitheses is hit upon and worked out. But the result is accomplished and attractive, and several run as if meant for song. Only one is known as a song: that beginning

> Now I finde, thy lookes were fained,
> Quickly lost, and quicklie gained:
> Softe thy skin, like wooll of Wethers,
> Hart vnstable, light as feathers:
> Toong vntrustie, subtill sighted:
> Wanton will with change delighted,
>> Sirene pleasant, foe to reason:
>> Cupid plague thee, for this treason.[24]

Feminine rhymes continue throughout the poem, and the last couplet recurs as refrain to each of the five verses. Thomas Ford set it, in his

---

[23] Ed. cit., Intro., p. xviii.
[24] For discussion of trochaic measures, which became widely used after Sidney had introduced them in some of his songs, see below, pp. 81–4.

Mvsicke of Svndrie Kindes, 1607, for four voices to sing to the lute, orpharion, or bass viol.[25]

Another of Lodge's lyrics is admirably made for lute-song, but no such setting of it is known: his 'Striue no more' calls to mind the pattern of 'Come againe: sweet loue doth now enuite', from Dowland's *First Booke of Songes*, and with its recurrence of stresses from verse to verse it could be well partnered by strophic setting (it could in fact be sung to Dowland's tune, if one phrase in the last line of each verse were repeated). He was clearly aware of madrigal verse too; in 'For pittie pretie eies surcease' he translates a madrigal ascribed to Guarini,[26] and 'My bonie Lasse thine eie' combines a line-structure suggesting influence from madrigal verse with masculine rhyme and disposition into several verses, which are characteristics of English lyric verse.

One of the finest lyrics in the book is probably by Ralegh: 'Praised be Dianas faire and harmles light' is assured and unforced in its movement, sound patterns, placing of pauses, and variety of phrasing.[27] Also possibly his is the far better known 'Like to a Hermite poore in place obscure', which had already appeared in *Brittons Bowre of Delights* and survives in several commonplace-books. It is a sonnet based on one by Desportes, but when Ferrabosco set it, in his *Ayres*, 1609, he used only the first quatrain and the closing couplet, so making from it a six-line verse.[28] He gave it a grave air, setting the whole opening line, until the last syllable, to one repeated note, a device that shows his bent for declamation, while the sureness of a contrapuntalist is shown in the interweaving threads of the accompaniment.[29]

Sonnet form is perhaps also evaded in a setting for another sonnet indebted to one by Desportes, 'Those eies which set my fancie on a

---

[25] See *ELS* 1st series, vol. 3.

[26] Noted by Alice Walker, 'Italian Sources of Lyrics of Thomas Lodge', *MLR* xxii (1927), 78.

[27] When it was later printed in *Englands Helicon* it was with the initials S. W. R. subscribed, but erased or pasted over. Agnes Latham suggests that the cancellation of this attribution of the poem to Sir Walter Ralegh may indicate that Ralegh objected to being named, not necessarily that the ascription was incorrect. See her Muses' Library edition of *The Poems of Sir Walter Ralegh* (1951, 1962), pp. 102–3.

[28] Lanier's later setting also avoids the sonnet form, using the last couplet after each quatrain to obtain three verses with a refrain. Several mid-seventeenth century manuscripts and printed versions give it this form (see Edward Doughtie, *Lyrics from English Airs 1596–1622* (Cambridge, Mass., 1970), pp. 561–2).

[29] See *ELS* 2nd series, vol. 16.

fire', in William Barley's *A new Booke of Tabliture, Containing sundrie easie and familiar Instructions, shewing howe to attaine to the knowledge, to guide and dispose thy hand to play on sundry Instruments, as the Lute, Orpharion, and Bandora: Together with diuers new Lessons to each of these Instruments* (1596). This was a timely, indeed opportunist, book,[30] providing instruction in skills that were soon to be widely cultivated with the rise to favour of singing to the lute, which received impetus from the publication of Dowland's first book of lute-songs the next year. The section for the bandora, a bass stringed instrument, includes besides instrumental pieces four songs for solo voice and bandora, the first English songs to be printed for this combination. The words of two of the songs are appended in full; for the other two only the opening words are given. The two with words in full are 'Those eies which set my fancie on a fire', and Lord Vaux's 'How can the tree but waste and wither away', poems already printed in, respectively, *The Phoenix Nest* and *The Paradyse*. The former poem is obtrusively patterned, with its four-item catalogue of eys, hairs, hands, and wit, repeated in each quatrain and recapitulated in the final couplet. The unknown composer has provided music for six lines of verse; so unless the second strain is reserved for the closing couplet, the sonnet becomes a song of three verses with refrain.[31] The text of this poem is followed by another from *The Phoenix Nest*, 'Short is my rest, whose toile is overlong', but no separate music for it is given; perhaps the same melody was meant to serve for both, or, more probably as the second poem is not well fitted by the music, its inclusion is intended to suggest it as suitable for setting.

Besides these settings by Ford and Ferrabosco and the one by an unknown composer published by Barley, a fourth poem from *The*

---

[30] It was 'Collected together out of the best Authors professing the practice of these Instruments'; Barley drew on Adrian Le Roy's *Instruction de partir toute musique des huits divers tons en tablature de luth*, 1557, for the lute instruction, and on compositions of the most celebrated lutenists of the time, John Dowland, Francis Cutting, Philip Rosseter, and Anthony Holborne, for the lessons. Seven pieces by Dowland were included, and the composer, who had not then published any of his music himself, registered his objection in introducing his book of songs the next year. Barley's book has been edited by Wilburn W. Newcomb, *Lute Music of Shakespeare's Time* (Pennsylvania State University Press, 1966).

[31] The text is accordingly printed with the closing couplet following the first quatrain. Ward suggests that 'Barley may have taken the words from a musical source in which the first quatrain and the final couplet were set out under the music, the second and third quatrains placed after the music', and considers that all the quatrains would be sung before the couplet ('Barley's Songs Without Words', *LSJ* xii (1970), 8).

Phoenix Nest was made into a lute-song by Robert Jones, and published in his *The Second Booke of Songs and Ayres*, 1601.[32] It is the accomplished if trifling lyric 'Now what is Loue, I praie thee tell', as welcome in its lightness as a soufflé after more solid fare. It was ascribed to Ralegh in *Englands Helicon* but this ascription too was cancelled, 'Ignoto' being pasted over the initials, and Francis Davison attributed it to Ralegh in his manuscript list of the poems in *Englands Helicon* but not when he put it into *A Poetical Rapsody*—withdrawals that may, as in the case of 'Praised be Dianas faire and harmles light', imply either correction or submission to Ralegh's wishes.[33] That the authors he drew on were unwitting and might be unwilling contributors to his publication is admitted in Jones's address 'To the Reader':

If the Ditties dislike thee, 'tis my fault that was so bold to publish the priuate contentments of diuers Gentlemen without their consents, though (I hope) not against their wils: wherein if thou find anie thing to meete with thy desire, thanke me; for they were neuer meant thee.

Poems thus published from unauthorized manuscript copies were liable to have variations both inadvertent and intended in their printed forms: in Jones's version of 'Now what is Loue' some of the metaphors for love are different or differently expressed, but the form is the same as in *The Phoenix Nest*, whereas in *Englands Helicon* the poem is the same in substance but is given pastoral garb as a dialogue between Meliboeus and Faustus: 'Sheepheard, what's Loue, I pray thee tell?' In all versions, each line opens with a variant of the same question, and ends with a variant of the same answer:

And this is Loue as I heard tell.

Jones reinforces the lyric's emphasis by giving the opening question a rising melodic phrase and partnering it with a falling one for the answer 'And this is Loue', which is then repeated a tone lower, and is each time anticipated in the accompaniment. The gay ingenuity of the music well matches that of the words.

It was not, then, composers of madrigals who turned to *The*

---

[32] *ELS* 2nd series, vol. 5.

[33] See Rollins, *The Phoenix Nest*, pp. 192–5. Miss Latham does not let it into her edition of Ralegh even amongst the Conjectural Poems, nor does she approve of it: 'For all its surface charm it is trivial and shallow'. (Her final dismissal, 'It seems to have had a certain popularity. Perhaps it had a good tune' (ed. cit., p. 171), is a good example of the unwillingness of literary editors to inform themselves about musical settings.)

Phoenix Nest for settable verse in the decade or so after its publication, but composers of lute-songs or ayres, songs for one voice or with parts for several voices, with lute and sometimes additional stringed accompaniment.[34] This kind of song spanned almost the same period as the madrigal, and held its own with it even at the height of the madrigal vogue; it rose to great favour at the close of the century, and the late Elizabethan miscellanies include an increasing number of lyrics that received lute-song setting. The ayre will be considered fairly fully in the next two chapters, but its presence alongside the madrigal needs recognition here, because, being strophic in form (that is, repeating the same music for each verse), it accommodates the English lyric's most typical form, of a few fairly short verses. And this form was never ousted by that of the madrigal. The madrigal has, typically, a single stanza from seven to eleven lines long; its lines are of seven or eleven syllables, and short and long lines are interspersed in any order; the rhymes too may come in any order, but almost all are feminine. Madrigal setting might of course be given to the octet or sestet of a sonnet, or to poems written in other kinds of stanza, but Italian verse made for madrigal setting used the single, intricately woven madrigal stanza.

This stanza proved unassimilable to English verse, and has rarely been used except for the specific purpose of providing grist for the madrigalist composer's mill; such verse makes no claim to stand alone and has mostly, and rightly, been left in the music-books where it belongs.[35] Not a single lyric in *The Phoenix Nest* has the form of the madrigal stanza: even Lodge's 'For pittie pretie eies surcease', the only one traced as a madrigal translation, is in octosyllabic couplets. Of course, the compiler of the anthology was exercising his taste, and may have chosen to exclude such madrigal verse as he knew; and his collection came out just too soon to reflect more than the first ripples of the madrigal's impact. But by 1600, far more madrigal verse was available, much of it already published in the madrigal composers' collections: the editor of *Englands Helicon*[36] could have filled his

---

[34] The spelling 'ayre' is worth retaining, to avoid other musical meanings of 'air'.

[35] It can most conveniently be read in *English Madrigal Verse 1588–1632*, ed. E. H. Fellowes, 3rd ed., rev. F. W. Sternfeld and D. Greer (Oxford, 1967). I quote madrigal texts not in Obertello from this edition.

[36] Probably the printer and bookseller Nicholas Ling was the editor, and John Bodenham the planner and patron of the enterprise. See *Englands Helicon*, ed. H. E. Rollins (Cambridge, Mass., 1935), 2 vols.: Intro., vol. 2, pp. 41–62. (There is also an edition by Hugh Macdonald (1925, 1949, 1962), and a Scolar Press facsimile (1970).)

book with it, and yet here too there is almost none to be found. This compiler is casting his net widely to gather an anthology of pastoral verse, collecting it from prose romance and drama and eclogue, from song-books and royal entertainments, and he presents five lyrics that are described as madrigals in their titles. But are they? Greene's 'Melicertus *Madrigale*' has four six-line verses, and his 'Montanus *his Madrigall*' has eleven; 'Damætas *Madrigall in praise of his* Daphnis' by Wotton has ten five-line verses, Lodge's 'Rosalindes *Madrigall*' has four nine-line verses, and 'Rowlands *Madrigall*', by Drayton, has three verses of twenty lines each. Not one is a madrigal in form. Even of the texts the anthologist drew from madrigalists' settings, only four are true madrigal stanzas. Of the three he chose from *Mvsica Transalpina*, the translation 'Zephirus *brings the time that sweetly senteth*'[37] preserves the sonnet form, and '*Thirsis* to die desired'[38] is a longer piece; the remaining one, '*Thirsis* enjoyed the graces',[39] is a madrigal stanza if taken alone, but he prints it after the other Thirsis lyric with the heading '*Another stanza added after*'. The three texts '*Out of M.* Morleyes *Madrigalls*' are true madrigal stanzas,[40] but those set by other English madrigal composers, Weelkes,[41] Bateson,[42] East,[43] and Ward,[44] are not.

It is worth comparing the choice of verse made by these other English composers with that made by Morley himself, to see how in practice they answer the questions that Morley left unasked and

[37] It was set in two sections (i.e. as two madrigals) by Conversi. (The octet was also set by Michael Cavendish, as one of the madrigals in his mixed volume, *14. Ayres in Tabletorie to the Lute expressed with two voyces and the base Violl or the voice and Lute only. 6. more to 4. voyces and in Tabletorie. And 8. Madrigalles to 5. voyces*, 1598.)

[38] Set in three sections by Marenzio.   [39] Set by Ferrabosco.

[40] '*Clorinda* false adieuw, thy loue torments me', 'In dewe of Roses, steeping her louely cheekes', and 'Harke iollie Sheepheards'; all in *Madrigalls to Fovre Voyces*, 1594.

[41] 'My Flocks feede not, my Ewes breede not'; *Madrigals To 3. 4. 5. and 6. voyces*, 1597. Weelkes's book gave the poem its first known appearance in print, but variants indicate that the compiler of *Englands Helicon* took it not from his text but from its subsequent printing in *The Passionate Pilgrim*, 1599, a collection of poems presented by Jaggard the printer, probably from a commonplace-book he had acquired, as sonnets by Shakespeare; it includes poems by Shakespeare, Marlowe, Ralegh, and Barnfield.

[42] 'The Nightingale so soone as Aprill bringeth'; *The first set of English Madrigales*, 1604.

[43] 'In the merry moneth of May', set as two madrigals in *Madrigales To 3. 4. and 5. parts: apt for Viols and voices*, 1604.

[44] 'A Satyre once did runne away for dread' and 'Neere to a bancke with Roses set about'; *The First Set of English Madrigals To 3. 4. 5. and 6. parts apt both for Viols and Voyces*, 1613.

unanswered in his text-book, concerning how madrigal texts might be made or found.[45] Each of the three texts used by Morley that appear in *Englands Helicon* consists of a single stanza that has long and short lines interlaced and that makes much use of feminine rhyme; none has much to offer a reader who knows only the printed page, and does not hear the madrigal's music, actually or in recollection; but even the slightest gives scope for musical embellishment:

> *Clorinda* false adiew, thy loue torments me:
> Let *Thirsis* haue thy hart, since he contents thee.
> Oh greefe and bitter anguish,
>   For thee I languish,
> Faine I (alas) would hide it,
>   Oh, but who can abide it?
> I can, I cannot I abide it.
> Adiew, adiew then,
>   Farewell,
> Leaue my death now desiring:
> For thou hast thy requiring.
> Thus spake *Philistus*, on his hooke relying:
>   And sweetly fell a dying.

The third and fourth lines here are too jingling to evoke feeling in a reader, but when Morley has given them the appropriate treatment for expressing 'a lamentable passion', the result may transport a listener.[46] 'In dewe of Roses' is equally trite as verse; but the deserted nymph's 'Aye me's become moving in musical lament. Morley's other choice, 'Harke iollie Sheepheards', the last poem in *Englands Helicon*, is better able to stand alone, because of its vigour and its vivid conjuring up of the rustic scene of the morris dance (which the next madrigal in his collection enacts). Its subject and expression leave little room for doubt that it is of English origin; the other two may also be English, although closer to Italian models, since no Italian sources for them have been found. Whether Morley made his own texts, or had them made or translated for him,[47] it is clear that all he wanted was an evocative trifle, lightly made, easily dividing into phrases that lend themselves to lively illustration in music: why turn to real poetry, which may be less obliging than this?

---

[45] See p. 48 above.

[46] His textbook instructions (quoted above, p. 46) are well exemplified in his setting (no. 2 in *EM* vol. 2).

[47] Italian originals are known for three texts in this 1594 book.

Other madrigal composers, however, chose less Italianate verse. Of those whose madrigals were drawn on for *Englands Helicon*, or who drew upon it for texts, Weelkes, although he composed in the Italianate musical style, took no texts at all from the Italian anthologies[48] and mostly set quatrain or sixain verse. The longer and more intricately patterned lyric 'My Flocks feede not', with three twelve-line verses making much use of internal rhyme and marked changes of movement and rhythm, was inviting but lengthy as a madrigal text, so he set it as three. Bateson used two texts drawn from the Italian collections, one from Watson's and one from Morley's 1598 selection, in his first book of madrigals. From *Englands Helicon* he took the first seven lines of a poem by Sidney, 'The Nightingale so soone as Aprill bringeth';[49] mostly his choice is of English-patterned verse.

East drew rather more on Italian texts, setting four from the 1588 and one from the 1597 volume of *Mvsica Transalpina*, one from Watson's *Italian Madrigalls Englished*, and one from Morley's Italian madrigal selection of 1598. He published, from 1604 to 1624, seven collections of compositions which became increasingly diverse, the first two books consisting of madrigals, the rest including anthems, instrumental fancies, and other kinds. His literary taste was equally wide-ranging, and also uneven. The first book contains settings of some very deftly written lyrics, notably Breton's 'In the merry moneth of May', which East probably drew from *Englands Helicon* but which had been previously published as part of the entertainment presented to the Queen when she stayed at the Earl of Hertford's estate at Elvetham in September 1591;[50] the first verse of a song from Greene's prose romance *Menaphon*; and Chidiock Tichborne's *tour de force* of antitheses, 'My prime of youth is but a frost of cares';[51] but it contains also some very ungainly quatrains. His last book contains only one setting of secular words, Wotton's 'You meaner beauties of the night', and consists otherwise of anthems.

---

[48] Two four-line texts in his 1597 book have Italian counterparts in his 1608 book; the sources are not known.

[49] The poem is one of the *Certain Sonnets*, published in the Countess of Pembroke's collected edition of her brother's writings in 1598, but Bateson drew his text from *Englands Helicon*. Sidney wrote the lyric to go to an Italian tune; see pp. 80–1 below.

[50] See below, p. 66.

[51] The first verse of this had been set by Mundy, in *Songs and Psalmes composed into 3. 4. and 5. parts, for the vse and delight of all such as either loue or learne Mvsicke*, 1594. Alison, in *An Howres Recreation in Musicke, apt for Instrumentes and Voyces*, 1606, set the same two verses as East did. The third verse remained unset.

Ward, who published only one set of madrigals, shows a more consistent literary taste. Four of his texts are drawn from Sidney: 'My true love hath my heart, and I have his', from the *Arcadia*; the first quatrain of the sonnet, 'A satyr once did run away for dread'; the last stanza of the tenth song from *Astrophil and Stella*, 'O my thoughts, my thoughts, surcease'; and five lines beginning 'How long shall I with mournful music stain', adapted from part of the dialogue 'As I behind a bush did sit', in *Arcadia*. His is the only madrigal set to use verse by Drayton (who is absent from the lute-song books too). 'Upon a bank with roses set about' is the first stanza of three in the second eclogue of Drayton's *Poemes lyrick and pastorall*, 1606, which had first been published in *Englands Helicon*;[52] there is a setting of a version of two quatrains from the second eclogue of *The Shepheards Garland*, 1593, 'O divine Love, which so aloft can raise'; and the two stanzas of 'If the deep sighs of an afflicted breast' are in part drawn from its ninth eclogue. Five others of Ward's madrigals draw upon poems by Francis Davison and his brother that appeared in *A Poetical Rapsody*, 1602, the last Elizabethan miscellany, which Davison edited. Another of Ward's texts is taken from Bartholomew Yong's translation of Montemayor's *Diana*, and one each from translations used in Morley's selected Italian canzonets of 1597, and selected Italian madrigals, 1598. In all, an unusually high proportion of Ward's texts are by known authors; and most bear being read, unadorned with the music, better than those set by others who composed in the Italianate madrigal vein. He was clearly more aware than most of the English composers of the poetic quality of a text, although, like the Italians, he would make changes in it to suit his musical purpose; perhaps his bent towards fuller-textured writing, for five and six voices, and the more serious approach that went with it, disinclined him to set much slight and frivolous verse.[53]

Of the madrigal composers who set texts that appear in *Englands Helicon*, then, Morley was alone in preferring Italian or Italianate texts. Even composers who adopted an Italianate musical style often chose to set lyrics that were English in form; and composers of other styles of song held more strongly this same preference. So the English lyric was not required to take upon itself an Italian shape, the shape of

---

[52] The first line there is 'Neere to a bancke with Roses set about'. Ward's version indicates that his source was Drayton's volume, not *Englands Helicon*.

[53] On Ward's choice and treatment of texts, see Helen Wilcox, ' "My Mournful Style": Poetry and Music in the Madrigals of John Ward', *M&L* 61 (1980), 60–70.

the madrigal stanza; it was transformed by the contact nevertheless, although more subtly. The effect of the Italian madrigal on the English lyric cannot be assessed by counting the number of madrigal stanzas that appear in *Englands Helicon* or in its successor, *A Poetical Rapsody*, or indeed in English verse at all; but by observing the change that has come over most late Elizabethan lyrics through the assimilation of features and qualities acquired from the contact.

Actual madrigal verse in English, made to translate or to imitate, was often awkward, even absurd: patterns that had dancing lightness in their native Italian use became flat and effortful as English words with their basically monosyllabic rhymes and iambic rhythms contorted themselves into the borrowed shapes. When they turned from making translations and versions to writing original madrigal stanzas, verse-writers did better, and gained by abandoning the solid tread of fourteener couplets and verses with lines all of equal length, for the lighter Italian pace. The thud of too regularly placed rhyme was avoided by the off-setting of shorter and longer lines interlaced, the metrical beat gave place to the fluid rhythms of vocal phrasing. The new patterns began to be used with more ease: the lyrics written, for instance, for *The Triumphes of Oriana* are mostly trifles, but the writers of some show skill in the new craft. For his contribution Wilbye set this stanza:

> The Lady Oriana
> Was dight in all the treasures of Guiana.
> And on her Grace a thousand Graces tended.
> And thus sang they: Fair Queen of peace and plenty,
>   The fairest Queen of twenty.
> Then with an olive wreath for peace renowned
>   Her virgin head they crowned.
>   Which ceremony ended
> Unto her Grace the thousand Graces bended.
>   Then sang the shepherds and nymphs of Diana:
>   Long live fair Oriana.

It observes the pattern of madrigal verse, with eleven lines of seven or eleven syllables, and its use of feminine rhyme throughout is managed with technical if not always conceptual ease. The writer of the stanza set by John Bennet, 'All creatures now are merry, merry-minded', has preferred twelve lines, but conforms in other respects to the madrigal pattern and frankly invites, and receives, illustrative setting with lines such as 'Yond bugle was well winded' and 'Music the time beguileth': he has spun a gossamer tissue of tribute to Oriana not meant to stand by itself as a poem, but to be partnered in correspondingly fanciful intricate sound.[54]

Composers clearly enjoyed setting such verse; here it was written for a special purpose, perhaps even a special occasion, for Morley was making an anthology to praise and cheer Queen Elizabeth;[55] but madrigal verse written with no such specific aim had still a good chance of receiving setting by professional composers in search of new texts. But the acquisition of the knack of writing neat madrigal stanzas would have been, in itself, of small importance to English lyric verse; if the English lyric had lost itself in adopting this form, English madrigal verse would have provided little poetic consolation. Much of it is deft, but derivative and slight: in content the Italian ingredients are present, love, nature, and legend, couched in emblems, conceits, and paradoxes; but the exquisite matching of concept and craft in the poetry of Petrarch, Ariosto, and Tasso is lacking. There is nothing surprising in this, for English poets of comparable stature wrote almost no madrigal verse. Major poets such as Sidney and Spenser were leading English poetry into new eloquence and power and were deeply influenced by the practice of Italian poets, but their contact was not only by way of madrigal settings but by extensive knowledge of their work. For lesser writers however, the madrigal was often the medium of their meeting with Italian verse; and its importance for English lyric poetry lies in the fact that so many minor writers learnt so much from it, and that these gains were not expressed only in madrigal stanzas, but went to the enrichment of the native forms of verse. The English lyric, like English vocal music, was not swamped by the madrigal's tidal wave, but took on new beauty from its sea-change. Even when writing for madrigal setting, most writers chose to produce several quatrain or sixain verses, and composers seemed happy to accept them.

Here Morley's influence and taste are again apparent; his predilection for the ballett and canzonet, both associated with strophic verse,

---

[54] *Madrigales The Triumphes of Oriana, to 5. and 6. voices: composed by diuers seuerall aucthors*, 1601 (*EM* vol. 32).

[55] The model for it was a famous Italian collection of 1592, *Il Trionfi di Dori*, commissioned to celebrate a Venetian bride. Roy C. Strong has pointed out that many of the madrigals suggest a pastoral entertainment or masque. ('Queen Elizabeth I as Oriana', *SR* vi (1959), 257–8.) Dart suggests the May Day celebrations of 1601 as the occasion (ed. cit., Reviser's Note). See Fellowes, *English Madrigal Verse*, ed. cit., pp. 698–700, and Kerman, *The Elizabethan Madrigal*, pp. 193–209.

led to the blurring of distinctions between them and the madrigal in English practice, both musical and poetic. The Italian canzonetta, which was polyphonic in musical texture, had several stanzas, most commonly with three eleven-syllable lines in each.[56] The Elizabethan anthologies gave only one translated stanza; so English canzonet verse often had only one; and English composers might treat the canzonet either as strophic or as a slighter kind of madrigal: Morley himself did both. The ballett, or balletto, remained strophic, with a fa-la refrain (with the verses set homophonically and the refrain contrapuntally); a form easily adopted by English verse.

Morley's fondness for Italianate rhythmical figures that partnered feminine rhymes also had its effect, on the verse written for his book of balletts for instance: the occasional resort to expedients such as

> Sing wee and chaunt it,
> While loue doth graunt it,

where the final syllables are meaningless but musically demanded, reveals the strain. The verse in his first book of canzonets too was all feminine-rhyming. So verse-writers learnt, when matching either Italian verse or Italianate musical rhythms, to perform such alien feats of necessity; but they learnt also the advantages of using some feminine rhymes to vary their measures, when writing without such pressures. Not all writers used double-endings with equal discretion: Lodge is sometimes carried away:

> Mvses helpe me, sorrow swarmeth,
> Eies are fraught with Seas of languish:
> Haplesse hope my solace harmeth,
> Mindes repast is bitter anguish

he begins, and rattles on throughout twenty quatrains without repeating his rhyme; the *tour de force* must have had its admirers, for the lyric is one of the nine that *Englands Helicon* took up from *The Phoenix Nest*. Another feature that Lodge uses here (and elsewhere) remorselessly is trochaic metre; again, the mere substitution of trochaic for iambic metre is not a gain, any more than the adoption of feminine in place of masculine rhymes; but the variety lent by occasional use is. 'Mvses helpe me, sorrow swarmeth' has the

---

[56] It came increasingly to have four or more lines, including seven-syllable ones. For discussion of these forms, and finer distinctions, see Kerman, op. cit., pp. 136–69. Morley defines them in his text-book; ed. cit., p. 295.

monotony that occurs whenever rhythm marches in step with metre; but *Englands Helicon* contains also lyrics that achieve fine rhythmic variety by exploiting their interplay:

> Beautie sate bathing by a Spring,
>> where fayrest shades did hide her.
> The winds blew calme, the birds did sing,
>> the coole streames ranne beside her.
> My wanton thoughts entic'd mine eye,
>> to see what was forbidden
> But better Memory said, fie,
>> so, vaine Desire was chidden.
>> hey nonnie, nonnie, &c.
>
> Into a slumber then I fell,
>> when fond imagination:
> Seemed to see, but could not tell
>> her feature or her fashion.
> But euen as Babes in dreames doo smile,
>> and sometime fall a weeping:
> So I awakt, as wise this while,
>> as when I fell a sleeping.
>> hey nonnie, nonnie, &c.

It is not that the poet is consciously reversing the metre, beginning the poem with a trochaic foot, but that he is allowing phrase rhythms to take precedence of metre. This too could be learned from the madrigal; for the Italian madrigal moulded its music to the verbal phrasing of the verse, and as English translators and writers in turn moulded their verse to match these freely varying vocal units, the shackling stiffness of iambic feet, and the cramping habit of thinking of verse as composed in units of metrical feet, were eased away. Their verse began to reflect the rhythms of natural speech phrasing, to counterpoint them flexibly with the metre:

> So I awakt, as wise this while

does not disrupt the underlying pattern but plays with refreshing naturalness over it.

This rhythmical freedom is one of the most notable qualities of late Elizabethan miscellany verse, and the evidence of their interests and practice strongly suggests that many minor writers acquired it largely by contact with madrigal verse. In this lyric, the old flat fourteener verse is only a hair's breadth away, and yet also a world away, for the feminine rhymes in alternate lines soften the pattern from eight syllables and six, to eight and seven, and the occasional trochaic rhythms allow a natural variety of phrasing.[57]

'Beautie sate bathing by a Spring' and many other lyrics in *Englands Helicon* show that the lyric has been transformed, and many readers and critics have found the transformation baffling. Even C. S. Lewis, who was more aware than most of the need to think of lyrics as songs, registers surprise. 'Nothing is more remarkable in the 1590s than the way in which excellence may suddenly flow from the meanest pen', he writes, and cites this lyric, finding it incredible that it was probably written by 'the wretched Munday'.[58] He continues: 'Poetic power is spread in such "commonalty" that if we were not on our guard we should come to take the "Spirit of the Age" for more than a figure of speech and believe that poetry could really be "in the air".'[59] But it was music, and more particularly the madrigal, that was in the air; wherever groups of friends met to sing in their houses, wherever social entertainment in the middle or upper classes was afoot, madrigals were being sung and listened to, madrigal books were circulating, madrigal verse was being written and set. By the time *Englands Helicon* was put together, the madrigals collected by Yonge and Watson had been known for a decade, and the English madrigal had established itself in its own right; not only Morley, but Weelkes, Kirbye, Wilbye, Farmer, and Bennet had all published sets, and Morley was able to draw on over twenty English composers for contributions (a few undistinguished, but most of them skilful) in compiling *The Triumphes of Oriana*. And as the verse-writers encountered and began to produce madrigal verse, they naturalized some of its features in their other verse, adopting its varied line-lengths, its lighter rhythms, above all, its flexible phrasing in place of earlier insistence on metre. All the features that Lewis observes as characteristic of 'golden lyrics' are there in the madrigal for the taking:[60] the fact does not constitute proof of influence, but the

---

[57] For an earlier appearance of a lyric with this pattern, written to a tune, see p. 17 above.

[58] In *Englands Helicon* it is subscribed 'Sheepheard Tonie'. It is in Anthony Munday's translation 'out of French and Italian' of the prose romance *The Famous and Renowned Historie of Primaleon of Greece*. For evidence supporting the identification of Shepherd Tony as Munday, see M. St. Clare Byrne, 'The Shepherd Tony—A Recapitulation', *MLR* xv (1920), 364–73, and her further articles in *The Library*, ser. 4, vols. 1 (1921), 225–6, and 4 (1923), 9–23.

[59] *English Literature in the Sixteenth Century* (Oxford, 1954), p. 479.

[60] It is hard to believe that he did not recognize the connection; yet he says of

juxtaposition is worth making. As so often in tracing the progress of lyric verse, it is worth while to follow the musical pointers: the parts of the puzzle fall into place. The ease and grace that set *Englands Helicon* apart from its courtly predecessors are seen to be largely the madrigal's endowment; *Mvsica Transalpina* and *Italian Madrigalls Englished* were the eggs from which the nestful of singing-birds hatched.

Once hatched, English singing-birds found their own voice: they learned to sing in forms traditional in English verse, and invited setting in styles that had kinship with the continuing vein of English part-song. 'Beautie sate bathing by a Spring' was made in two verses with a refrain, and was chosen for lute-song setting by three composers; Jones and Corkine dropped the refrain, Pilkington retained it.[61] Twelve other lyrics in *Englands Helicon* are known as lute-songs: four had appeared in Dowland's *The First Booke of Songes or Ayres of fowre partes with Tableture for the Lute,* 1597,[62] one was published in Morley's *The First Booke Of Ayres. Or Little Short Songs, To Sing And Play to the Lvte, With the Base Viole,* 1600,[63] and one of the lyrics from *A Poetical Rapsody* added to the anthology in the 1614 edition had been set by Jones in *Vltimvm Vale.*[64] The rest had appeared in the miscellany before they were printed as songs;[65]

Watson that he 'has the distinction of being the earliest of the poets who are golden from their first word' (p. 483), but in his account of Watson's output makes no reference at all to his *Italian Madrigalls Englished,* which evidence an interest worth considering for light on his own writing. Again, he remarks that 'Lady Pembroke's "Alas, with what tormenting fyre" would be pure Gnomic Drab if you removed the third and sixth lines of each stanza with their feminine rhymes' (p. 482), without comment on the familiarity madrigals had brought with such rhymes.

[61] Pilkington, *The First Booke of Songs or Ayres of 4. parts,* 1605, Jones, *Vltimvm Vale, with a triplicity of Musicke,* 1605, Corkine, *Ayres, To Sing and Play to the Lvte And Basse Violl,* 1610.

[62] 'Burst foorth my teares, assist my forward greefe', 'Come away, come sweet Loue', 'Away with these selfe-louing-Lads', and 'My thoughts are wingde with hopes, my hopes with loue'.

[63] 'Faire in a morne, (ô fairest morne).'

[64] 'Now haue I learn'd with much adoe at last.'

[65] 'Goe my flocke, goe get hence', the ninth song in Sidney's *Astrophil and Stella,* is in Robert Dowland's *A Mvsicall Banqvet,* 1610, with music by an unknown composer. Pilkington printed settings of three other lyrics from *Englands Helicon,* besides 'Beautie sate bathing', in his book of ayres: 'With fragrant flowers we strew the way', by Thomas Watson, 'Downe a downe', from Lodge's *Rosalynde,* 1590; and 'Diaphenia like the Daffadown-dillie', by H. C. (now presumed to be Henry Chettle). 'Sheepheard, what's Loue, I pray thee tell?' was set by Jones (for comments see above, p. 54, and Doughtie, *Lyrics from English Airs,* pp. 504–10). Detailed notes on most of these texts and settings are provided by Doughtie, and by Fellowes, *English*

but some of the songs were composed and performed long before the music was printed.

One kind of source that provides evidence of this is of special interest, because it records the musical contexts of songs which now have lost their music: the printed descriptions of royal progresses and entertainments.[66] Madrigals and lute-songs preserved by their composers and later printed survive; songs made for a special occasion often do not, for the printed records give only the words. Sometimes music for them survives in manuscript, and scholarly search and good fortune may still combine to reunite words and music. The contemporary account of the entertainment presented to the Queen at Elvetham, for instance, gives the text of five songs;[67] for one of them the music is lost, for two it survives in manuscript, for another it has recently been found, and the remaining song is still a puzzle.[68] For Breton's lyric 'In the merry moneth of May' Ernest Brennecke has found and published what is no doubt the setting made for and used in the entertainment, by John Baldwin; so now we can appreciate the Queen's enjoyment, when

On Wednesday morning, about nine of the clock, as her Majesty opened a casement of her gallerie window, there were three excellent musicians, who, being disguised in auncient countrey attire, did greet her with a pleasant song of Coridon and Phyllida, made in three parts of purpose. The song, as well for the worth of the dittie, as for the aptnes of the note thereto applied, it pleased her Highnesse, after it had beene once sung, to command it againe, and highly to grace it with her chearefull acceptance and commendation.[69]

But we do not know what music the Queen heard when, two days earlier, to welcome her on her arrival, Graces and Hours went before her 'strewing the way with flowers, and singing a sweete song of six parts, to this dittie which followeth'—'With fragrant flowers we strew the way'. Only Pilkington's setting of Watson's lyric is known

---

Madrigal Verse, ed. cit.). 'My hart and tongue were twinnes, at once conceaved' was set by John Dowland, and published in *A Pilgrimes Solace*, 1612.

[66] See John Nichols, *The Progresses and Public Processions of Queen Elizabeth*, 3 vols. (1788–1805), David M. Bergeron, *English Civic Pageantry 1558–1642* (1971), and Jean Wilson, *Entertainments for Elizabeth I* (Woodbridge, 1980).

[67] *The Honorable Entertainement gieven to the Quenes Majestie, in Progresse, at Elvetham in Hampshire, by the Right Honourable the Earle of Hertford*, 1591. Reprinted by John Nichols, op. cit., vol. 2; 23 pp.

[68] See Ernest Brennecke, 'The Entertainment at Elvetham, 1591', in *Music in English Renaissance Drama*, ed. J. H. Long (Lexington, 1968).

[69] *The Honorable Entertainement . . .*, p. 18.

today, and it is not a six-part madrigal, but is for one voice and lute; if the earlier madrigal setting was his, it seems not to have survived.

The next year, 1592, Queen Elizabeth was entertained whilst on a progress, at Bisham, Sudeley Castle, and Rycote, and the record of the festivities in her honour this time brings a lyric in *Englands Helicon* vividly to life. As the Queen approached Bisham, a wild man emerged from the woods and paid tribute to her civilizing power, Pan left wooing two shepherdesses and promised to keep all safe in the woods and valleys and fields, and Ceres, entering with her nymphs, in a harvest cart, sang a song 'Swel *Ceres* now, for other Gods are shrinking'. *Englands Helicon* reprints the words, and notes that the author is unknown; and for this lyric the music too is lost. But on the Sunday of the progress, at Sudeley, a shepherd came running to tell of Apollo's pursuit of Daphne, and her turning into a laurel: 'This speech ended, her Majesty sawe Apollo with the tree, having on the one side one that sung, on the other one that plaide', and the song is 'My hart and tongue were twinnes, at once conceaved'.[70] Who wrote the music? The 'one that plaide' most probably; for who he is becomes clear from a parley amongst shepherds and shepherdesses on the third day. The dramatis personae are listed as '*Meliboeus. Nisa. Cutter of Cootsholde*', but as they riddle, Nisa commands Cutter to sing, and then turns to a fourth person present:[71]

> And you sir, a question, or commaundement?
> *Do.*   A commaundement I; and glad that I am!
> *Nis.*   Then play.
> *Do.*   I have plaide so long with my fingers, that I have beaten out of play al my good fortunes.

There follows a song, 'Hearbes, wordes, and stones, all maladies have cured'. If '*Do.*' is John Dowland, famed for his lute-playing, well might Meliboeus say after it 'Well song, and wel plaide; seldome so well amonge shepheards'. If Dowland made the music for this, it has perished for lack of being printed, but in his 1612 song-book he preserved what is in all probability the setting of 'My hart and tongue

---

[70] *Speeches delivered to Her Majestie This Last Progresse, at the Right Honourable the Lady RUSSELS, at Bissam; the Right Honourable the Lorde CHANDOS, at Sudley; at the Right Honourable the Lord NORRIS, at Ricorte*, 1592. Reprinted by Nichols, op. cit., vol. 2, 14 pp.

[71] The significance of this extra person's presence was observed by Robert Spencer, and pointed out by him to Diana Poulton; see her *John Dowland* (1972), pp. 29–30 and 309–10.

were twinnes' that he composed, and performed, for this celebration before the Queen.

Dowland dedicated his 1612 book to Lord Walden, with whom he then had a post, and it may be that the last songs in it were written for Lord Walden's wedding festivities.[72] This points to another range of occasions for the making of special songs—family celebrations of weddings, betrothals, and comings-of-age,—when the words might be noted down in the family records, or in the commonplace-book of a guest, but the music would not. Such songs were creations of and for a day, ephemeral as dragonflies unless pinned down by some such record.

Royal entertainments were a fruitful resource for Ling in compiling *Englands Helicon* because compliment is often couched in pastoral guise, and he was in search of pastoral verse wherever it was to be found; from the sonnet-sequences of Sidney, Drayton, Lodge, and Watson, from the songs in pastoral plays and romances—*Arcadia*, *Love's Labour's Lost*, Lodge's *Rosalynde*, Greene's *Menaphon*—contributions are culled. In earlier collections, pastorals had been present, in *Brittons Bowre of Delights* and *The Arbor of amorous Deuises*, still more in *The Phoenix Nest*; now they fill the scene. Roundelay, madrigal, carol and dump, lute-song, dialogue, echo-song, consort and branle, all in pastoral vein, follow one another; the woods resound with the warblings of shepherdesses and swains. If too many are read at a time today, they pall, for the contrasts of texture and further levels of meaning that many had in their original contexts of prose or verse narrative, or of drama, are missing; furthermore, for the most part this is pastoral simple and unironic, hiding nothing more complex than compliment.

There is some variety and refreshment, however, as lyrics of a freshness that comes from the native tradition of carol and song, with its direct description and unaffected expressions of love and joy, are interspersed with others overlaid with the enamel of Petrarchan praise; and there are verse-forms that fit easily to ballad-tune measures, not only quatrains but all the patterns based on divided fourteeners. So some lyrics have links not with the artistic musical forms of madrigal and ayre, but with ballad and dance tunes; it is difficult to date the beginning of such associations, but some were probably formed as soon as the words became known, whilst others

---

[72] Suggested in *English Madrigal Verse*, ed. cit., p. 743.

were made later. 'Come liue with mee, and be my loue' gave its name to 'a sweet new tune', as the broadside ballad version of this 'most excellent Ditty of the Lover's promises to his beloved', and its answer, described it; the ballad registered on 11 June 1603 as 'ye louers promises to his beloved' supplies an early date for it.[73] 'In Pescod time, when Hound to horne' similarly gave its name to a tune, one popular for broadside ballads.[74] One of the poems added in the 1614 edition, 'On a hill that grac'd the plaine', was registered as a broadside ballad, 'The Shepheards Delight. To the tune of *Frog Galliard*', on 14 December 1624; the partnership may have begun before then, for the tune was a favourite considerably earlier: Dowland based a solo lute piece on it, as well as his setting of 'Now O now I needs must part' in his first book of ayres of 1597.

'*Coridon*, arise my *Coridon*' appears with music in a manuscript of about 1598–9, as Rollins noted;[75] Coridon and Philida answer each other in simple, tuneful dialogue. Rollins also observed that in the British Library copy of the first edition of *Englands Helicon* a seventeenth-century hand has written in 'tune of crimson ueluet' after the title of 'Sheepheard, saw you not', and the next poem, '*Venus* faire did ride', has 'same tune';[76] when this latter poem was published in the 1612 edition of Deloney's *Strange Histories*, the tune was named with it again. One of the several sets of verse that the tune has partnered is a lament put into the mouth of Queen Mary at the return of her husband King Philip to Spain, and presumably this would be written about the time of his departure, in 1555. 'Onely joy, now heere you are' was sung to the tune 'Shall I wrastle in dispair', and 'As it fell vpon a day' went 'To a pleasant new tune', but these associations belong to about 1620.

Ballads and courtly songs, madrigals and ayres: all kinds of musical alliance are here, traditional, old-fashioned, and new. In his pursuit of pastoral, Nicholas Ling ranged over several decades for his material, gleaning from earlier anthologies as far back as *Songes and Sonettes* as well as gathering manuscript verse; he drew on a royal entertainment of about 1578 as well as those of 1591 and 1592; and he

[73] See W. Chappell, *Popular Music of the Olden Time*, 2 vols. (1885–9), vol. 1, pp. 213–15 for the tune. (Repr., intro. Sternfeld, New York, 1965.) See *Englands Helicon*, ed. cit., for details of ballad associations.

[74] See Chappell, op. cit., vol. 1, pp. 196–8.

[75] Bod. MS Rawlinson Poet. 148, ff. 88ᵛ–90; *Englands Helicon*, ed. cit., vol. 2, p. 126.

[76] See Chappell, op. cit., vol. 1, pp. 178–81 for the tune.

took texts from the song-books of Byrd in the 1580s[77] as well as from the newest publications of the madrigal and lute-song composers.

The last of the Elizabethan miscellanies, published in 1602, covered a shorter time-span, of twenty years or so, but was wider in scope than its pastoral predecessor; the full title indicates its range: *A Poetical Rapsody Containing, Diuerse Sonnets, Odes, Elegies, Madrigalls, and other Poesies, both in Rime, and Measured Verse. Neuer yet published.* The last words were no doubt the publisher's, not the editor's, boast, and the claim is telling and substantially true. More than three-quarters of the contents of *Englands Helicon* had been printed before, but most of the new miscellany's verse had previously existed only in handwritten copies. The editor, Francis Davison, in putting together his own poems and some by his youngest brother Walter, was able to gather many by friends and other writers too, and his collection shows what a rich harvest of unpublished verse could be reaped by one who belonged to literary and professional circles. A commercial printer compiling a miscellany was largely dependent on chance or audacity for obtaining copies of poems, but Davison was likely to have them given to him, or to have the authors' consent or at least acquiescence in printing their verse, perhaps with a proviso of anonymity. He blamed the printer for publishing even his own and his brother's names, as well as for enhancing the book with 'diuerse thinges written by great and learned Personages', notably the two pastorals by Sidney with which the book, in its first edition, opened; but the disavowals may be merely formal.

In 1593 Davison had been admitted to membership of Gray's Inn, of which Campion was already a member of seven years' standing, and he commemorates their parts in its extensive revels for the winter of 1594. His sonnet to his mistress, 'Who in these lines may better claime a parte', is headed '*Vpon presenting her with the speech of Grayes-Inne Maske at the Court 1594. consisting of three partes, The Story of Proteus Transformations, the wonders of the Adamantine Rocke, and a speech to her Maiestie*'. He both wrote and acted in the masque of Proteus, with Campion apparently providing '*A Hymne in praise of Neptune*' to open it; he printed this with the subscription

---

[77] Three lyrics are from Byrd's *Psalmes, Sonets, & songs of sadnes and pietie*, 1588: 'What pleasure haue great Princes', 'Though *Amarillis* daunce in greene', and 'As I beheld, I saw a Heardman wilde'. One, 'While that the Sunne with his beames hot', is from his *Songs of sundrie natures*, 1589. Byrd's songs are discussed in Chapter 3, pp. 87–90.

'*Th. Campion. This Hymne was sung by Amphitryte Thamesis, and other Sea-Nimphes in Grayes-Inne Maske, at the Court.* 1594.'[78]

Other entertainments presented before the Queen also furnished pieces for the anthology: the fourth poem in its first edition, 'I Sing diuine ASTREAS praise', is '*A* DIALOGVE *betweene two shepheards,* Thenot, *and* Piers, *in praise of* ASTREA, *made by the excellent Lady, the Lady* Mary *Countesse of* Pembrook, *at the Queenes Maiesties being at her house at* [——] Anno 15[——]'—that is, at Wilton, in 1599. The following year the Earl of Cumberland presented the Queen with 'a shew on horsebacke' on May Day which included the song 'Th'Ancient Readers of Heauens Booke', with which the first edition ended. In the second edition, of 1608, sixty-four new items were added, more than half of them ascribed to Davison himself, most of his being epigrams. The two pieces that open this edition, probably both by Sir John Davies, also show the vogue for witty brief verses. The second is from another royal entertainment, that presented to the Queen in July 1602 at Harefield House, the home of Sir Thomas Egerton, the Lord Chancellor, and his wife, the Countess of Derby. On the first of June that year a merchant ship carrying from the East Indies a cargo valued at a million ducats was captured by the English fleet, and this inspired the device for 'A Lotterie':[79]

A Marriner with a Box vnder his arme, containing all the seuerall things following, supposed to come from the Carrick, came into the presence singing this Song.

Cynthia Queene of seas and lands,

and then declared he had found various trifles, which he would divide among them by lots: a mask, a ring, a pair of gloves, and so on. Each was presented to a lady with a rhymed couplet comment: thus, with a dozen points, or laces:

You are in euery point a louer true,
And therefore Fortune giues the points to you.

The mariner's song was already in print when this piece was added to the miscellany, as Robert Jones had included his setting of it, which

[78] Campion probably also wrote the other song for the masque, 'Shadowes before the shining sunne do vanish'; see W. R. Davis, *The Works of Thomas Campion* (1969), pp. 475 and 507–8. The settings of the songs seem not to have survived.

[79] The entertainment must therefore belong to 1602, not 1601, as the miscellany prints. See *A Poetical Rhapsody*, ed. H. E. Rollins, 2 vols. (Cambridge, Mass., 1931): vol. 1, p. 247, and vol. 2, pp. 202–10.

may well be the one made for the occasion, in his *Vltimvm Vale* of 1605.

A few of the first edition's texts, too, had already been printed with music: Michael Cavendish's book of ayres and madrigals, of 1598, contained 'Faustina hath the fairer face' as a madrigal, and this was probably Davison's source for it; 'Lady, my flame still burning, and my consuming anguish' and its answering stanza, translating Ferrabosco's madrigals 'Donna, l'ardente fiamma' and 'Signor, la vostra fiamma', were in Yonge's second volume of *Mvsica Transalpina*, and were set also by John Farmer in his book of madrigals of 1599; and in 1601 Richard Carlton included in his book of madrigals a setting of one stanza of the anonymous lyric, 'The loue of change hath changed the world throughout'. As well as these madrigals, four lyrics had been published as lute-songs: 'Absence heare thou my Protestation' in Morley's book of ayres of 1600, and three in *A Booke of Ayres* by Rosseter and Campion, 'And would you see my Mistres face?' in Rosseter's part, and 'Blame not my Cheeks, though pale with loue they bee' and 'When to her Lute *Corinna* sings' in Campion's.

For the most part, the borrowing is the other way about: Davison's anthology furnished composers with a rich source of texts. One minor lutenist composer, John Maynard, made a whole song-book, *The XII. Wonders of the World*, 1611, by setting the opening item of the second edition for one voice to sing to the lute and bass viol. The twelve six-line epigrams were written by Sir John Davies and inscribed on a set of trenchers he gave as a New Year's gift, probably in 1600, to the Lord Treasurer, the Earl of Dorset.[80] (The wonder of 'The Courtier', 'The Diuine', 'The Widowe' and the others presented in these brief characters is that each is virtuous.) Of other composers, Robert Jones was the one who drew on the miscellany most extensively, both for his lute-songs and for his madrigals. It was not hard to come by lyrics to make into ayres, but not easy to get consent for publishing them; in the address to the reader in his first book, of 1600, he gave the impression of being almost importuned by gentlemen who

were earnest to haue me apparell these ditties for them; which though they intended for their priuate recreation, neuer meaning they should come into the light, were yet content vpon intreaty to make the incouragements of this my first aduenture . . .[81]

[80] See Doughtie, *Lyrics from English Airs*, pp. 596–7.
[81] Ibid., p. 115.

In his second book, the following year, he admonished the reader, perhaps salving his conscience for not having this time secured consent, as well as shrewdly whetting desire to see what was current in coteries, 'the Ditties . . . were neuer meant thee'.[82] *A Poetical Rapsody* brought many such lyrics 'into the light', and in his next book, *Vltimvm Vale*, Jones set nine that appeared there,[83] including one by Francis and one by Walter Davison, and Campion's 'Blame not my Cheeks, though pale with loue they bee'. He could have got the last of these from *A Booke of Ayres*, but he may have obtained some of Campion's lyrics from the poet himself, since for *Vltimvm Vale* he also set 'There is a Garden in her face' and 'Now let her change & spare not', which Campion did not publish with settings of his own until about 1618; and Jones's fourth book of ayres opens with 'Though your strangenes frets my heart', which Campion published with his own setting about 1613.[84]

Far less abundant than lyrics for ayres were stanzas shaped for madrigal setting; few poets chose to write in madrigal stanzas, or to solicit this kind of setting. *A Poetical Rapsody* however included a considerable number of pieces called madrigals, some close to epigrams, which several of them translate, some in true madrigal stanzas, and for his one set of madrigals, published in 1607, Jones was indebted to it for seven or eight of his texts. He set five of Davison's own pieces (one of them translated from Guarini's *Il Pastor Fido*, and one from Groto)[85] and two anonymous ones, as well as Campion's 'When to her Lute *Corinna* sings', which could have come from the anthology, or from *A Booke of Ayres*, or from the poet himself. Campion had shaped this lyric suitably for lute-song setting, and set it so himself; Jones used it effectively for madrigals, by giving each stanza a separate setting. Usually he differentiated clearly between madrigalian and non-madrigalian texts, giving each the appropriate style of setting. His choice of verse is very diverse in quality, ranging from some that is trite and jingling to some highly accomplished anonymous lyrics, and those by Campion and Sidney.[86] Apart from

[82] Ibid., p. 149. See above, p. 54.

[83] A setting by him of another text that appeared in the miscellany survives in manuscript; see below, p. 91, note 37.

[84] 'My loue bound me with a kisse', in Jones's second book of ayres, is probably also by Campion; and 'Doe not, O doe not prize thy beauty at too high a rate' may be his: see Davis, ed., *Works*, p. 508.

[85] This latter, 'Loue, if a God thou art', appears in Bod. MS Mus. Sch. F 575 in a lute-song setting. (*English Madrigal Verse*, ed. cit., p. 692.)

[86] For Sidney's see below, pp. 79–80 and 81.

A Poetical Rapsody, he drew little on any poetic miscellany; in his 1601 book of ayres he set 'Now what is loue I pray thee tell', which had appeared in *The Phoenix Nest* and *Englands Helicon*,[87] and Munday's 'Beauty sate bathing by a spring', which he set in his 1605 book, was also available in *Englands Helicon*,[88] but both were widely known lyrics.

John Ward too turned to *A Poetical Rapsody* for madrigal texts, setting two that Davison, their author, presented as madrigals and devising three others from poems in different forms. From Davison's ode 'My onely starre', which has seven eight-line stanzas, he took the second stanza only, 'Hope of my Hart'; and he adapted parts of Davison's sonnet 'To Pitty', and of Walter Davison's sonnet, 'I haue entreated, and I haue complained'.[89]

A few other songs owe their texts to the miscellany: John Dowland probably took his of 'The lowest Trees haue tops, the Ante her gall', in his third book of ayres, from it, and Thomas Ford set Davison's dialogue 'Shut not (sweet Breast) to see me all of fire' in his *Mvsicke of Svndrie Kindes*, 1607, for two voices and two bass viols.[90] Martin Peerson made three songs on lyrics from it in *Priuate Musicke*, 1620, setting two poems and the first two stanzas of a third.[91]

Song-verse, sought after as it was, was not all that Davison's collection had to offer; translations or imitations of odes of Anacreon, epigrams of Martial and Luigi Groto, sonnets by Petrarch and others, reflect his interest in classical and Continental verse and, especially, in verse forms. Some poems exhibit elaborate ingenuity, including his brother's 'A Roundelay in inuerted Rimes', and the pair of poems in sixains (the second Davison's, the first left anonymous), Strephon's palinode, and Urania's answer in which the rhymes of the first are returned inverted. The fashion for writing in classical measures, current chiefly in the 1570s and 1580s, when Sidney and

---

[87] In this case Davison, or the publisher, in adding the poem in the second edition, may have taken his text from Jones; Doughtie (*Lyrics from English Airs*, p. 504) notes that their texts agree in some variants from the text in *The Phoenix Nest*.

[88] Probably also in Munday's *Primaleon of Greece*, 1596; Doughtie (op. cit., p. 527) notes that this survives only in one imperfect copy, in the British Library, which does not contain the lyric, but the second edition, of 1619, does.

[89] Ward's texts indicate that he was using the second edition, of 1608, or the third, 1611. On his choice of verse, see above, p. 59.

[90] Part of the anonymous dialogue 'Come gentle Heard-man, sit by mee' is set, for singing to lute accompaniment, in BL Add. MS 15117.

[91] Jones had set all three in his *Vltimvm Vale*, but Peerson's texts are closer to those of the anthology.

Spenser and Harvey were experimenting with it, was well represented:[92] there were ten quantitative poems, including Spenser's 'Iambicum Trimetrum', four anonymous tributes in memory of Sidney, one an epigram in elegiac verse and the other three elegies in hexameter verse, and four poems in 'Phaleuciacks', one with the haunting beginning:

> Time nor place did I want, what held me tongtide?
> What Charmes, what magicall abused Altars?

Here the unknown writer has not only mastered the phalaecian metre, but made finely controlled use of alliteration and assonance, tolling monosyllables, and rhetorical patterning throughout the poem; if he took Sidney's 'Reason, tell me thy Mynde, yf here be Reason?' as his model, he observed it well.

In all, Davison's book provided for many tastes, and pleased them enough to be kept in demand well into a new poetic age: it went into four editions, with Davison himself probably providing the extra material, or much of it, for the second edition of 1608, but not being involved in the third, of 1611; the last, in 1621, came after his death. Meanwhile, in 1614, *Englands Helicon* was reprinted, with seven poems from *A Poetical Rapsody* among the nine additions. By this time the purely poetic miscellanies had strong rivals in the song-books, with their wealth of verse; even by 1602 at least twenty-one books of madrigals and eight books of ayres had been published, and by 1608 there were seven more of madrigals and ten more of ayres. The long line of miscellanies came to an end with the Elizabethan age, but it ended in climax, not in decline: the last two, *Englands Helicon* and *A Poetical Rapsody*, together display the span and achievement of the Elizabethan lyric in almost all its many developments and forms.

---

[92] For discussion of the interest in quantitative verse, see below, pp. 85–9 and 96–101.

3

Sidney and Campion: verse and music

As the poetic miscellanies show, by 1600 many poets had acquired lyric skills. Twenty years before then, however, Sir Philip Sidney was exploring and practising almost all that lesser poets learned in the century's last two decades. At the time of his death none of his poems had been printed (with the possible exception of two sonnets that may be his); many of them would be circulating among his friends, and being copied into their commonplace-books, but the circle of people who knew them cannot have been wide. Yet 'that Incomparable Sidney', as his sister well termed him, was renowned as a poet, as for so much else. His presence hovers about *The Phoenix Nest* although none of his poems are in it; the 1597 edition of *Brittons Bowre of Delights* opens with Breton's lengthy lament for him, and contains five other tributes; and *Englands Helicon*, drawing upon the 1598 edition of Sidney's work, includes more poems by him than by any other author except Bartholomew Yong, a writer prolific of pastoral verse.

Born into a time when the way ahead for English poetry was far from clear, Sidney was prepared to widen the range of lyric forms and patterns by every possibly fruitful kind of experiment. His *Arcadia* was ideal ground for such experiment. The heroic and courtly characters of its main action, as well as characters encountered in its pastoral setting, express themselves in song as the prose narrative progresses, and the eclogues, interludes of pastoral entertainment amongst true country-born shepherds, give scope for contests and songs that range from comic flyting to love lament in tone, from debate to hymn and epithalamium in kind, and from quatrain to double sestina and various classical measures in versification. In its first state, the *Arcadia* contained well over seventy songs and poems and other pieces of verse, and they provide an unsurpassed conspectus of the possibilities for Elizabethan lyric verse. The romance gives a natural context for songs; but they are songs within the fiction only, for the romance is meant for reading, not acting, despite the original

description of its divisions as five 'books or acts'.[1] Parts of it might be
read aloud in a household gathering; but it would suffice that the
shape of a lyric commended it to the imagination as song. In book
three of the original *Arcadia*, at the sight of the sun speedily setting,
Basilius's 'Inwarde Muses made hym in his best Musick singe this
Madrigall',[2] 'Why doost thou haste away'. Ringler remarks, 'This
appears to be the earliest appearance of the word and the type in
English';[3] Sidney would almost certainly have heard madrigals
during his stay in Italy, both in entertainments and in his study of
music there, and he is probably presuming that his readers will have
heard imported Italian madrigals sung, or at least have heard of the
kind. The length and variations of line-length he uses here, and in
Basilius's further praise of Cleophila the same night, 'When two
Sunnes do appeare', which has the same pattern, lead the reader to
accept that these are madrigals. Other songs are presented as being
sung to the lute, or harp, the lyre or bass lyre, or the gittern; the
madrigal for Sidney is simply one dart in a full-stocked lyrical quiver.
He revels in the opportunities his romance framework affords for
using and devising verse-patterns of all kinds; the eclogues especially
show his fascination with technical aspects of versifying. The song
contest between Lalus and Dorus in the first eclogues, for instance, is
a *tour de force*, a series of challenges of versification, met and
outdone, to be savoured as verse, not set to music;[4] indeed none of

---

[1] The fact that Dametas's song 'Now thanked be the great God *Pan*' is to be found
in Ravenscroft's *Pammelia*, 1609, set as a six-voice canon, prompted John P. Cutts to
speculate on the possibility of some kind of dramatic presentation. 'Is it possible that
the first book of *The Arcadia* was given some sort of rhetorical and semi-dramatical
presentation? . . . Is it possible that behind the first book there is the shadow of an
earlier masque-like entertainment such as Sidney gave us in *The Lady of the May*; or is
it possible that the manuscript of the first book as it circulated amongst friends inspired
a semi-dramatic presentation?' ('Dametas' Song in Sidney's Arcadia', *RN* xi (1958),
183–8.) 'All is possible', as Wyatt said, and some of the music collected by Ravenscroft
belonged to an earlier time; but the appearance of the words as text for a canon thirty
years after the romance was written is slight ground for such speculations.

[2] *The Complete Works of Sir Philip Sidney*, ed. A. Feuillerat, 4 vols. (Cambridge,
1912–26), vol. iv, p. 195. Prose quotations are from this edition unless otherwise noted;
poems are cited as in *The Poems of Sir Philip Sidney*, ed. W. A. Ringler (Oxford, 1962).
The songs in *Arcadia* are discussed as they occurred in Sidney's original version; some
were later omitted, and some differently placed.

[3] *Poems*, p. 408.

[4] On the eclogues, their versification, and Sidney's models for them, see Ringler's
Commentary, *Poems*, pp. 383–422. Frank J. Fabry, 'Sidney's Poetry and Italian Song-
Form', *ELR* 3 (1973), 232–48, notes that the fifth exchange between Lalus and Dorus
(lines 73–96) consists of eight feminine-rhymed tercets and that these 'could have been

the eclogues are designed for setting, and none have been set, except for a few lines excerpted from them.[5]

In their context, it is enough for the songs in *Arcadia* to be introduced as if they had music; and comparatively few were later chosen by composers in search of texts to set. No setting of a song from *Arcadia* that pre-dates the romance's first printed appearance is known, although Puttenham, writing in or before 1589, knew 'My true love hath my hart, and I have his' in a ten-line version that uses the first line as a refrain, which suggests an arrangement for song.[6] Only four other printed settings of songs from the *Arcadia*, besides those so far mentioned, are known;[7] two of them are of Musidorus's song after he and Pamela have eloped, 'Locke up, faire liddes, the treasures of my harte'.[8] Both of these, and one of the other two settings,[9] were made forty years or so after the poems; the earliest known is of 1601, and oddly this one, by Robert Jones,[10] is of a lyric from book two that was not presented in the narrative as a song: the

---

sung to the music of any *capitoli* in the *frottola* collections'. The frottola was framed to so many poetic patterns that it would be surprising if Sidney did not use some of them, and I do not think the observation is significant. Fabry also directs attention to eight tercets in the dialogue between Plangus and Boulon in the Second Eclogues, lines 158–81, saying that these, 'ending as they do at a break in the sense and tone of Boulon's response, are appropriate for singing not only in form and content, but they also satisfy the informal conventions of singing *capitoli* for entertainment in Italy'. But the phrase 'Can I forget' with which they begin has also opened the two previous tercets; also the hearer is plunged into an unexplained situation, and will be further confused by there being two speakers. It seems improbable that Sidney planned or would have welcomed such an extraction.

[5] Lines 38–41 of the dialogue between Plangus and Boulon, as mentioned at p. 59 above, are made into a five-line text set by John Ward in *The First Set of English Madrigals*, 1613. The first two lines of 'O sweet woods the delight of solitarines!', also from the second eclogues, provide the opening lines of each stanza, and the refrain, of a song in John Dowland's *The Second Booke of Songs or Ayres*, 1600: the poem is in a quantitative measure, but Dowland was never beguiled by measured music, and he does not match its quantities in his setting. Henry Lawes also set this composite text (Autograph MS, BL Add. MS 53723, f. 11ᵛ).

[6] Noted by Ringler, *Poems*, p. 407. 'My true love hath my hart, and I have his' was later set, in two sections, by John Ward in his madrigal book (see p. 59 above); and BL Add. MS 15117, of *c.*1616, contains another setting (f. 18ᵛ). For a list of known settings of poems by Sidney, see Ringler, pp. 566–8.

[7] There is also an unpublished setting of 'My Lute within thy selfe thy tunes enclose' by Henry Lawes (Autograph MS, f. 3ᵛ).

[8] By Thomas Vautor, *The First Set: Beeing Songs of diuers Ayres and Natures*, 1619–20, nos. 8 and 9, for five voices, and by Martin Peerson, *Priuate Musicke*, 1620, no. 13.

[9] Pilkington set the latter part of the song Musidorus sang as he dressed himself to become Dorus, 'Come shepheard's weedes, become your master's mind', for five voices, in *The Second Set of Madrigals and Pastorals*, 1624, no. 14.

[10] In *The Second Booke of Songs and Ayres*, 1601, no. 11.

disguised Pyrocles 'tooke a willowe stick, and wrote in a sandie banke these fewe verses' beginning 'Over these brookes trusting to ease mine eyes'.

In the years in which he was writing his romance, Sidney was writing separate lyrics and occasional pieces too. His entertainment presented to 'Her Most Excellent Majestie walking in Wansteed Garden' in 1578 has as its centrepiece a contest in song between the rival suitors for the May Lady,[11] the forester Therion and the shepherd Espilus, with Therion supported by his fellow foresters playing cornets, and Espilus by the other shepherds on their recorders; and after the Queen has given judgement in favour of Espilus, 'the shepheards and forresters made a full consort of their cornets and recorders', and Espilus sang '*Silvanus* long in love, and long in vaine'.[12] But, as with so many entertainments, no music is known, for the singing-match, which appears in *Englands Helicon*, or for the final consort and song.[13] Yet settings may one day be found or identified, as in the case of two songs in Sidney's *Certain Sonnets*. Eight of the poems he gathered together under this title were written to specified tunes, but in the course of time these musical links were lost, until only one of the tunes he wrote for was known. This was 'Wilhelmus van Nassau' (which was adopted for the Dutch national anthem), and from it not much could be learnt of how Sidney wrote words for music because of its stolid regularity; he could do little but accept its terms, and his lyric for it, 'Who hath his fancie pleased', reflects its rhythmical staidness. But two pieces of polyphonic music (not simply 'tunes') have recently come to light, identified in a manuscript collection of Italian madrigals and villanellas at Winchester College by Frank J. Fabry.[14] To one of them, 'Non credo già che più infelice amante', Sidney wrote two lyrics, and comparison of these,

---

[11] Ringler believes this to be the earliest example in English of a singing-match, a feature of Greek and Latin pastoral, and the whole piece to be the earliest conventionalized pastoral drama in English (*Poems*, pp. 361–2).

[12] *Works*, ii. 337–8.

[13] Similarly, in the mock tournament presented before the French ambassadors to the Queen in the tiltyard at Whitehall in May 1581, when the Earl of Arundel, Lord Windsor, Fulke Greville, and Sidney as the Four Foster Children of Desire attacked the Fortress of Perfect Beauty, the gallery where Queen Elizabeth sat, the sonnets 'Yeelde yeelde, O yeelde, you that this FORTE do holde' and 'Allarme allarme, here will no yeelding be', which may both be by Sidney, were sung, but the music has not survived with the text.

[14] See his article, 'Sidney's Verse Adaptations to Two Sixteenth-Century Italian Art Songs', *RQ* xxiii (1970), 237–55, which includes the music.

'the fire to see my wrongs for anger burneth'[15] and 'The Nightingale, as soone as Aprill bringeth',[16] with each other and with the music, reveals his grasp of both the demands and the latitude of writing to music. He suits speech rhythms to the musical phrasing, and takes advantage of the extra options the varied rhythms of the lower voices provide, with the result that he is able to write two lyrics which are not identical with the Italian song-verse or with each other in their accentuation, and do not even adhere to their own initial rhythmic patterns in their second stanzas, yet can both be sung acceptably to the music.

This shows his practical response to music; but far more particular interest attaches to the lyric he wrote to the other recovered tune. The lyric 'No, no, no, no, I cannot hate my foe' was written *'To the tune of a* Neapolitan *song, which beginneth*: No, no, no, no', and it is trochaic in rhythm. So are two others of the *Certain Sonnets*, and both of them were written to music: 'O faire, ô sweet, when I do looke on thee' has the form of a villancico, and is written 'To the tune of the Spanish song, 'Se tu señora no dueles de mi'; in the other, 'Al my sense thy sweetnesse gained',[17] written 'To the tune of a Neapolitan Villanell', Sidney introduced the villanella into English verse. The music for both of these is so far unknown,[18] but the Winchester College manuscript contains music for four voices, and Italian words, beginning 'No, no, no, no', and both words and music throw light on the rhythm of Sidney's lyric. For the refrain, the Italian words provide accentual iambic and trochaic lines alternately, but Sidney, writing 'to the tune' and not to the model of the Italian verses, chooses a different, but appropriate, pattern, substituting an iambic quatrain. The music will accommodate this in the refrain, but

---

[15] Sidney put this into his revised *Arcadia* (in Book 3, ch. 15), as part of the water-music presented by Amphialus, and performed by five viols and five voices. Richard Jones included it in *The Arbor of amorous Deuises*, 1597; but Corkine drew his text not from this but from the *Arcadia* when he gave it three-part setting in *The Second Booke of Ayres*, 1612.

[16] Bateson set this in *The first set of English Madrigales*, 1604, taking the words from *Englands Helicon*.

[17] Subsequently set by Robert Jones, in *The Muses Gardin for Delights*, 1610.

[18] Two other poems in *Certain Sonnets*, besides these, were written to tunes that are not now known. No. 6, 'Sleepe Babie mine, Desire, nurse Beautie singeth', was to go 'To the tune of *Basciami vita mia*': several settings with this name survive, and Sidney's model has not been identified. No. 24, 'Who hath ever felt the change of love', was 'To the tune of *The smokes of Melancholy*'. (No. 16, the sonnet 'A Satyre once did runne away for dread', was not written for music, but John Ward, who set three other texts from Sidney, gave the first quatrain four-part setting in his book of madrigals.)

for the stanza it requires trochaic measure, as in the Italian words:

> Perche quel dolor ch'io sento,
> Quel tormiento . . .

and Sidney frames his words to match:

> For so faire a flame embraces
> All the places . . .

In the context, he is not innovating; because he is writing to specific music, he frames his words in an answering pattern. It is an entirely natural way for new rhythms to enter lyric verse, and it is odd that it should be found surprising. Ringler, for instance, recognized that the rhythms of the songs written to music would derive from their tunes, and yet wrote:

An especially tantalizing problem is raised by CS7, 26, and 27 [the three trochaic lyrics], the first to a Spanish and the last two to Neapolitan tunes, for they bring a new rhythm into Elizabethan verse . . . his greatest triumph was naturalizing an entirely new rhythm, the accentual trochaic,[19]

experimentally in *Certain Sonnets*, and with assurance in *Astrophil and Stella*. He noted that 'after Sidney accentual trochaics became exceedingly popular and were used by many poets of the 1590s', and went on to observe Sidney's use of feminine rhyme in songs, including all those in trochaic measures, and his avoidance of it in sonnets:

This distinction in its use may be the result of some privately formulated and as yet unexplained principle of decorum. Though feminine rhyme almost never appears in the poetry of the mid century, by the 1590s, probably in part as a result of Sidney's example, it had become an accepted feature of English verse.[20]

If the relations of poets and poetry with music are borne in mind—not only the particular fact that Sidney wrote some poems to go to named tunes, but wider aspects of reciprocal influence in the 1580s and 1590s too—these matters may all be seen as natural developments

---

[19] *Poems*, pp. xliii (where he notes an exceptional earlier occurrence of the rhythm, in Henry VIII's 1545 Primer), and lv.

[20] *Poems*, pp. xliii note 1, and lvi. Fabry ('Sidney's Poetry and Italian Song-Form') also quotes from these passages, and relates Sidney's practice chiefly to the frottola and its texts. I find more ground for relating it to the later forms, the popular villanella and the more literary madrigal, than to the frottola, which was losing favour in Italy by the time of Sidney's birth.

and not as unfathomed phenomena. Sidney's example may well have contributed to the acceptance of feminine rhyme; but another, and major, factor of influence emerged from the consideration of the later song-books in the last chapter: the spreading familiarity with Italian music and verse in the 1590s. This illuminates the other two problems too, the 'unexplained principle of decorum' and the ready acceptance of accentual trochaics. The musical associations of feminine rhymes, not only with madrigals but with slight and trivial Italian kinds, may have contributed to Sidney's selectiveness in their use; they were admirable in lending lightness to verse designed either for singing or for fictionally presenting as song, but masculine rhymes are more fit for English verse of more gravity, such as his sonnets. And there is reason to suggest that the concurrence of feminine rhymes with trochaic rhythms is not fortuitous: the rhymes have prompted the rhythms. Lines of seven or eleven syllables come easily to Italian verse; lines of eight or ten are more natural in English. Where only the effect of song is needed, or where the actual music permits it, there is scope for an English verse-writer to compromise, by combining disyllabic rhyme with an even-syllabled line. The rhyme ends the line with a falling rhythm; the rhythm affords a pattern for the whole line, and for the whole stanza, although not all of its lines are even-syllabled. All the *Astrophil and Stella* songs that are in trochaic measures combine lines of seven and eight syllables, and in all but one of these, the eight-syllable lines have feminine endings. The exception, the fourth song, 'Onely joy, now here you are', is especially interesting; the last couplet of each six-line stanza is a refrain, which is iambic in movement; only the first line of the refrain has eight syllables, the other five lines having seven, and there are no feminine rhymes: so the trochaic movement has been selected solely for its own rhythmic effect.

This highlights a progression that may often be traced, although it cannot always be proven: the introduction of a pattern into verse by way of music, and its continuing use as a verse-pattern in its own right. The songs in *Astrophil and Stella*, like those in *Arcadia*, do not expect to be sung; they fulfil their purposes within the sonnet-sequence, contributing to its structural patterns, providing contrasts in verse texture and pace, supplying by lyric implication what the explicit narrative leaves out, and allowing Stella a voice; actual music is not called for. But by the time Sidney turned to his sonnet-sequence, he had experimented with trochaic rhythms in songs; and if they commended themselves to him as useful for carrying a suggestion of singing that would enhance his songs-without-music, or as being enjoyable in themselves, it is not surprising that he should explore them as a welcome resource for increasing the range of lyric measures.[21]

Although the songs in the sequence serve their purpose without performance, composers found some of them inviting and rewarding to set. In the first few decades after Sidney's death, the second, fourth, sixth, eighth, ninth, tenth, and eleventh songs were all set, or fitted to music.[22] One feature shared by these lyrics chosen for setting appears at a glance: they are the short-lined ones; the long-lined ones remained unset. But six of them share another distinction: they are the six in trochaic measures. Sidney's instinct in using them for their suggestion of song has proved right: they have suggested it also to composers. In his writing of verse so that it implies and invites singing, as in his skill in writing for music already made, it seems that

---

[21] Sidney used trochaic measures also for five of the forty-three psalms he versified (nos. 16, 28, 38, 42, and 43). The French metrical versions by Clement Marot and Theodore Beza, published in 1562 with musical settings by Claude Goudimel, were among his main models, but he seems not to have intended his versions for music, for the partial stanzas with which some of them end make them unsuitable.

[22] The setting of the second song, 'Have I caught my heav'nly jewell', in BL Add. MS 15117, f. 19, is of unknown authorship (it has been printed by J. P. Cutts, *SQ* xi (1960), and by D. Greer, *Songs from Manuscript Sources*, 1 (1979)). Henry Youll set the first stanza of the fourth song, 'Onely joy, now here you are', in *Canzonets To Three Voyces*, 1608. The Italian composer Gastoldi also set the fourth song, drawing his text from *Englands Helicon*; an entry in the Rylands Library copy of *Englands Helicon* indicating that the lyric was sung to 'Shall I wrastle in disp. [despair]', suggests its continuing popularity. (Noted by Pattison, who prints the tune, *Music and Poetry of the English Renaissance*, pp. 175–6.) Gastoldi also set a medley made from the eighth song and the opening lines of the tenth. Byrd set the sixth song, 'O you that heere this voice', in *Psalmes, Sonets, & songs of sadnes and pietie*, 1588, and the first three stanzas of the tenth song, 'O deere life, when shall it be' in *Songs of sundrie natures*, 1589. Robert Dowland published settings of the eighth, ninth, and tenth songs in *A Musicall Banquet*, 1610: the music for the eighth, formerly assumed to be by Charles Tessier, is by Guillaume Tessier: in his *Primo Libro Dell'Arie* (Paris, 1582) its text is Ronsard's 'Le petit enfant amour'. Doughtie (*Lyrics from English Airs*, p. 587) comments: 'Apparently Robert Dowland found that Tessier's tune would fit Sidney's poem, and then fashioned a lute accompaniment from the three lower voices of Tessier's song.' It is not known who composed the settings Robert Dowland gives for the ninth and tenth songs. A different setting of the first stanza of the ninth song, 'Go my flocke, go get you hence', for treble and bass, in a manuscript of c.1620 (Christ Church, Oxford, MS 439), is ascribed to Robert Taylor (Doughtie, p. 585). John Ward's setting of the last stanza only of the tenth song, in his book of madrigals, has already been noticed (p. 59 above). Thomas Morley set the eleventh song, 'Who is it that this darke night', in *The First Booke of Ayres*, 1600, apparently prompted by the publication of Sidney's collected writings in 1598.

he illustrates his own well-known description of a poet in *The Defence of Poesie*:

hee commeth to you with words set in delightfull proportion, either accompanied with, or prepared for the well enchanting skill of *Musicke*.[23]

But it is probable that he intended a particular meaning by 'delightfull proportion', and that the poems in which he aimed at it are not only the ones that were written to tunes or made into songs. He was prepared to experiment with any ways of constructing or patterning verse that would extend the resources available to English poetry; and he enjoyed exercising himself under poetic restraints, finding stimulus in meeting their requirements, and even laying more rigorous restrictions upon himself, as in going beyond the sestina itself to accomplish a double sestina and a rhymed sestina, in the *Arcadia* eclogues. There was the attraction of challenge, as well as the promise of increased metrical variety, in trying to naturalize the measures of classical verse into the vernacular. It was being attempted in Italy and France; in England it had been discussed at Cambridge in the 1540s by Cheke and Ascham and Thomas Watson,[24] and at Cambridge again, Thomas Drant, who entered St John's College in 1558, formulated some rules for determining quantity in English scansion, which he communicated to Sidney, who passed them on to Spenser, who in turn wrote to Gabriel Harvey, in April 1580,

I would hartily wish you would either send me the Rules and Precepts of Arte, which you obserue in Quantities, or else followe mine, that M. Philip Sidney gaue me, being the very same which M. Drant deuised, but enlarged with M. Sidneys own iudgement, and augmented with my Obseruations, that we might both accorde and agree in one, leaste we ouerthrowe one an other, and be ouerthrown of the rest.[25]

His tone shows the concern and uncertainty that many Elizabethans felt on the matter, which was much debated and variously understood and misunderstood. Sidney's judgement was far better informed than most; he was aware both that Latin was incorrectly

---

[23] *Works*, iii. 20.
[24] A meticulous classical scholar, later Bishop of Lincoln, who lived 1513–84; Thomas Watson the poet and compiler of *Italian Madrigalls Englished* lived c.1557–92.
[25] *Elizabethan Critical Essays*, vol. i, pp. 99–100. No copy of Drant's rules is known; for Sidney's, see Ringler, *Poems*, p. 391. For a detailed study of the Elizabethan understanding of classical prosody, see Derek Attridge, *Well-weighed Syllables* (Cambridge, 1974).

pronounced in his day in England, and that Latin verse was incorrectly read, being read either by word-accent as if it were prose, or when memorizing or scanning, by stressing the ictus (the initial beat of each foot). He valued the discipline and artifice of an abstract metrical system, valid to the mind even if not audible to the ear; English verse, with its small number of patterns, mostly iambic, and its governance by speech-stress, which needs no scholarship to perceive, had nothing comparably complex to offer. He would be aware too, through his contact with Continental scholars such as Ramus and Lipsius, that Latin poetry had in its own time probably been read in a way that made quantity more than purely theoretical; and his interest was caught by the implications for English verse of adopting a consistent convention for syllabic quantities, whereby also a basis for alliance with music is provided.

This last consideration, the possibilities for the matching of words and music in song, seems to have come foremost for Sidney. It predominates in his prose references to measured verse; and the eclogues in elegiac, sapphic, hexameter, anacreontic, phalaecian, and asclepiadic verse written for *Arcadia* are without exception presented as songs.[26] At the close of the first eclogues, '*Dorus* . . . sange wth a sorowyng voyce, these *Elegian* verses'; Cleophila 'tooke out of his hande the Lute, and . . . sange these Sapphistes'; then Dorus 'began this provoking songe, in Exameter verse, unto her'.[27] At this point two early manuscripts make explicit the aptness of such measures for musical setting, for Dicus and Lalus argue the respective merits of measured and rhymed verse:

Dicus said that since verses had ther chefe ornament, if not eand, in musike, those which were just appropriated to musicke did best obtaine ther ende, or at lest were the most adorned; but those must needes most agree with musicke, since musike standing principally upon the sound and the quantitie, to answere the sound they brought wordes, and to answer the quantity they brought measure. So that for every sem[i]brefe or minam, it had his silable matched unto it with a long foote or a short foote, whereon they drew on

---

[26] Ringler, *Poems*, pp. xl and 493, observes that such metres served, in the original *Arcadia*, to distinguish princely sojourners from rustic inhabitants; hence in giving the uncouth Dametas a hexameter line for inscription on his *impresa*

Miso mine owne pigsnie, thou shalt heere news o' Dametas

when revising the romance Sidney perhaps wittily expresses disenchantment with quantitative measures.

[27] *Works*, iv. 75-7.

certaine names (as dactylus, spondeus, trocheas, etc.), and without wresting the word did as it were kindly accompanie the time, so that eyther by [the] tune a poet should strayght know how every word should be measured unto it, or by the verse as soone find out the full quantity of the musike.[28]

Lalus replied, defending rhyme and affirming the supremacy of words over music. The echo of their debate can be heard in *The Defence of Poesie*:

Now of versefying, there are two sorts, the one auncient, the other moderne. The auncient marked the quantitie of each sillable and according to that, framed his verse: The moderne, observing onely number, with some regard of the accent; the chiefe life of it, standeth in that like sounding of the words, which we call Rime. Whether of these be the more excellent, wold bear many speeches, the ancient no doubt more fit for Musick, both words and time observing quantitie, and more fit, lively to expresse divers passions by the low or loftie sound of the well-wayed sillable. The latter likewise with his rime striketh a certaine Musicke to the eare: and in fine, since it dooth delight, though by another way, it obtaineth the same purpose, there being in either sweetnesse, and wanting in neither, majestie. Truly the English, before any Vulgare language, I know is fit for both sorts . . .[29]

Fit for music the ancient sort of versifying might be, but if Sidney hoped that some of his own verse would be matched with measured music, he was to be disappointed. In France, such views were being not only propounded but embodied: Jean-Antoine de Baïf, a member of the Pléiade, had already introduced classical prosody into French verse, linked with an attempt to establish a system of orthography indicating syllabic length by signs. The purpose of this double innovation was to achieve the closer alliance of French music and lyric poetry, and Baïf worked in constant collaboration with a musician, writing his *vers mesurés* to be set by Thibault de Courville. One wishes vainly that Sidney had done the same, especially that his path in life, and its span, had made possible a partnership with Byrd. The association of these two is not random: Byrd's settings of two songs from *Astrophil and Stella* were the closest in time to Sidney's lifetime, and his 1588 book of songs contained not only one of these, of 'O you that heere this voice', the earliest printing of a whole poem known to be Sidney's, but also two funeral songs for him.[30] It has

<hr>

[28] Quoted from Ringler, *Poems*, pp. 389–90, who edits the passage from MSS Je and Qu.

[29] *Works*, iii. 44.

[30] *Psalmes, Sonets, & songs of sadnes and pietie*, nos. 16, 34, 35; see *EM* 14.

been suggested that these elegies may have been written by Thomas Watson,[31] who refers to Sidney's death in three of the texts he wrote for his *Italian Madrigalls Englished*. Certainly there is evidence of quantitative skill in the funeral song, 'Come to me, grief, for ever': like Sidney's poem 'When to my deadlie pleasure', which it is clearly designed to bring to mind, it is in Aristophanean (or first Pherecratean) metre, — ∪ ∪ — ∪ — —, with some use of permitted variants, such as — — — ∪ ∪ — —, (second) Pherecratean.[32] The fourth stanza, for instance, runs:

> Sidney, the hope of land strange,
> Sidney, the flower of England,
> Sidney, the spirit heroic,
> Sidney is dead, O dead, dead.

Byrd picked up the cue in his setting: as Kerman remarks,

It is possible that Byrd wrote it in a style that he knew Sidney would have appreciated; in the melody a uniform metrical pattern is applied to each line, rather in the style of the French *musique mesurée*:

[Ex. 8]

and he notes

Another song in this set, 'Constant Penelope', no. 23 is in fact in strict *musique mesurée* as far as the 'first singing part' is concerned. An English hexameter translation from Ovid (by Watson ?), its quantities are rendered literally by Byrd with half- and quarter-notes. We must associate this musical idea with Byrd's literary acquaintances. Sidney and Watson were surely well acquainted with Baïf's classicizing musical experiments and probably regarded them with sympathy.[33]

The qualifying 'surely' is needed, for evidence of direct contact between Sidney and Baïf's *Académie de Poésie et de Musique* is lacking, but there are indirect links: both Sidney and Baïf knew the

[31] By Kerman, *The Elizabethan Madrigal*, p. 10.

[32] Aristophanean and Pherecratean, both Aeolic metres, were often used in later classical poetry for lyrics of a sombre or pathetic nature; if the author was aware of this, he may have felt his pattern to be intrinsically appropriate for an elegy, as well as a tribute to Sidney's use. (I am indebted to Profesor E. K. Borthwick for helpful comment on Greek lyric metres.)

[33] *The Elizabethan Madrigal*, p. 113.

neo-Latin poet Daniel Rogers, and in Heidelberg Sidney had met the German court poet Melissus (Paul Schede), who knew of the French poets' writings and theories, and they kept up a correspondence for some years.[34]

Baïf and his associates had more in mind than the mechanical matching of long and short syllables in minims and crotchets; they were interested in exploring affective aspects of the alliance of music and poetry, and recovering the powers attributed to them in ancient belief and legend, but it is doubtful if such concepts were grasped as the style of their experiments became known in England. Seen as a mere method for partnering words and music, *musique mesurée* had little to offer composers to compare with the madrigal's scope for technique, and English composers were not drawn to accept it.

Byrd was as able to practise the one style as the other, matching a piece of hexameter verse in the French manner in his 1588 song-book, whilst both Yonge the same year, and Watson two years later, on the title-pages of their madrigal collections drew attention to contributions from him. For the latter he 'composed after the Italian vayne, at the request of the sayd Thomas Watson' two settings of a lyric probably by Watson, 'This sweet and merry moneth of May', for six voices and for four. The six-part setting shows him using the madrigal's illustrative technique with zest, playing on words such as 'merry' and 'wanton', enacting 'sing' and 'play', punning upon the 'joyful time' with a shift from triple to duple measure, and introducing voices in turn at 'I choose' and in greeting to 'Eliza' before they combine to begin their address to the Queen.[35]

Byrd's own inclination however, was towards neither madrigal nor *musique mesurée*: the native consort song was his chosen kind, with its strophic setting of lyrics consisting of two or more stanzas. He absorbed from the madrigal what he could turn to the purpose of his own style of song, and he was willing to make provision for the new preference for several voices singing without viols, but he

[34] Much is now known about the many contacts between French and English men of letters made during their travels, stays at embassies abroad, and meetings with foreign ambassadors in England; from his first tour abroad, Sidney had contacts with what J. A. van Dorsten terms 'the great yet intimate world of continental humanism'. See his illuminating study, *Poets, Patrons, and Professors* (Leiden, 1962).

[35] *Italian Madrigalls Englished*, no. xxviii. This madrigal is appended to Byrd's 1611 book in *The Collected Works of William Byrd*, ed. Fellowes, rev. Dart and Brett, vol. 14, and is in *The Byrd Edition*, ed. Brett, vol. 16. The four-part setting is in *The Collected Works*, vol. 14, and *EM* 16.

eschewed some features of madrigal style. When he arranged the songs of his first book, originally written for solo voice and viols, to be sung by five voices, he ensured that the words should still be intelligibly heard by maintaining the clarity of the 'first singing part' while admitting some repetition of phrases in other voices. Many of the songs in his later sets were expressly written for several voices, and there is contrapuntal play between them, but the madrigal's point-by-point word-painting and its tossing of phrases to and fro are absent from his polyphony. Byrd's aim was music 'framed to the life of the words', as his 1611 title-page put it. That life he considered to inhere more in sense and mood than in shape: he did not feel bound to preserve the poem's original proportions if changing them produced better balance: when setting a sonnet of English pattern, for instance, he repeats the final couplet, both words and music, so giving the sestet an eight-line length in performance. He does this with 'As I beheld, I saw a herdman wild', and also repeats the last line of the octet, slightly changing the music in response to the words

> And weeping sore these woeful words he said:

which lead into the shepherd's complaint.[36] By means of such modifications of its structure, Byrd came to musical terms with the sonnet, a form almost wholly shunned by English composers in its own heyday: his three song-books contain eight sonnets, whereas no Italianate English composer set more than one. But for most of his secular songs he chose lyrics of several stanzas, often six-lined.

In his choice and sources of texts Byrd ranged widely: his first book contains psalm-settings and devotional songs for domestic use, serious songs with moral texts, the two funeral songs for Sidney, and sixteen 'Sonnets and Pastorals'. His later books likewise contain pieces both sacred and secular, including moral verses from the earliest English emblem-book, Geoffrey Whitney's *A Choice of Emblemes*, 1586. His approach to song-writing was basically serious; he preferred to apply his art to verse of some worth, and sometimes, as with Whitney, the worth is more moral than poetic. But for his secular songs he drew, amongst others, not only on Sidney but on Sidney's friend Edward Dyer, the Earl of Oxford, and Ralegh.

---

[36] *Psalmes, Sonets, & songs of sadnes and pietie*, no. 20. Commented on by H. K. Andrews, *The Technique of Byrd's Vocal Polyphony* (1966), p. 265. On Byrd's styles of song, and choice of texts, see this book, Kerman, *The Elizabethan Madrigal*, pp. 101–8, and Brett's editorial prefaces.

A similarly serious literary taste is shown by other composers who, like Byrd, remained basically unmadrigalian in style. Richard Alison's texts differ widely in quality; in *An Howres Recreation in Musicke*, 1606, he includes a moralizing alliterative piece from *A gorgious Gallery, of gallant Inuentions*, 'O heavy heart whose harms are hid', and two sententious sixains from *The Paradyse of daynty deuises*, but also Psalm 134, two stanzas of Chidiock Tichborne's 'My prime of youth is but a frost of cares', and three fine lyrics by Campion. Richard Carlton expresses a defiant conservatism both in the prefatory matter to his *Madrigals To Fiue voyces*, of 1601, and through the sentiment of his choice of opening verse. In 'A Preface to the skillful Musitian' he writes rather querulously,

I have laboured somewhat to imitate the *Italian*, they being in these dayes (with the most) in high respect, yet may I not nor cannot forget that I am an English man

and his first text is this:

> The love of change hath changed the world throughout;
>   And what is counted good but that is strange?
> New things wax old, old new, all turns about,
>   And all things change except the love of change.
> Yet find I not that love of change in me,
> But as I am so will I always be.[37]

His collection of verse is sombre, severe, and undistinguished except for four stanzas from *The Faerie Queene*.

Only two other composers of the period set verse by Spenser; one was a madrigalist in the Italian style, George Kirbye, whose *The first set of English Madrigalls*, 1597, is filled with laments for unrequited love, but contains two stanzas from Colin's elegy for Dido in the November eclogue of *The Shepheards Calender* (the first and thirteenth) that chime well with his mournful strain. The other, Orlando Gibbons, was the only outstanding composer to follow Byrd in the English tradition of abstract, non-pictorial polyphony. He composed many anthems and instrumental pieces, but only one book of secular compositions, *The First Set of Madrigals And Mottets of 5. Parts*, 1612. Its texts include one stanza from *The Faerie Queene*

---

[37] *A Poetical Rapsody* prints this anonymous poem of six stanzas, of which this is the first. A setting of two stanzas for solo voice and bass accompaniment, by Robert Jones, survives in manuscript in the Folger Shakespeare Library; see *English Madrigal Verse*, ed. cit., p. 686.

(III. i. 49), which he divided and set in two sections, five lines and four; a poem on the theme of the quiet mind by Joshua Sylvester; a stanza of a poem that may be by Donne, 'Ah, dear heart, why do you rise?';[38] and that favourite for copying into commonplace-books, most commonly ascribed to Ralegh, 'What is our life? a play of passion'. The second text in the book makes explicit the preference for serious themes; it consists of one stanza of a poem attributed to Breton:

> O that the learned poets of this time,
> > Who in a love-sick line so well can speak,
> Would not consume good wit in hateful rhyme,
> > But with deep care some better subject find.
> For if their music please in earthly things,
> How would it sound if strung with heavenly strings?[39]

It may be that the choice of poems is not the composer's, but made by Sir Christopher Hatton for him, for Gibbons says in dedicating these compositions to Hatton, 'that language they speake, you prouided them'; Hatton perhaps knew they would accord with the composer's taste. Gibbons is far from the madrigalists in mood and manner; he sets one poem that in form is a madrigal stanza, but divides it into two sections and does not, here or elsewhere, adopt madrigalian style. The first and best-known song in his book, 'The silver swan, who living had no note', draws its plangency from a sustained melodic movement that has no kinship with the madrigal's short vocal interchanges.

These composers, notably Byrd and Gibbons, kept the English tradition of polyphonic song alive whilst the madrigal reached the crest of its wave, and their songs found an eager public. The same desire for more songs for domestic and friendly performing that led Yonge and Watson to gather and publish the newly available Italian kind kept others employed in copying consort and part-songs. Many of the songs in Byrd's published sets survive also anonymously in manuscript part-books which preserve their consort song form, underlaying the words to the solo voice part, and study of these and related manuscripts has led Brett and Dart to posit 'the existence of a small but very active group of professional copyists working in

[38] Dowland's setting, in *A Pilgrimes Solace*, 1612, gives two stanzas, and begins 'Sweet stay a while; why will you rise?' See below, pp. 121–2 and 148.

[39] Dowland set three stanzas of this poem, which begins 'From silent night, true register of moans', also in *A Pilgrimes Solace*.

London, to meet a considerable demand for part-books of this rather
specialized kind' between at least about 1590 and 1615.[40] As they
observe, these manuscripts 'provide important evidence that, at least
in some circles of music lovers, songs were still performed in this
manner well into the seventeenth century, despite the almost over-
whelming popularity of the English madrigal and lute-song'.

New styles came in, the older lived on while the two most famous
kinds spread and flourished together, sharing the same time-span.
The year of Byrd's and of Yonge's first publications, 1588, was the
year of two notable graduations too: Thomas Morley and John
Dowland both gained their Mus. Bac. degrees at Oxford, the one to
become the leading exponent of the madrigal and other Italian forms,
the other the most outstanding composer of lute-songs. The two
kinds are distinct, but several composers practised both, although
with a predilection for one or the other. Morley, a pupil of Byrd,
turned almost wholly to the Italian forms, but published a lute part
with his canzonets of 1597 'for one to sing and play alone when your
Lordship would retire yourself and be more private', as he wrote in
dedicating them to Sir George Carey; and later he published a book
of ayres. Robert Jones published five books of lute-songs, but also
one book of madrigals 'for Viols and Voices, or for Voices alone; or
as you please'. A few composers published mixed collections; two
such are Michael Cavendish's *14. Ayres in Tabletorie to the Lute
expressed with two voyces and the base Violl or the voice & Lute only.
6. more to 4. voyces and in Tabletorie. And 8. Madrigalles to 5. voyces,*
1598, and Thomas Greaves's *Songes of sundrie kindes: First, Aires To
be Svng To the Lute, and Base Violl. Next, Songes of sadnesse, for the
Viols and Voyce. Lastly, Madrigalles, for fiue voyces,* 1604.

The opportunity for singing and playing alone that Morley wrote
of to Sir George Carey was one of the distinctive attractions the lute-
song offered. Making music with others is one kind of pleasure;
making music that is artistically satisfying and complete alone is
another, and the lute-song, unlike the madrigal, could provide both.
In place of the madrigal's polyphony, in which each voice has its own
melodic line, it was conceived around one primary melody, with the
other part or parts providing essentially harmonic support. It was

---

[40] One set of such books, with the cantus missing, is now in Harvard College
Library, MS Mus. 30, and two are in the British Library, Egerton MSS 2009–12, and
Add. MSS 29401–5. See P. Brett and T. Dart, 'Songs by William Byrd in Manuscripts at
Harvard', *Harvard Library Bulletin*, 14 (1960), 343–65.

usually as solo song that the major lutenist composers first framed their ayres: the songs in Campion's and Rosseter's *A Booke of Ayres* are for solo voice, so are those of Campion's third and fourth books, and those of his first and second books too 'were for the most part framed at first for one voyce with the Lute, or Violl', and other parts were supplied, not primarily because the composer was thinking in terms of part-song, but because, as he said in his address to the reader,

When any shall sing a Treble to an Instrument, the standers by will be offring at an inward part out of their owne nature; and, true or false, out it must, though to the peruerting of the whole harmonie.

Dowland seems usually to have composed his ayres for solo voice and lute first, and then made part-songs of most, with inner parts that are sometimes instrumental rather than vocal in texture; he published some for one voice and instruments only. Both of Corkine's books of ayres are for one voice, except for one duet; so are two of Jones's books (the second and the last), Morley's book, and, with a few exceptions, the songs in Danyel's and Ferrabosco's books. Some composers, on the other hand, seem to have made at least some of their ayres expressly as part-songs; some present them for performing in either way, or group their songs according to the number of vocal parts.

There is diversity in the prescriptions or suggestions for accompanying instruments too. By far the most usual provision is for lute and bass viol, or lute and lyra viol, a small bass viol played from tablature like the lute, not from staff notation like other viols. The orpharion, a kind of cittern, is often mentioned as an alternative to the lute; or the bass viol could be used alone, without the lute.[41] But essentially and sufficiently, the Elizabethan ayre was for voice and lute; although delicate and evanescent in its sound, the lute gives enough support for a single voice, and can provide a satisfying musical texture. It was music to make by oneself, or with one companion or more.

For a composer, as for a performer, both lute-song and madrigal had their attractions; for a poet, the choice between them was clear. The English madrigal had little to offer a poet; for a hearer it was more likely to destroy than enhance the verse it set, for as it picked up

---

[41] Corkine set most of the songs in his second book to be sung to the bass viol alone, and Tobias Hume proclaimed its merits; a generation later, songs were usually written for voice and bass viol.

a phrase here, another there, to adorn with musical detail, the words were tossed in the air like so many rose-petals; and what had become of the rose? The high regard the Italian composers had for their texts was lacking,[42] and the word-painting taught by Morley fostered fragmentation. A sensitive composer could render multiple nuances of the verbal phrase rhythms in the several voices, and a singer could delight in such niceties, but even a perceptive listener would catch only fractions of this rich particularity. Words fell on the hearer's ear with moment-by-moment delight, but the intricate web of counterpoint obscured the poem's shape and scale. The ayre, on the other hand, respected a lyric's shape, setting it so that the words could be intelligibly heard in music made to match the verse structure. Like the consort song, it gave verse strophic setting, which better serves lyrics of several stanzas than the madrigal's method of throughsetting; the vivid embodiment of a single word or phrase may have to be forgone, but mood and meaning can be interpreted by other means, and some composers were ready to explore alternatives to the madrigal's musical literalism and complexity. In *A Booke of Ayres*, 1601, the joint venture of Rosseter and Campion comprising twentyone songs by each of them, the preface contains this manifesto against excessive pictorialism:

But there are some, who to appeare the more deepe, and singular in their iudgement, will admit no Musicke but that which is long, intricate, bated with fuge, chaind with sincopation, and where the nature of euerie word is precisely exprest in the Note, like the old exploided action in Comedies, when if they did pronounce *Memeni*, they would point to the hinder part of their heads, if *Video*, put their finger in their eye. But such childish obseruing of words is altogether ridiculous, and we ought to maintaine as well in Notes, as in action a manly cariage, gracing no word, but that which is eminent, and emphaticall.

The chief problem arising from the rejection of literal illustration as a principle for setting was what should replace it: how words 'eminent, and emphaticall' were to be graced. One line to explore further was the systematic relation of length and shortness of note values to syllabic values; but this proved to be an approach that bristled with ambiguities. Morley himself had not overlooked the matter of length: in his treatise he warned:

---

[42] On the reversal of relationship between words and music as the madrigal was introduced in England, see above, pp. 42–5.

We must also have a care so to apply the notes to the words as in singing there be no barbarism committed; that is that we cause no syllable which is by nature short be expressed by many notes or one long note, nor no long syllables be expressed with a short note.[43]

Campion too noted:

In joyning of words to harmony there is nothing more offensive to the eare then to place a long sillable with a short note, or a short sillable with a long note, though in the last the vowell often beares it out.[44]

The statements seem simple, but the implications are complex, for the terms are those of quantitative verse: Campion's remark indeed comes from his *Observations in the Art of English Poesie*, in which he tried to establish by exposition and example the feasibility of adapting some classical metres to English verse. The treatise, published in 1602 (but entered in the Stationers' Register eleven years earlier), failed to do much for its cause, but the thinking and experimenting that went into it may have done much both to clarify his understanding of the nature of English verse, and to sharpen his perception of a natural and fruitful basis for the matching of English verse and music in strophic song.

Campion's approach to the naturalization of quantitative prosody was a practical and sensitive one. He was intuitively aware that principles of accentuation, as yet not clearly identified and defined by Elizabethan poets or theorists, govern the spoken English language and therefore its native verse, and he did not wish to oppose or overlay them; his aim was to increase the variety of metres available for English verse by drawing upon classical measures, but only those 'which by my long observation I have found agreeable with the nature of our sillables'.[45] In his last chapter, on quantity, before setting out his rules, he declares:

But above all the accent of our words is diligently to be observ'd, for chiefly by the accent in any language the true value of the sillables is to be measured.

He continues:

Neither can I remember any impediment except position that can alter the accent of any sillable in our English verse. For though we accent the second

[43] Ed. cit., p. 291.
[44] *The Works of Thomas Campion*, ed. W. R. Davis (1969), p. 293. Verse and prose quotations of Campion follow this edition; lyrics set by other lutenist composers are quoted as in Edward Doughtie, *Lyrics from English Airs 1596–1622* (Cambridge, Mass., 1970).   [45] *Works*, p. 312.

of *Trumpington* short, yet is it naturally long, and so of necessity must be held of every composer. Wherefore the first rule that is to be observed is the nature of the accent, which we must ever follow.[46]

This is not confusion, but exposition: word-accent is of primary importance in English verse, but in the making of 'artificial' quantitative verse in English, the classical rules for syllabic length must also be borne in mind.[47] His enterprise was to select only those classical metres in which it was possible to bring the two kinds of requirement into concordance, and to compose examples that would sound acceptably English to the ear whilst presenting a classical quantitative pattern to the mind.

It was a move further in the same direction that Sidney had taken, and Campion probably had Sidney's practice in this kind of verse, and his rules, in mind. Part of the attraction of writing quantitative verse for Sidney lay in the artifice it required, and appreciation of the artifice was part of the pleasure it was designed to give. If the sound of the verse was to give pleasure too, it must be amenable to reading with normal accentuation, and this in some degree he achieved by such means as matching word-accent to ictus. Occasionally he went further and held two systems in poise, in poems that answer both to rules of quantity and to the dictates of natural speech-stress, notably in 'My muse what ails this ardour' and 'O my thoughtes' sweete foode, my my onely owner', but he knew this was not part, so to speak, of the quantitative game. (Still less was it playing the game to keep no rules of quantity at all but to borrow a classical pattern with stress taking the place of quantity; he did this in 'Get hence foule Griefe, the canker of the minde', which is after the sapphic pattern.)

With Campion the weighting of the attempt was changed; he was still further than Sidney from the rigorous classicizing intentions of Drant or Stanyhurst, and aimed at verse that could hold its own in the terms of the native accentual tradition, but was more subtle and various because of its quantitative dimension. The examples he gave to support his *Observations* show the high degree of his success, especially two of those illustrating the eighth chapter, 'Just beguiler' and the more famous 'Rose-cheekt *Lawra*, come'. He begins the chapter by describing the prosodic elements to be used in making

---

[46] *Works*, p. 313.

[47] Campion's use of the word 'accent' is multiplex here, and with 'Trumpington ' (as with 'carpenter' in the Spenser–Harvey letters) the matter of the penultimate rule, clashing here with the rule of position, is raised; but the main point stands.

'The English *Sapphick*', and gives a poetic example, and then proceeds to describe dimeter,

whose first foote may either be a *Sponde* or a *Trochy*. The two verses following ['verse' = line] are both of them *Trochaical*, and consist of foure feete, the first of either of them being a *Spondee* or *Trochy*, the other three only Trochyes. The fourth and last verse is made of two *Trochyes*. The number is voluble, and fit to expresse any amorous conceit.

THE EXAMPLE

Rose-cheekt *Lawra*, come,
Sing thou smoothly with thy beawties
Silent musick, either other
Sweetely gracing.
Lovely formes do flowe
From concent devinely framed;
Heav'n is musick, and thy beawties
Birth is heavenly.
These dull notes we sing
Discords neede for helps to grace them;
Only beawty purely loving
Knowes no discord:
But still mooves delight,
Like cleare springs renu'd by flowing,
Ever perfect, ever in them—
selves eternall.

The third kind begins as the second kind ended, with a verse consisting of two *Trochy* feete, and then as the second kind had in the middle two *Trochaick* verses of foure feete, so this hath three of the same nature, and ends in a *Dimeter* as the second began. The *Dimeter* may allow in the first place a *Trochy* or a *Spondee*, but no *Iambick*.

THE EXAMPLE

Just beguiler,
Kindest love, yet only chastest,
Royall in thy smooth denyals,
Frowning or demurely smiling,
Still my pure delight.

Let me view thee
With thoughts and with eyes affected,
And if then the flames do murmur,
Quench them with thy vertue, charme them
With thy stormy browes.

> Heav'n so cheerefull
> Laughs not ever, hory winter
> Knowes his season, even the freshest
> Sommer mornes from angry thunder
> Jet not still secure.[48]

Both poems read well as accentual verse as well as embodying the quantitative patterns they are made to exemplify; but the two systems do not merely function as separate or superimposed levels: they interweave like warp and woof to produce a new and exquisite texture, with the strength of speech-stress refined by heightened syllabic awareness.

This quality is one of the permanent gains to English poetry of the excursion into classical prosody; Sidney, Spenser, and Campion all returned to the writing of verse in the native accentual manner, but returned enriched by what they had learnt of the artful disposition of syllables, and this enrichment made part of the beauty of late Elizabethan verse.

There was gain too in another direction, through the much more limited trial, and the rejection, of quantitative song. 'Just beguiler' and 'Rose-cheekt *Lawra*, come' are from the chapter in which Campion dealt with 'such verses as are fit for *Ditties* or *Odes*, which we may call *Lyricall*, because they are apt to be soong to an instrument, if they were adorn'd with convenient notes'.[49] He seems not to have set the examples made for his treatise, but his last song in *A Booke of Ayres* is in sapphic verse, the first kind he proposed as fit for song. It begins

> Come, let us sound with melody the praises
> Of the kings king, th'omnipotent creator,
> Author of number, that hath all the world in
> Harmonie framed.

The metre is handled with some freedom, but variations of foot are within the permitted range. To set it he used the strict form of *musique mesurée*, allowing himself only two lengths of note, except for the last one. Ex. 9 gives the whole song, from the first edition. (The bass part is given above the voice part and tablature, facing the other way, enabling the bass viol player to use the same book.) The result, as he must have realized, was musically wanting—wanting in

---

[48] *Works*, pp. 310–11.   [49] *Works*, p. 309.

XXI.

Come let vs found with melody the praises of the kings king, Th'omni-

potent cre-a-tor, Author of number, that hath all the world in harmonie framed.

Heau'n is his throne perpetually shining,
His deuine power and glorie thence he thunders,
One in all, and all still in one abiding,
  Both Father, and Sonne.

O sacred sprite inuisible, eternall,
Eu'ry where, yet vnlimited, that all things
Canst in one moment penetrate, reuiue me
  O holy Spirit.

Rescue, O rescue me from earthly darknes,
Banish hence all these elementall obiects,

Guide my soule, that thirsts, to the liuely Fountaine
  Of thy deuinenes.

Cleanse my soule, O God, thy bespotted Image,
Altered with sinne, so that heau'nly purenes
Cannot acknowledge me but in thy mercies
  O Father of grace.

But when once thy beames do remoue my darknes,
O then I'le shine forth as an Angell of light,
And record with more than an earthly voice thy
  Infinite honours.

FINIS.

rhythmic variety, in fluency, and in sense of direction. And far from enhancing the verse, it impoverished it, for Campion's poem combined with its quantitative pattern the accentual rhythm that characterized Horace's use of sapphic, and this was annulled by the purely quantitative setting. The address to the reader in this song-book states:

The Lyricke Poets among the Greekes and Latines were first inventers of Ayres, tying themselues strictly to the number and value of their sillables, of which sort, you shall find here onely one song in Saphicke verse; the rest are after the fascion of the time, ear-pleasing rimes without Arte.

But when Campion published his *Two Bookes of Ayres* about 1613, in his address to the reader he said,

But some there are who admit onely *French* or *Italian* Ayres, as if every Country had not his proper Ayre, which the people thereof naturally usurpe in their Musicke.

He had discovered, by experiment both as poet and composer, that strict tying to the length of syllables ran counter to the nature of the 'proper Ayre' born of the English language. He had tied himself strictly to certain carefully selected quantitative verse patterns, and used them with accentual subtlety and success; but when he tied himself strictly in length of notes too, the method proved both poetically and musically stultifying. Moreover, it had nothing to offer in place of the madrigal's illustration; what was needed was a way of setting that had selectivity, 'gracing no word, but that which is eminent, and emphaticall', as Rosseter's preface said. In music, length confers emphasis, and in measured music, every long syllable is given this emphasis. Even if composers had adapted the system, and underlined not syllabic length but syllabic accentual stress, the 'English ayre' would not have been heard, for only the metre would have been matched, and not every syllable that bears metrical ictus is otherwise 'eminent or emphaticall'. Measured music could not be 'framed to the life of the words' of English verse, for part of that life inheres in the interplay between metre, the basic accentual pattern that underlies a poem, and rhythm, which is made up of the varying sequences of emphatic stress that the sense suggests; and this interplay is significantly felt not in syllables nor in words alone, but in phrases.

The recognition of this was hard for Elizabethans to formulate, for terms such as 'rhythm' did not bear single and definite meanings, but many poets and theorists show awareness of it, and that Sidney, Spenser, and Campion sensed it is clear. Campion's practice as a maker of ayres, in both poems and settings, is based upon phrase rhythms; and not only Campion's: the lively and sensitive embodiment of verbal phrase rhythms is one of the most consummate achievements of the English ayre.

The madrigal too had shaped its melodic and rhythmic phrasing to the length and rhythms of verbal phrases, but its music was heard only once, matching one set of words. The challenge to both poet and composer is far greater in strophic setting, where the same music must serve for every stanza. From a purely poetic point of view, there is no structural or aesthetic reason why the rhythms arising from words and phrases within the time-lengths of line and stanza should recur in identical position in succeeding stanzas; there may be good reason to change or contrast them, as in this anonymous lyric in *A Poetical Rapsody*, where in the first four lines the bold breaking of the disyllabic rising-stress pattern underlying the poem emphasizes the strain on the lover's endurance:

> When will the fountaine of my Teares be drie?
> When will my sighes be spent?
> When will Desire agree to let me die?
> When will thy hart relent?
> It is not for my life I pleade,
> Since death the way to rest doth leade,
> But stay for thy consent,
> Lest thou be discontent.
>
> For if my selfe without thy leaue I kill,
> My Ghost will neuer rest:
> So hath it sworne to worke thine only will,
> And holds that euer best.
> For since it only liues by thee,
> Good reason thou the ruler bee:
> Then giue me leaue to die,
> And shew thy powre thereby.

But how is a composer to fit both stanzas in strophic setting? If he reproduces the forceful falling rhythms of the opening lines, there will be clashes between musical and verbal rhythm when the corresponding lines of the second stanza are sung. The only composer who chose to set this lyric was Robert Jones, in his *Vltimum Vale*, 1605, and he rose well to the challenge. The openings of the second and fourth lines are the chief obstacles to devising a setting to fit both stanzas well, and his solution was to give notes of equal length to the first and second syllables and avoid the rhythmic stolidity this might produce by a prefatory rest:

Ex. 10

stanza 1, line 2: When will   my sighs be   spent
and line 4:   When will   thy heart re - lent

stanza 2, line 2: My   Ghost will neu - er   rest
and line 4:   And   holdes it   eu - er   best

Only the 'And' is unduly stressed.

Far more felicitous matching of words and music is possible when the poet has framed his verses with the composer's task in mind, holding himself free to use what rhythmical patterns he chooses for the first stanza, but bound in succeeding stanzas to repeat them nearly enough for one setting to give just accentuation to all; and composers of ayres in search of texts looked for lyrics that showed some degree of such correspondence. When poet and composer are one, the opportunities for the complementing of words and music in strophic song are at their greatest; and Campion indeed excels all other lutenist composers in the perfect matching of words and music. Dowland and Danyel excelled him in purely musical art, but in the composite art of the ayre the balance and blend Campion achieves is unique. The poems of his song-books were made expressly for setting and singing, and, more than the poems of any other Elizabethan writer, they reward being sung or listened to rather than merely read. This is not to say that they cannot stand alone as poems, but that their particular excellencies can most fully be appreciated in their own designed context and mode, and the purposes, as well as the effects, of their subtleties of rhythm be enjoyed.[50] If the lyrics of his

50 The combining of 'genuine complexity with genuine simplicity' which characterizes Campion's art of song is spelled out by Stephen Ratcliffe, *Campion: 'On Song'*
(Boston, London and Henley, 1981); exhaustive analysis of 'Now winter nights
enlarge' occupies four chapters.

songs in *A Booke of Ayres* are described in terms of metrical patterns, nine of the twenty-one prove to be iambic in movement and three trochaic (using the classical terms but to denote patterns of accentual stress not length); but for several this kind of classification breaks down, and we find that a description adequate and relevant to the poems must be in terms of phrase rhythms rather than metrical feet. Beneath the apparently spontaneous flow of varying rhythms lies consummate control of rhythmical phrasing, and it is this that primarily deserves responsive attention. In the tenth song, for instance, the accentual patterns, phrasing, and placing of pauses in the first stanza are all matched in the second:

> Fóllow your Saínt,|fóllow with accents sweét,
> Haste you, sad noátes,|fáll at her flýing feéte;
> Thére, wrapt in cloúd of sórrowe,|pítie móve,
> And téll the rávisher of my soúle|I pérish for her lóve.
> But if she scórns my néver-ceásing paíne,
> Then búrst with sighing in her síght,|and nére retúrne agaíne.
>
> Áll that I soóng|still to her práise did ténd,
> Stíll she was first,|stíll she my sóngs did énd.
> Yét she my lóve and Músicke|bóth doeth flíe,
> The Músicke that her Eccho is,|and beáuties símpathie;
> Then let my Noátes pursué her scórnfull flíght:
> It shall suffice that they were breáth'd,|and dyéd, for hér delíght.

The heavy stresses fall similarly throughout the two stanzas, except in the fourth lines, where the turbulent feeling in the first stanza and the wistfulness of the second are individually rendered. Major pauses are identically placed, even in their absence from the fifth lines. The contrast with such a lyric as 'When will the fountaine of my Teares be drie?' is marked. Campion's lyric is an invitation to music, for a setting framed in rhythm and melody to the phrasing of either stanza would clothe the other with equal grace. In his own setting (Ex. 11), the voice takes up the phrasing in fluent melodic curves.[51] The song is

Ex. 11

[51] For the whole song, see *ELS* 1st series, vol. 4.

hauntingly eloquent, and Campion, no doubt recognizing himself its
success, with craftsman's economy turned both verbal rhythms and
music to further use. In his last book of ayres, of about sixteen years
later, the languishing opening rhythms reappear:

> Love me or not, love her I must or dye;
> Leave me or not, follow her needs must I.

and they are set to the same 'dying fall'. All three of the poem's
stanzas begin with phrases and pauses moulded and placed exactly as
in the earlier lyric, so the same music, with its slight descending
sequences, matches them well. Then the two songs diverge, and the
second half of the later song's quatrains is given its own setting.[52]

Another fine lyric in *A Booke of Ayres* that like 'Follow your Saint'
cannot appropriately be assessed in terms of normal scansion is
'Followe thy faire sunne, unhappy shaddowe'; one might describe its
quatrains as comprising one trochaic line followed by three iambic
ones, in the scheme 10*a*, 6*b*, 6*b*, 11*a*, but the impetus behind them is
not metrical but vocal, even melodic, as if music were already framing
itself as Campion wrote. It is set for the most part with striking
felicity, the melodic phrasing flowing with that of the words. In its
turn, the melody, it seems, drew Campion to write further words,
translating its mood into loftier terms: his next collection of songs
contains a hymn to the same music:[53]

> Seeke the Lord, and in his wayes persever;
> O faint not, but as Eagles flye,
> For his steepe hill is high;
> Then, striving, gaine the top, and triumph ever.

The provision of eight syllables in the second line of each stanza here
removes the need to repeat a phrase, which flawed the other partnership, and the felicities of this one are far more striking, especially in
this first stanza, for the second line of the melody opens with long
descending notes, then gains impetus and leads into the steady ascent
of the third line, which is succeeded by a scramble of jerky upward
intervals to the triumphant height and length of the final phrase, in
vivid fulfilment of the words. Ex. 12 gives the whole song, from the
first edition. This use of pictorial illustration (here in mirror-image of

---

[52] See *ELS* 2nd series, vol. 11.
[53] The melody and bass are the same in both songs but the inner parts are different,
the later setting being sparer. See *ELS* 1st series, vol. 4, and 2nd series, vol. 1.

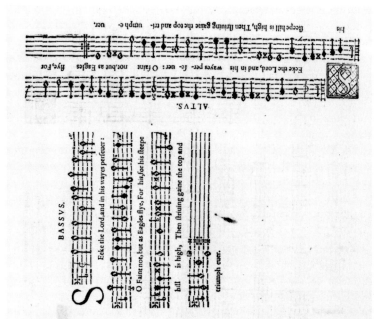

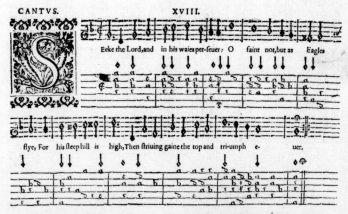

1 Seeke the Lord, and in his wayes perseuer:
   O faint not, but as Eagles flye,
   For his steepe hill is high;
   Then striuing gaine the top, and triumph euer.

2 When with glory there thy browes are crowned,
   New ioyes so shall abound in thee,
   Such sights thy soule shall see,
   That worldly thoughts shall by their beames be drowned.

3 Farewell World, thou masse of meere confusion,
   False light with many shadowes dimm'd,
   Old Witch with new foyles trimm'd,
   Thou deadly sleepe of soule, and charm'd illusion.

4 I the King will seeke of Kings adored,
   Spring of light, tree of grace and blisse,
   Whose fruit so fou'raigne is,
   That all who taste it are from death restored.

G

the usual procedure, the music apparently being made first, for the secular words) is such as Rosseter would accept, for it serves an interpretative, not merely descriptive purpose, and is selective in its gracing of words.

The same criterion, of serving to interpret the words, controls Campion's use of other musical resources, such as repetition. Dowland, in his later songs especially, was prepared to repeat words and phrases to the detriment of the verse structure for the sake of musical sequences or instrumental elaboration of a strand of melody; Campion rarely used repetition without expressive purpose. In 'Shall I come, sweet Love, to thee', in his third book of ayres, the slight repetition near the end gently mocks the lover's pleading, as long hours, long love, and cold nights in turn are lamented in the sly setting.[54] There are many instances of enhancing repetition in his songs: part of the charm of 'There is a Garden in her face', in the fourth book, arises from the contrast between the quiet grace of the opening lines of the melody and the gay street-call, 'Cherry ripe', that rings and echoes at its close. In 'Never weather-beaten Saile more willing bent to shore', in his first book of ayres, after the steadily moving melody that serves for each of the first two verse lines, and the sequential setting of the long third line, the music gives fervour to the last line's plea, 'O come quickly', by sequential rising repetitions.

A device favoured by some lutenist composers more for the scope it gives the accompaniment than for its value in interpreting the words is to give the voice a monotone chant and weave round it strands of instrumental melody. In the middle section of Dowland's 'Goe nightly cares, the enemy to rest', in *A Pilgrimes Solace*, for instance, it is clear that the composer's interest lies not with the voice, which merely gets on with the necessary task of uttering the words, but with the musical texture of lute, viol, and viola da gamba in counterpoint. Campion, on the contrary, is prepared at times to subdue the setting in order to give prominence to the words, as in 'Come, chearfull day, part of my life, to mee', in the first book, where the vocal line soars into relief against the drone-like accompaniment. If he holds the voice to a repeated note and restricted range, it is to serve the whole song's expressive purpose, as at the beginning of 'The Sypres curten of the night is spread', in *A Booke of Ayres* (Ex. 13). The throbbing monotony of the first phrase of the melody, the

---

[54] See below, pp. 109–11, and *ELS* 2nd series, vol. 10.

Ex. 13

VOICE

The cy - press cur - tain of the night is
The weak - er cares by sleep are con - quer -

LUTE

spread, And ov - er all a si - - lent dew is
- ed, But I a - lone with hi - - deous grief a -

cast.
- ghast,

The lute-part (a tone lower in the tablature) has been transposed to fit the vocal line (printed, as here, in G minor — to avoid the use of a remote key-signature); in Campion's time the song would have been heard in F minor.

momentary upsurge at the start of the second and its drooping close, embody the despair expressed in the words, and the accompaniment has enough rhythmic variety to be interesting but not distracting. The melody has essentially musical coherence and shapeliness, but its curves are implicit in the intonation of the speaking voice, and its rhythms accommodate all three stanzas; music is simply endowing the words with a fuller, more flowing eloquence than they attain alone. The acuteness of Campion's ear has led him to achieve a perfect matching of words and music, such as Baïf and de Courville were seeking, without imposing alien conventions on English verse, without restricting the rhythmical options of music. He has hit upon the 'proper Ayre' for English verse and music and bodied it forth by realizing the relationship that is its essence: the relationship between musical rhythm and verbal phrase rhythm.

The range and release afforded to both poets and composers by this basis of setting is in marked contrast to the limitations imposed by the binding of musical time to verse metre. The song from Campion's third book already mentioned makes the difference clear: here is the poem:

> Shall I come, sweet Love, to thee,
>   When the ev'ning beames are set?
> Shall I not excluded be?
>   Will you find no fained lett?
>   Let me not, for pitty, more,
>   Tell the long houres at your dore.
>
> Who can tell what theefe or foe,
>   In the covert of the night,
> For his prey, will worke my woe,
>   Or through wicked foule despight:
>   So may I dye unredrest,
>   Ere my long love be possest.
>
> But, to let such dangers passe,
>   Which a lovers thoughts disdaine,
> 'Tis enough in such a place
>   To attend loves joyes in vaine.
>   Doe not mocke me in thy bed,
>   While these cold nights freeze me dead.

In metrical terms, it is in accentual trochaics; and if it were set to music that modelled its note values on verse metre, the basic pattern would be

Ex. 14

The fifth line of the opening stanza would be well served; almost all
the rest would be falsified. For the poem asks to be rendered by the
rhythms of its phrases, and these set up a quite different pattern; and
the music responds to this pattern. Ex. 15 reproduces the song from
the first edition. As poet, Campion has evolved a pattern of rhythms
that carries a seemingly spontaneous sequence of questions and pleas,
and carries it right through the poem. To write lyrics in which phrase
rhythms recur only because they are slavishly close to the metre is
easy, and makes strophic setting simple, but dull; to write lyrics in
which they run against the metre without recurring is easy, but
obstructs strophic setting. To write lyrics in which phrase rhythms
seem to ride freely, and yet virtually recur in succeeding stanzas,
requires care and skill; and it makes possible strophic setting that
responds to the poem's rhythms with ease and success; and as
composer Campion achieved such setting.

The matching of musical and verbal phrase rhythms that characterizes the ayre proved a splendidly fruitful approach to English
song, because it made use both of the endlessly rich variety of
rhythms arising in verbal phrasing, and of the freedom of music to
express these rhythms with answering flexibility and flow. This kind
of alliance was not sustained for long; on the whole song-composers
of the middle decades of the seventeenth century took as their basis
for setting verse in strophic song the linking of musical stress to verse
metre. Elizabethan and Jacobean composers took the more richly
expressive way of partnering verse rhythms; and lyric poets were
prepared to take thought for the needs of strophic setting. Many
anonymous lyrics set by lutenist composers show fine rhythmical
power and strophic control, as in this one:

> Deare if you change ile neuer chuse againe,
> sweete if you shrinke Ile neuer thinke of loue,
> Fayre if you faile, ile iudge all beauty vaine,
> wise if to weake moe wits ile neuer proue.
> > Deare, sweete, faire, wise, change shrinke nor be not weake,
> > and on my faith, my faith shall neuer breake.

Shall I come sweet Loue to thee, When the eu'ning beames are set?
Shall I not ex- cluded be? Will you finde no fained lett? Let me not for pit- ty
more, Tell the long, long houres, tel the long houres at your dore.

BASSVS.

2 Who can tell what theefe or foe,
  In the couert of the night,
  For his prey will worke my woe;
  Or through wicked foule despight :
  So may I dye vnredrest,
  Ere my long loue be possest.

3 But to let such dangers passe,
  Which a louers thoughts disdaine :
  'Tis enough in such a place
  To attend loues ioyes in vaine.
  Doe not mocke me in thy bed,
  While these cold nights freeze me dead.

> Earth with her flowers shall sooner heau'n adorne,
> Heauen her bright stars through earths dim globe shall moue,
> Fire heate shall loose and frosts of flames be borne,
> Ayre made to shine as blacke as hell shall proue:
>> Earth, heauen, fire, ayre, the world transform'd shall vew,
>> E're I proue false to faith, or strange to you.

In metre it is accentually iambic, but from the first line the syntactic parallels set up their strongly marked rhythms, and it is the rhythms, not the five feet of the metre, that John Dowland took up in setting it in his first book of ayres, giving the first line a musical phrase of two bars of unequal length (Ex. 16). The whole setting moves with

Ex. 16

Deare if — — you .hange ile ne - uer chuse a - gaine

evolving flow, no two lines given identical time values, each individually rendered;[55] and in the second stanza the writer has reproduced the rhythmical patterns sufficiently closely for it to be fitly accentuated too: in the last couplet, the apostrophes to the lady in the first stanza ask for emphasis to be given to each, and Dowland has been able to meet this demand, because in the second stanza the roll-call of earth, heaven, fire, air, rings out equally tellingly.

Such scope for artistry, allied to such discipline, made the ayre a shapely yet flexible form of song that respected the lyric a poet had made and yet took the impress of each composer's style. The combination of freedom and control it offered and required is the source of much of the lute-song's special appeal and success.

[55] See *ELS* 1st series, vol. 1.

4

Dowland, Ferrabosco, and Jonson: ayres and masque songs

IT was with the publication in 1597 of Dowland's *The First Booke of Songes or Ayres of fowre partes with Tableture for the Lute* that the ayre rose to high favour in England. His song-books spanned most of the prime period of the English lute-song, his last collection appearing in 1612. Fuller declared:

He was the *rarest Musician* that his *Age* did behold: Having travailed beyond the Seas, and compounded *English* with *Forreign Skill* in that *faculty*, it is questionable whether he excell'd in *Vocal* or *Instrumental Musick*.[1]

Questionable as some of Fuller's statements are, this one is true and pertinent, for Dowland, renowned for his skill as a lutenist, brought his practical experience to bear when composing, and not only in instrumental pieces but also in songs. For sheer musical beauty and power, no other composer of ayres was his equal. Many songs in his first book have settings closely responsive to the words, moulded in careful detail to support and interpret individual phrases. Diana Poulton has pointed out how in 'Come heauy sleepe, the Image of true death'

Dowland makes use of his knowledge of the special sonorities of the lute with moving effect, particularly at the junction of the fourth and fifth lines. The last words of line four 'sorrows sigh swoln cries' end on a full close with a chord of G major; a chord which on the lute is mainly composed of notes on the open strings, giving a clear ringing quality. This will support a considerable volume of tone from the singer. The next line begins on a B major chord which, by the position of the notes on the strings of the instrument, has a somewhat more muted tone colour. If the singer drops his voice to match the natural change of quality in the accompaniment the repeated notes of the invocation to sleep then take on a kind of hushed urgency . . .[2]

---

[1] *The History of the Worthies of England* (1662), p. 244.
[2] *John Dowland*, p. 241. For the songs in *The First Booke*, see *ELS* 1st series, vols. 1 and 2.

The same modulation of tone is fitting in the second stanza too, at '. . . doth my mind affright./O come sweet sleepe'; and this is worth observing, because the more fully individual phrases of the first stanza are mirrored in the music, the more important it is that both rhythms and nuances in other stanzas should be similarly patterned if strophic setting is to succeed. In the setting of another song in this book, 'Come againe: sweet loue doth now enuite', the climactic fourth line of the first stanza is vividly presented in a series of rising fourths divided by rests (Ex. 17):

Ex. 17

To see,   to hear,   to touch,   to kiss,   to die,

and the corresponding line in the second stanza is also well matched:

I sit,   I sigh,   I weepe,   I faint,   I die,

but the four remaining stanzas do not proffer such a series of brief phrases, and when sung produce rhythmical infelicities such as this:

Her eies—of fire,—her hart—of flint—is made.

This in itself should arouse one's suspicions: it would be surprising if Dowland had accepted the invitation of the first two stanzas if it betrayed him into this; the lack of strophic conformity, the final lines of the last four stanzas having eight syllables instead of ten as in the first two stanzas, and the original numbering of the stanzas, 1,2,1,2,3,4, strongly indicate that they were added to the song after Dowland composed it. Doughtie suggests that they formed a separate poem;[3] Diana Poulton defends their singability,[4] and it is true that with some repetition of phrase in the last line of the stanzas, and prolongation of the minims on the line quoted above to replace inappropriate rests, they can be sung; and Dowland let them stand in later editions. But I question whether his setting would have been so closely modelled on the first two stanzas if he had been composing with all six before him.[5]

---

[3] *Lyrics from English Airs*, p. 465.   [4] *John Dowland*, pp. 236–7.

[5] It is sometimes asserted that only the first stanza of an ayre was meant to be sung, or that composers bothered only to fit the first. (See my p. 128.) The evidence of the song-books suggests that this is far from being generally true: not only Campion but lesser poets showed care and skill in fitting their verse for strophic setting; and

It is no wonder that Dowland's first song-book was so well received that it was still reappearing after his last collection came out, being reprinted in 1600 and 1603, and, with revisions probably by Dowland himself, in 1606 and 1613, because it contains songs with several overlapping but distinguishable kinds of appeal. Besides songs in which the melody springs from and is shaped for the specific poem it sets, there are songs made on tunes, some already familiar, in currently fashionable dance rhythms, and songs with personal connections or ceremonial or dramatic contexts.

Dowland's favourite dance form was that of the galliard; he composed at least thirty galliard tunes, probably more, re-scoring many of them for various modes of performance. The tunes of the third, fourth, and fifth songs of the first book, for instance, he arranged also for solo lute, and for instrumental consort as 'Sir Iohn Souch his Galiard', 'Captaine Piper his Galiard', and 'The Earle of Essex Galiard' in his *Lachrimae, or Seaven Teares Figvred in Seaven Passionate Pauans, with diuers other Pauans, Galiards, and Almands, set forth for the Lute, Viols, or Violons, in fiue parts* of 1604. Inferences may be drawn from the nature of a tune and its setting as to whether it seems vocal or instrumental in conception; and, more generally, it seems probable that where dance tunes are found in both instrumental and song arrangements the tune would more often be made first, and words be written to fit it, than vice versa; but firm evidence as to which form a composition of Dowland's was first given is often lacking. Miss Poulton suggests grounds for thinking that the tune of the nineteenth song, 'Awake sweet loue thou art returnd', was first written as a galliard for solo lute.[6] The sixth song, 'Now O now I needs must part', goes to his 'Frog Galliard', which he arranged also for solo lute, and which became immensely popular;[7] this alone of Dowland's galliards has the trochaic movement that for Morley characterized this dance; it does indeed

go by a measure which the learned call 'trochaicam rationem', consisting of a long and short stroke successively, for as the foot *trochaeus* consisteth of one syllable of two times and another of one time so is the first of these two

although composers varied in their concern for succeeding stanzas, and Dowland himself was not constant in this respect, the high number of settings which achieve good expression of most or all stanzas, and the printing of all stanzas in the song-books, support the view that effective performance of whole poems was the aim.

[6] *John Dowland*, pp. 143–4.
[7] One of the lyrics put to it was by Breton; see p. 49 and p. 69 above.

strokes double to the latter, the first being in time of a semibreve and the latter of a minim.[8]

The lyric needs only a regular trochaic pattern of stresses to be carried on the melody's steady swing: Ex. 18 gives the beginning of the melody.

Ex. 18

Now O now I needs must part, par-ting though I ab-sent mourne,

It was his dance tunes that became the most famous of Dowland's compositions, both in England, where they were sung as well as played and danced to, and on the Continent, where they were borrowed for anthologies and printed without words. The most celebrated of all is not a galliard, but its graver counterpart, a pavan: the tune 'Lachrimae' itself. Miss Poulton considers that Dowland composed it first for solo lute; then it became a song for two voices in *The Second Booke of Songs or Ayres* of 1600, and lastly he arranged it for viols and lute, as 'Lachrimae Antiquae', in *Lachrimae, or Seaven Teares*.[9] Its success was phenomenal: lutenists both English and Continental copied it into their music-books for decades, some basing fresh compositions on it; Byrd, Morley, Farnaby, and other composers made keyboard arrangements of it;[10] and as a song it had a long run, appearing in collections down to the 1682 edition of John Forbes's *Songs and Fancies*.

In his text-book Thomas Morley described the pavan as 'a kind of staid music ordained for grave dancing and most commonly made of three strains, whereof every strain is played or sung twice',[11] and his description points to two features, both influential on lyrics written to pavans: the stateliness of the dance, and its structure. The second is the more readily observed; a verse-writer making a lyric to go to a pavan of three sections or strains will respond to its threefold musical pattern: if he writes six stanzas, he may use three different patterns, repeating each: *aa bb cc*. But he may make modifications, for whereas a dance must repeat its patterns so that the corresponding dance

[8] Ed. cit., p. 296.
[9] *John Dowland*, pp. 125–6. For the song, see *ELS* 1st series, vol. 5.
[10] For detailed listing, see Poulton, *John Dowland*, pp. 123–4 and p. 481.
[11] Ed. cit., p. 296.

figures may all be performed, repetition of each strain is not essential when the music is used for a song. The lyric that accompanies 'Lachrimae' in Dowland's song-book exemplifies this; it has three stanza patterns, but only five stanzas, the last pattern being used only once.[12] First come two alternate-rhyme quatrains, unusual only in their line-lengths, of 7, 8, 10, and 6 syllables; then two stanzas that make no metrical sense on their own but when sung to the second strain take shape;[13] and lastly, a single quatrain, its phrases taking up the tune's rhythmical patterns. The music shows a repeat sign for the accompaniment, but not for the melody, which suggests that the music alone would be played again as a coda. Here are the words:

> Flow my teares fall from your springs,
> Exilde for euer: Let mee morne
> where nights black bird hir sad infamy sings,
> there let mee liue forlorne.

> Downe vaine lights shine you no more,
> No nights are dark enough for those
> that in dispaire their last fortuns deplore,
> light doth but shame disclose.

> Neuer may my woes be relieued,
> since pittie is fled,
> and teares, and sighes, and grones my wearie dayes,
> of all ioyes haue depriued.

> From the highest spire of contentment,
> my fortune is throwne,
> and feare, and griefe, and paine for my deserts,
> are my hopes since hope is gone.

> Harke you shadowes that in darcknesse dwell,
> learne to contemne light,
> Happie, happie they that in hell
> feele not the worlds despite.

That lyric is indeed grave, like the music of a pavan; and this suggests one of the less tangible, more subtle ways in which dancing

---

[12] Similarly, the fifth song of *A Pilgrimes Solace*, 'Shall I striue with wordes to moue', which goes to galliard music ('M. Henry Noell his Galiard', in *Lachrimae*), has five stanzas, two to each of the first two strains, and one to the third.

[13] This is a pointer to musical partnership (not, of course, a proof) that is worth noting: many lyrics written to tunes may have survived in separation from them, and when one encounters a lyric that seems to require some missing metrical prop, it is worth while to look for a musical alliance or link.

has left its mark on lyrics. Courtly dancing in Queen Elizabeth's day was not only a matter of steps and movements: it implied a whole world of social grace and decorum. Of all dances the pavan was the most dignified; as 'Thoinot Arbeau' (Jehan Tabourot) informed his pupil Capriol:

And as for the *Pavane*, it is used by kings, princes and great lords, to display themselves on some day of solemn festival with their fine mantles and robes of ceremony; and then the queens and the princesses and the great ladies accompany them with the long trains of their dresses let down and trailing behind them, or sometimes carried by damsels. . . . These *Pavanes* are also used in a masquerade when there is a procession of triumphal chariots of gods and goddesses, emperors or kings resplendent with majesty.[14]

Poems written to a pavan tune are likely to catch some of this atmosphere of courtliness, and contemporaries would expect appropriate qualities in such lyrics; it is significant that despite the wide currency of the 'Lachrimae' pavan and the many contemporary references to it—in plays by Fletcher, Massinger, Middleton, and Webster, for instance[15]—not a single ballad is known to have been written to it.

   A pavan carries with it a sense of occasion, because it was used to open court balls, and in masques, and also solemn ceremonies; more specific associations with the court and its celebrations attach to one of the songs, not in a dance-rhythm, in Dowland's first book. The lyric clearly implies either a real or a dramatic occasion:

> His golden locks time hath to siluer turnde,
> O time too swift, O swiftnes neuer ceasing,
> his youth gainst time & age hath euer spurnd,
> but spurnd in vaine, youth waneth by encreasing:
> Beautie, strength, youth are flowers but fading seene,
> Duty, Faith, Loue are roots and euer greene.

> His helmet now shall make a hiue for bees,
> And louers sonets turne to holy psalmes:
> A man at armes must now serue on his knees,
> And feed on prayers which are ages almes,
> > But though from court to cotage he departe
> > His saint is sure of his vnspotted hart.

---

[14] In *Orchésographie*, 1588; tr. Cyril W. Beaumont (1925), p. 58.
[15] See Doughtie, *Lyrics from English Airs*, pp. 475–6.

And when he saddest sits in homely Cell,
Hele teach his swaines this Caroll for a songe,
Blest be the harts that wish my soueraigne well,
Curst be the soule that thinke her any wrong:
Goddes allow this aged man his right,
To be your beadsman now that was your knight.

The occasion proves to have been a real situation, its treatment
vividly displaying the Elizabethan flair for heightening the drama of
life. Sir Henry Lea or Lee, master of the Queen's armoury, had
vowed to present himself as her champion each year at the tilt on the
anniversary of her accession to the throne, 17 November, so initiating an annual ceremonial assembly of lords and gentlemen in arms.
On 17 November 1590, wishing to resign the performance of this
vow because of his age, he presented himself to the Queen and her
company at the Tiltyard in Westminster, with the Earl of Cumberland for acceptance as his successor, in an elaborate device. To the
sound of sweet music, the earth appeared to open, revealing a
pavilion of white taffeta, with an altar on which were gifts, which
three virgins presented to the Queen.

These presents and prayer being with great reuerence deliuered into her
Maiesties owne hands, and he himselfe disarmed, offered vp his armour at the
foot of her Maiesties crowned pillar; and kneeling vpon his knees, presented
the Earl of Cumberland, humbly beseeching she would be pleased to accept
him for Knight, to continue the yeerely exercises aforesaid. Her Maiesty
gratiously accepting of that offer, this aged Knight armed the Earle, and
mounted him vpon his horse. That being done, he put vpon his owne person
a side coat of blacke Veluet pointed vnder the arme, and couered his head (in
lieu of an helmet) with a buttoned cap of the countrey fashion.[16]

The song 'His golden locks time hath to siluer turnde' accompanied
the sweet music; and the symbolic change it enacts, from knight to
hermit, is poignant both in itself and in the reminiscence it evoked,
for when the Queen had visited Sir Henry Lee's house at Woodstock
fifteen years earlier, the entertainment he gave for her was narrated
by one Hemetes the Hermit. It seems probable that the words of 'His
golden locks', which Robert Hales sang before the Queen, were
written by Lee himself, or for him, and that Dowland's is the original

---

[16] From the account by Sir William Segar, Principal King at Arms, in his *Honor,
Military and Civill*, 1602, sigs. R3-4ᵛ. Quoted by Poulton, *John Dowland*, pp. 237–9;
see also Nichols, *The Progresses and Public Processions of Queen Elizabeth*, vol. 3, pp.
60–2, and Doughtie, *Lyrics from English Airs*, pp. 466–8.

2. Sir Henry Lee's tournament armour.

setting. The beauty of the poem and the sustained plangency of the music combine to make the song a moving one for any hearer; for contemporaries who had been present at that Accession Day tilt in 1590, or heard about it, the blended pomp and pathos of the situation must have made it unforgettable.

There are grounds for associating Lee too with the poem on old age, 'Times eldest sonne, olde age and heyre of ease', set by Dowland as a sequence of three songs in his second book, which also contrasts the retired and the public life.[17] More positively, one of the songs by John Dowland printed by his son Robert Dowland in *A Mvsicall Banqvet*, 1610, 'Farre from triumphing Court and wonted glory', which is there ascribed to Lee and is full of verbal echoes of 'His golden locks', clearly refers to a visit Queen Anne paid him, which greatly heartened the old knight.[18]

The quality of the lyrics Dowland set is high, yet few of them can be traced to their authors. The first two books contain only three of known authorship, all by Fulke Greville.[19] The third book contains Campion's 'I must complaine, yet do enioy my loue' (which the poet also set and included in his fourth book of ayres about fifteen years later), and one or two by Essex.[20] Dowland's last book, *A Pilgrimes Solace*, 1612, contains a version of a sonnet by Breton, and other poems in it, as in the other books, have been uncertainly ascribed to various authors.[21] The second song, 'Sweet stay a while, why will you rise?', clearly suggested Donne's poem 'Breake of Day' to many who heard or read it, and a number of manuscript copies of Donne's poem, mostly made twenty or more years after the song-book's

---

[17] See Doughtie, op. cit., pp. 478–9, and Poulton, op. cit., pp. 259–60.

[18] The occasion is described in a letter from John Chamberlaine to Dudley Carleton, 29 September 1608, quoted by Poulton, p. 316.

[19] 'Who euer thinks or hopes of loue for loue' and 'Away with these selfe louing lads' in the first book, and 'Faction that euer dwels' in the second. Only two other composers chose poems of his for setting; Martin Peerson produced a whole volume, *Mottects Or Grave Chamber Mvsique*, in 1630, as a memorial tribute to Greville, who had died in 1628. All its texts, except for an elegy on the poet, are from *Caelica*; four of the settings are of whole sonnets. In musical style, as in date, these five-part songs stand apart from both madrigal and ayre. The first poem in *Caelica*, one of those chosen by Peerson, was set also by Cavendish in his *14. Ayres in Tabletorie*.

[20] 'It was a time when silly Bees could speake' is ascribed to Essex in fourteen manuscript sources (see Doughtie, op. cit., pp. 518–20). 'Behold a wonder here' may have been part of an entertainment arranged or made by Essex for the Queen (ibid., pp. 513–14).

[21] Details are given by Doughtie, pp. 607–18. The song-book is in *ELS* 1st series, vols. 12 and 14.

appearance, give its first stanza before Donne's poem, or intermix them in some way.[22] The 1669 edition of Donne's *Poems* also gave a version of the first stanza as the opening of 'Breake of Day', despite the difference in length of the last couplet, the difference of tone between the two poems—there is no argumentative note in the plea and praise of the anonymous lyric—and the difference of sex of the speakers. The third song in *A Pilgrimes Solace* also has similarities to a poem of Donne's: 'To aske for all thy loue, and thy whole heart' reads like a recasting of 'Love's Infiniteness' into shorter lines and stanzas, with less complex thought, to fit it for strophic setting, but it is unlikely that Donne himself made it.

Thematically, most of the lyrics in Dowland's song-books are variations on familiar aspects of the fruits or fruitlessness of love, especially the latter: complaints of denial and cruelty predominate, some of them voicing extreme grief or despair. A few lyrics affirm steadfast faith and even hope, a few are praises, but only two or three celebrate mutual love. Life at court, as well as women's kindness and constancy, is viewed with disenchantment, and a group of songs in *A Pilgrimes Solace* shows the turning from worldly to heavenly desires that the title suggests, expressing praise of God, repentance, prayer for relief from suffering, and thanksgiving for grace.[23] The tone of Dowland's texts is not unvaryingly sombre; light-heartedness occasionally breaks in, and the range of moods and personae is extended by the songs that imply dramatic contexts. But compared with the songs of Campion, Dowland's are noticeably darker and sadder, and narrower in emotional range. The first of Campion's *Two Bookes of Ayres* consists chiefly of songs that are, as he says, 'graue and pious'; his other collections are full of love-songs of praise, of invitations tender and gay, or impudent and mocking; his lovers are playful and joyful, as well as complaining.

Musically, it is Dowland who has the wider range; his song-books show him varying and expanding his treatment of the ayre. The first book already contains hints of adventurous handling: in the last section of 'Can shee excuse my wrongs with vertues cloake:' interest

---

[22] For details, see Doughtie, pp. 608–10. The song text, like others of unknown authorship set by Dowland, is sometimes ascribed to the composer. It was set also by Gibbons in his *The First Set of Madrigals and Mottets of 5. Parts*, 1612 (the first stanza only), and later by Henry Lawes (Autograph MS, f.10ᵛ); and by anonymous composers.

[23] Nos. XII to XVII. Of these, XIV to XVI share the text of Breton's sonnet 'When *Iob* had lost his Children, Lands and goods', with two prefatory lines not his.

centres not in the vocal line, which until its last phrases sustains monotone chant, but in the tuneful accompaniment, which embodies the popular song 'Shall I go walk the woods so wild?'. This fore-shadows the independent accompaniments of later songs, of 'Dye not beefore thy day, poore man condemned', in the second book, where in the final section two-part counterpoint holds the attention; even of 'Goe nightly cares, the enemy to rest', in his last book, with its chanted fifth and sixth lines around which viol, viola da gamba, and lute weave a web of polyphonic texture. In *The Second Booke of Songs or Ayres*, of 1600, an instrumental phrase often opens an ayre, and appears between lines of the lyric, and the symmetrical style is replaced by more extended setting, sometimes non-strophic: the three six-line stanzas of 'Times eldest sonne, olde age the heyre of ease' are through-set. The songs in *The Third and Last Booke of Songs or Aires*, 1603, range in style from the limpid melody of 'Time stands still with gazing on her face', which clothes the long lines of the verse with a sustained long-breathed flow, through the rather square-cut, or sectional, setting of the much shorter-lined stanzas of 'Behold a wonder here', well-suited for public performance, to the last song's use of two voices in dialogue (a form much favoured by the next generation of song-writers), with some imitation between the voices and a lute and bass lute, and with parts also for three viols, doubled by voices at the chorus.

A Pilgrimes Solace, Dowland's fourth and truly last book of ayres, of 1612, is rich in variety. It contains two songs that look back to his earlier use of dance measures, and several that look forward to the declamatory vein that was soon to prevail. The eighth song, 'Tell me true Loue where shall I seeke thy being', shows the care to match verbal rhythms in the vocal line that was to take precedence of intrinsically musical considerations with the next generation of composers, whilst the three following songs, for which Dowland added to the musical texture a descant part for treble viol, show that none the less his interest in extending the lute-song's musical dimensions was still increasing. In the tenth song, 'From silent night, true register of moanes', the interests of words and music are finely united: the flowing melody is built on the words, its chromatic progressions intensifying their impact, and lute, bass viol, and treble viol obbligato provide an accompaniment full of complementary instrumental interest.

In contrast to this contrapuntal richness, the settings of the last

3. Masque presented at Sir Henry Unton's wedding banquet, with a broken
consort playing.

three songs are harmonically conceived, the accompaniments simply providing mainly chordal support for the voices; and in seeking the reason for their difference of style, it is worth noting that all three imply a context of masque or ceremony. The first of them, 'Vp merry mates, to *Neptunes* prayse', is a sailors' song, and the other two are the wedding songs that may have been made for the marriage of Lord Walden in March 1612. These and some other songs of Dowland with a framework of public performance have already been mentioned: those connected with Sir Henry Lee, and 'My heart and tongue were twinnes, at once conceiued', probably the setting sung in the pageant given for the Queen at Sudley.[24] Several more songs of Dowland seem, by their import and manner, to come from masques or entertainments. In the second book alone, five or six songs besides the 'Times eldest sonne' sequence imply dramatic contexts: the third, fourth, and fifth seem to form a sequence, the plaint of a 'woefull wretched wight', followed by Hope offering comfort to a man condemned, and then a lament at the passing of his last day. 'Come yee heauy states of night,/Doe my fathers spirit right' is a dirge; the dialogue 'Hvmor say what mak'st thou heere,/In the presence of a Queene' suggests a masque; and 'Fine knacks for ladies, cheape choise braue and new' suggests a pedlar's guise, perhaps in an outdoor entertainment.[25]

Such links with drama and court entertainments encouraged the development of a declamatory style in the ayre. The lute-song, with its subtle, fluid rhythms, was ideal for purely private entertainment, for singing alone or in a domestic circle: informal and unemphatic in style, it was as if overheard rather than presented. But songs designed to be projected as part of an entertainment of large scope and more formal intent called for some adaptation of manner.

In effect, composers writing ayres for a more public purpose inclined to one of the two approaches to the matching of words and music that were being more consciously and explicitly worked out elsewhere, one chiefly in France, the other in Italy. It is with the manner of the Italian experiments that Dowland's practice shows more affinity. The Camerata, a group of musicians and musical amateurs, poets and scholars who met in the house of Count Bardi in

---

[24] See above, pp. 67–8 and 118–21.
[25] Other songs that imply dramatic contexts are the third, fourteenth (and perhaps thirteenth), and last in the third book, and the sailors' song, the nineteenth song in the fourth book.

Florence in the closing decades of the sixteenth century, debated the
principles of the declamatory style in music, formulated their findings, and composed music exemplifying their views. Like the
exponents of 'la musique mesurée a l'antique' in France, they were
intrigued by the affective power attributed to music by the Greeks,
and were trying to rediscover the lost art of the musical declamation
they supposed to have been employed in Greek drama, and reawaken
or release anew such power. Some of their premisses were ill-
founded, but the style they evolved was rich in dramatic potentialities. The precedence given by Plato to words over rhythm and
harmoniousness they took literally to mean that Greek poetry would
be declaimed according to natural verbal inflexions, the varying
pitches of the speaking voice being embodied in music and so
amplified in power and intensity. On this basis Galilei and Cavalieri
began to write music for solo voice with viol accompaniment, and
this monody *in stile rappresentativo* soon led to the evolving of
opera: Peri's *Dafne* was performed in Florence in 1597, and his
Euridice in 1600, and Caccini composed his rival opera *Euridice* also
in 1600. In the preface to his collection of songs in the new style, or
'new musics', *Le Nuove Musiche*, Caccini wrote:

poi che non poteuano esse mouere l'intelletto senza l'intelligenza della
parole, mi vēne pensiero introdurre vna sorte di musica, per cui altri potesse
quasi che in armonia fauellare, usando in essa (come altre volte ho detto) vna
certa nobile sprezzatura di canto.[26]

Even the earliest operas show the dramatic scope of thus 'talking in
music'; and Monteverdi's *Orfeo*, produced in 1607, showed what
emotional power and musical beauty could be achieved through
music closely responsive, in details of accentuation and intonation as
well as in mood, to its text.

In England the declamatory style never achieved such musical
stature; as the Italian monody was naturalized by Nicholas Lanier,
Henry Lawes, and other and lesser composers, the results were often
thin in musical texture and fettered by syllabically close subservience

---

[26] Florence, 1602 (facsimile, Rome, 1934). 'Since the mind cannot be moved unless
the words are understood, I thought of introducing a kind of music in which one
might, as it were, talk in harmony and, in so doing, cultivate (as I have said at other
times) an attitude of fine disdain towards the [actual process of] singing.' (I am
indebted to Miss Deirdre M. Keaney for advice in translating this passage and that cited
in note 38, below.)

to the words. But Dowland, and the younger Ferrabosco, were already developing a declamatory kind of ayre suited for masques and other dramatic use as well as for independent songs, and Dowland combined it with rich musical resources. In his song 'In darknesse let mee dwell', for example, well-accented declamation, flowing counterpoint, limpid melody, and strident chromatic harmony coalesce to body forth despair, and the restraint imposed by strophic setting is thrown off, only one of the lyric's two stanzas being set. It is one of the three songs by Dowland that appeared in his son's compilation of 1610, *A Mvsicall Banqvet. Furnished with varietie of delicious Ayres, Collected out of the best Authors in English, French, Spanish and Italian*, which included two songs from *Le Nuove Musiche* (one of them the moving 'Amarilli, mia bella'). Clearly some of the music of the Italian monodists was in circulation soon after the turn of the century, if not earlier, and probably awareness of their ideas too,[27] but the movement of English composers of Dowland's generation towards a more declamatory style seems parallel rather than derivative, predominantly practical in impetus, and unhampered by emulative intent: songs of Dowland and Ferrabosco that show heightened attention to declamation, and the masque songs of Campion too, in their different vein, have a musical robustness that the music of English composers who deliberately followed the Italian way largely lacks.

One of the earliest composers to develop a markedly declamatory style was Alfonso Ferrabosco the younger, son of the madrigalist Alfonso Ferrabosco who had spent much of his life in England and had been connected with masques at court in 1572 and 1576. His son lived wholly in England, and became celebrated as a composer of fantasies and pavans for viols, and renowned too for his lyra-viol playing. His *Ayres*, published in 1609, shows considerable range of musical style and form: melodic ayre, masque song, declamatory song, and dialogue, all with accompaniments for both lute and viol. He made an accomplished lute-song of the anonymous lyric 'Shall I seeke to ease my griefe?' and gave Campion's 'Young and simple

---

[27] Dowland's description of his first book of ayres, in the dedication, as 'containing the consent of speaking harmony, ioyned with the most musicall instrument the Lute' may indicate familiarity with the intention behind Caccini's songs. Doughtie observes that 'the presence of declamatory passages in an earlier song like "Sorrow stay" [from the second book, 1600] may reflect an encounter with Caccini's songs during Dowland's visit to the Florentine court in 1595' (*Lyrics from English Airs*, p. 9).

though I am'[28] a square-cut setting rather like some of Campion's own. For Johnson's 'Come my Celia, let vs proue', a version of Catallus's famous lyric 'Vivamus, mea Lesbia atque amemus' which Jonson later included in *The Forrest*, Ferrabosco used a style close to lutenist ayre too; heard by itself the song is uncomplicated in its appeal, but in its dramatic context, heard as part of the would-be seduction of Celia by Volpone as he flings off the disguise of a dying old man, it evokes more complex responses.[29] But for setting Donne's poem 'The Expiration' he used a declamatory manner, breaking the text into phrases strongly marked by rests; and since Donne is not Campion, and his rhythms are prompted by other concerns than care for strophic correspondence, the result is a notably bad fit between verbal and musical patterns in the second stanza, especially in its third line (Ex. 19). Ex. 20 gives the whole song, from

Ex. 19

the first edition. John Hollander cites this setting as 'a startling, but typical case' of the disregard of lute-song composers for stanzas other than the first.[30] It is, however, far from typical of the style of lutenist ayres, being unusually declamatory; nor is it typical of declamatory ayre, for by the time this manner was generally practised, in the middle decades of the seventeenth century, the rhythms of most lyrics were much more in step with their metres, and strophic correspondence was therefore common. Donne's lyric is not framed

---

[28] Campion himself set it, in his fourth book of ayres. (Lanier also set it.) For Ferrabosco's *Ayres*, see *ELS* 2nd series, vol. 16.

[29] It is probable, although not ascertained, that Ferrabosco's setting was composed for performance in *Volpone*; Volpone may have accompanied himself on either the lute or the viol. (For non-dramatic performance, both lute and viol accompaniments could be used.) The fullest study of Jonson's songs is Mary Chan's *Music in the Theatre of Ben Jonson* (Oxford, 1980): see this for analytical and contextual discussion, sources and reproduction of musical settings of the songs in both plays and masques. See also David Fuller, 'Ben Jonson's Plays and their Contemporary Music', *M&L* 58 (1977), 60–75; and Vincent Duckles, 'The Music for the Lyrics in Early Seventeenth-Century English Drama: a Bibliography of the Primary Sources', in *Music in English Renaissance Drama*, pp. 143–7.

[30] *The Untuning of the Sky: Ideas of Music in English Poetry, 1500–1700* (Princeton, 1961), p. 188; also *Vision and Resonance* (New York, 1975), pp. 46–8.

to reward strophic setting; Ferrabosco perhaps wished to print it whole in his book, but he would have served himself better by presenting only the first stanza with his music.[31]

Ferrabosco included in his *Ayres* several songs composed for masques written by Jonson, so preserving them, whilst most of his other masque-songs are now lost. With the accession of King James, the splendour of court masques greatly increased. Queen Elizabeth had enjoyed entertainments and masques, especially those presented to her as gifts, but she grudged the huge expense involved in mounting elaborate masques at court; Queen Anne of Denmark revelled in pageantry and masquing, even taking part in court masques herself, unlike Queen Elizabeth, and King James, whilst not taking part himself, indulged her enthusiasm. The first Christmastide masque of his reign was provided by Samuel Daniel, but by the next year Jonson had ousted him, and begun his long run in favour as writer of court masques. Dowland at this time was abroad, holding the post of lutenist at the court of Denmark; he was able to have his song-books published in England and his fame stood high, but he was not at hand, and it was Ferrabosco who became Jonson's musical partner.

The first masque in which they were associated, presented on Twelfth Night, 1605, was *The Masque of Blackness*.[32] In it, to the shock of the beholders, the Queen and the noblest ladies of the court, the Countess of Bedford, Lady Herbert, the Countess of Derby, and eight others, appeared with blackened face and arms, as the daughters of Niger; the indecorum was forced upon Jonson, as his prefatory comments make clear, 'because it was her Maiesties will, to haue them *Black-mores* at first'. The text contains four songs, but Ferrabosco printed only one in his book of ayres, and it alone survives with its music: it is the second song, sung by a tenor voice from the sea, calling the sea-maidens back. Ex. 21 reproduces it from the first edition. The accompaniment gives simple harmonic support to the voice, which declaims the words clearly and, with only minor exceptions, with natural accentuation. The song is well made for its

---

[31] The anonymous setting, for voice and lute, in Bodleian Library MS Mus. Sch. F. 575, f.8ᵛ, gives the first stanza only. For the music, see *Poèmes de Donne, Herbert et Crashaw mis en musique par leurs contemporains*, transcribed by André Souris (Paris, 1961). See below, pp. 146–9, for further discussion of settings of poems by Donne.

[32] For full headings or titles, and the texts of the masques, see *Ben Jonson*, ed. C. H. Herford and P. and E. M. Simpson, 11 vols. (Oxford, 1925–52), vol. vii.

Ex. 20

VII.

O, fo, leaue off, this laft lamen- ting kiffe, which fucks two foules and vapours both a- way, Turne thou ghoft that way, And let me turne this, and let our felues be-night our happy day, we aske none leaue to loue, nor will we owe any fo cheape a death as faying goe. We aske none leaue to loue, nor wil we owe a- ny fo cheape a death as faying goe.

Goe, goe, and if that word haue not quite kild thee,
Eafe me with death by bidding me goe to :
O, if it haue let my word worke on me,
And a iuft office on a murderer doe.
　　Except it be too late to kill me fo,
　　Being double dead, going and bidding goe.

III

Ome away, come away, we grow ielous of your ftay, If you doe not ftoppe your eare, We fhall haue more caufe to feare, Sirens of the land then they, to doubt the Sirens of the Sea.

purpose; if one observes that it has not the melodic shapeliness of a typical lute-song by Campion, or the musical strength and inventiveness of one by Dowland, this is partly to recognize that Ferrabosco is not their equal in their special excellencies, but partly to notice that he is consciously composing for the conditions of masque, and that the declamatory style that resulted is capable of strong dramatic effect in performance but is usually of lesser intrinsic musical appeal than melodic ayre. Such settings belong in their context, with the speeches and dances they were interspersed with in the composite and complex form of the masque, and Ferrabosco's selectivity in compiling his book of ayres suggests recognition of this: there were usually four or five songs in a masque, but from the Haddington masque, of 1608, and *The Masque of Queens*, 1609, as from the 1605 masque, he included only one song each.

For one masque, however, he made an exception, preserving all but the opening and closing 'full' songs, or choruses, in his song-book; and in this, *The Masque of Beauty*, music and dancing and the symbolism they carry are central to Jonson's conception. In the *Masque of Blackness*, the moon goddess Aethiopia promised that one year thence the daughters of Niger would be transformed from their blackness to radiant fairness. It was three years before they appeared to claim fulfilment of the promise, delayed in the fiction by their compassionate search for four other Ethiop maidens, in fact by the intervening of 'other rites', the wedding of the Earl of Essex in 1606, celebrated by Jonson's *Hymenaei*, and that of Lord Hay, or Hayes, in 1607, celebrated by Campion's *Lord Hayes' Masque*. But for the Twelfth Night festivities of 1608, Jonson and Ferrabosco prepared the sequel, *The Masque of Beauty*, and in it Jonson presented the very apotheosis of music: Harmonia herself, a lyre in her hand, appeared on top of the throne, which itself was upon a floating island:

This Throne, (as the whole *Iland* mou'd forward, on the water,) had a circular motion of it[s] owne, imitating that which wee call *Motum mundi*, from the *East* to the *West*, or the right to the left side. . . . The steps, whereon the *Cupids* sate, had a motion contrary, with *Analogy*, *ad motum Planetarum*, from the *West* to the *East*: both which turned with their seuerall lights.

Loud music accompanied the splendid scene, followed by a 'full song' (that is, one sung by several voices), with two echoes rising from fountains within a maze:

> When *Loue*, at first, did mooue
> From out of *Chaos*, brightned
> So was the world, and lightned,
> As now! *Eccho*. As now! *Ecch*. As now!

Vulturnus, the east wind, addressed the Thames:

> Rise, aged *Thames*, and by the hand
> Receiue these *Nymphes*, within the land:
> And, in those curious *Squares* and *Rounds*,
> Wherewith thou flow'st betwixt the grounds
>
> Of fruitfull *Kent*, and *Essex* faire,
> That lend thee gyrlands for thy hayre;
> Instruct their siluer feete to tread,
> Whilst we, againe to sea, are fled.

So the first dance is introduced, and since the River Thames 'was personated by Master Thomas Giles, who made the dances', it was indeed he who instructed their feet, in 'a most curious dance full of excellent device and change', which left the dancers standing still in the form of a diamond, while a tenor voice, accompanied by musicians, sang:

> So beautie on the waters stood,
> When loue had seuer'd earth, from flood!
> So when he parted ayre, from fire,
> He did with concord all inspire!
> And then a *motion* he them taught,
> That elder then himselfe was thought.
> Which thought was, yet, the child of earth,
> For loue is elder then his birth.

Jonson's comment on the dance serves as a needed reminder that dancing was the very core of masquing, the element around which it developed, and that the figures and patterns traced out, and the dancers' grace and skill, conveyed subtleties and significances beyond what the music alone could suggest. Much of the dance music for Stuart masques has been lost; much survives, but almost all of it is anonymous, and difficult to assign with certainty to specific masques. Music for the main masque and antimasque dances was usually specially made by composers or dancing-masters preparing particular masques; some may have been drawn from the existing corpus of dance tunes, as the music for the revels presumably was.[33]

The sequence of dances and songs proceeds, with the audience alerted to respond with more than eye and ear. Each element of the masque's many-stranded art is being used by Jonson to awaken awareness of the mysterious correspondences of music and dancing with the movements and meaning of the universe itself; and it is possible that he divined more truly than the French and Italian theorists and musicians the mode of truth of the old legends of the power of music, and reawakened that power. If the myths were evolved to embody concepts born of musical and mathematical correspondences, correspondences which suggested that harmony, number, and proportion had more than metaphoric relationship to the nature and functioning of the universe,[34] the kind of validity they had for the Greeks may have been far more truly re-created and renewed in the imaginative life and potency Jonson evokes for these concepts than in most of the *musica instrumentalis*—the actual music composed and performed—that resulted from more literal belief and practical endeavour, in *musique mesurée* or Italian monody.[35]

Or in English declamatory ayre, as practised by Ferrabosco or by his successors, and recitative. No English composer of that age could embody in music conceptions as deep as those sounded by Jonson's words, as, forty years or so earlier, Tallis in his forty-part motet 'Spem in alium' had so marvellously conjured up the cosmic harmony. Jonson's poem 'So beautie on the waters stood' tells of

[33] The most important surviving collection of masque dances, compiled by Sir Nicholas L'Estrange, probably c.1624–6, is in BL Add. MS 10444. These dance tunes, together with many others from manuscript and printed sources, and virtually all known masque songs for the period 1604–40, are edited by Andrew J. Sabol, *Four Hundred Songs and Dances from the Stuart Masque* (Providence, Rhode Island, 1978). For a study of masque music, see Peter Walls, 'Music in the English Masque in the First Half of the Seventeenth Century', unpub. D. Phil. thesis, Oxford, 1975. The ephemerality of the masque is stressed in Walls's essay, 'Insubstantial Pageants Preserved: the Literary and Musical Sources for the Jonsonian Masque', *Jonson and Shakespeare*, ed. Ian Donaldson (1983).

[34] See Leo Spitzer, *Classical and Christian Ideas of World Harmony* (Baltimore, 1963).

[35] The 1589 Florentine *Intermedi*, created to frame the five acts of a comedy (Bargaglio's *La Pellegrina*) as part of the festivities celebrating the marriage of Ferdinando de' Medici and Christine of Lorraine, had for their theme the power of music, and here indeed the Platonic myth is powerfully represented, in music, dance, and spectacle. The first intermedio presents the harmony of the spheres, and in the last, rhythm and harmony descend to earth. Cavalieri, Marenzio, Peri, and other composers provided a rich range of instrumental and vocal music—solos, madrigals, large choruses and ensembles—for the sirens, fates, modes, planets, and Jove himself.

divine love creating the world, parting the elements, inspiring concord: this is the love that moves the sun and the other stars.[36]
Ferrabosco's melody is poised and moves serenely, but it is hard to
feel that it catches the overtones of the words. Exasperation as well as
acerbity may underlie the fact that Jonson both gave praise to
Ferrabosco and others who worked with him on his masques, and
rescinded it,[37] for his exaltation of the nature and function of the
masque, and of the poet's part in it, gave them exacting and yet
subservient roles. He brought to it a grandeur of concept and content
that the court masque never carried before him or after. Only Milton
gave it greater weight, and his *A Maske (Comus)* stands apart from
the court masque tradition. For Daniel, a masque's *raison d'être* was
to celebrate majesty, and spectacle afforded the most splendid means
of achieving that end; but for Jonson, a masque might serve a further
end, by displaying an ideal order and beauty towards which the real
world may aspire. The ideas of universal harmony the masque of
Beauty invokes give a pattern for earthly concord in state and society
which the king and the court may be moved to promote.

Hence the masque for Jonson was no mere spectacle: the author's
invention was as the soul of the enterprise, depending on the arts of
designer, composer, and choreographer for 'the bodily part', but
yielding to none its integrity. The coherence he gave to it won
approval, but the precedence he claimed for the poetry led to conflict,
notably and notoriously with the one supreme, indispensable
designer, Inigo Jones, and so to the poet's eventual replacement by
Davenant and others.

With his musical collaborators the problem was lesser, but none
the less real, for Jonson's high view of the masque led him to write
texts he was unwilling to see die when the masque's brief brilliant
night was done. His masque for the wedding festivities of Lord
Haddington at court on Shrove Tuesday, 1608, shows him preparing
a continuous literary text, openly meant for reading, and grudging
the adaptations needed to make place for songs and dances; it does

---

[36] 'L'amor che move il sole e l'altre stelle.' Dante, last line of *Paradiso*.

[37] A notable example is his praise of Ferrabosco in the quarto edition of *Hymenaei*,
1606, as 'a Man, planted by himselfe, in that divine *Spheare*; & mastring all the spirits of
Musique: To whose iudiciall Care, and as absolute Performance, were committed all
those Difficulties both of *Song*, and otherwise. Wherein, what his Merit made to the
Soule of our *Invention*, would ask to be exprest in Tunes, no lesse ravishing then his'
(*Ben Jonson*, ed. cit. vii. 232). The passage, which also acknowledged Inigo Jones as
designer and Thomas Giles for his choreography, did not survive to the 1616 folio text.

not contain lyrics made for singing, but ends with an epithalamion of seven stanzas. In performance, the epithalamion was broken up and sung interspersed with dances; and Jonson comments sourly that it '*because it was sung in pieces, betweene the daunces, shew'd to be so many seuerall songs; but was made to be read an intire Poeme*'. So much the worse for it as part of a masque text, Ferrabosco and the choreographers, Thomas Giles and Hierome Herne, must have thought; for it was songs and dances, especially dances, that together with spectacle most pleased the court.[38] Ferrabosco's book of ayres gives his setting of only one stanza of it, and that one truncated, the invocation to Hesperus that recurs as the poem's refrain being left off.[39]

Ferrabosco was succeeded by Nicholas Lanier as chief composer for Johnson's later masques. Ferrabosco's songs show declamatory features, but combined with the tunefulness characteristic of lute-songs; Lanier went further, to develop the fully declamatory ayre, with strong demarcation of verbal phrasing taking priority over melodic flow, and harmonic support for the voice provided by an instrumental bass. He was the first English composer, so far as can be established at present, to evolve declamatory ayre, which he was composing by 1613;[40] and also the first to go beyond it, discarding its balanced musical structure in favour of the unrestricted forward movement of recitative as early as 1617 if Jonson's recollection is right. Lanier composed music for two masques by Jonson performed that year, *The Vision of Delight*, presented twice at court in January, and *Lovers made Men*, presented in the house of Lord Hay in February, and the 1640 Folio of Jonson's *Works* mentions recitative in connection with both, as being used for one song in the former, and for the whole of the latter. The music for *Lovers made Men* is

---

[38] The king's famous outburst during *Pleasure Reconciled to Virtue*—'Why don't they dance? Why have you brought me here? The Devil take every man-Jack of you! Dance!'—occurred towards the end of the revels, not during the main dance, but still suggests a gap between the significance of the masque and the beholder's 'powre to rise to it'. (It is related by the Venetian embassy chaplain; a translation of his whole description is given in Sabol, *Four Hundred Songs and Dances*, Appendix B.)

[39] The stanza is the fifth, 'Why stayes the bridegroome to inuade'. The *Ayres* also contains one song for *The Masque of Queens*, 'If all the ages of the earth'. Some songs for *Oberon* and *Love Freed from Ignorance and Folly* survive in manuscript (St Michael's College, Tenbury, MS 1018): see *Songs from Manuscript Sources* ed. Spink (*ELS* 2nd series, vol. 19), Sabol, op. cit., pp. 62–71, and Chan, *Music in the Theatre of Ben Jonson*, pp. 235–8 and 267–72.

[40] See below, pp. 139–42.

lost, and for *The Vision of Delight* the one vocal fragment now known, anonymous but possibly Lanier's, is not recitative; Jonson's references may record after-impressions.[41] In August the same year an entertainment presented to King James by the Earl of Cumberland contained settings by George Mason, a musician in the earl's service, and the otherwise unknown John Earsdon,[42] and two of these, 'Come follow me, my wandring mates' and 'The shadowes darkning out intents', are in the style of recitative. The first recitative piece to be widely noticed and praised however was Lanier's 'Hero and Leander', which has survived; it was probably composed in 1628 or soon after, on his return from travelling in Italy to buy pictures for King Charles I.[43]

Recitative was obviously a valuable resource for a masque composer; used, not for setting a text throughout as in opera, but for short passages, it made possible very natural transitions between speech and song, and Henry Lawes was not far behind Lanier in employing it. In his music for Milton's *A Maske Presented at Ludlow Castle*, he achieved considerable diversity of effect within the declamatory style, using recitative for the entry and departure of the Attendant Spirit, but shapely declamatory melody for the invocation of Sabrina and for the Lady's song, 'Sweet echo'; and embodying appropriate dance rhythms in the Spirit's bidding to the country dancers, 'Back, shepheards, back, enough your play', and his presentation of the children to their parents in a measure suited for introducing the main masque dance.[44] A few years later, he composed a recitative piece, 'Ariadne', which was much acclaimed, and which he placed first in his first printed collection, *Ayres and Dialogues*, of 1653.

The music of Lanier and Lawes shows masque songs moving away from the treatment of lyrics as songs that contrast with their spoken context towards the view of the text as libretto, with some to be spoken, some given the heightened delivery of recitative, some set in declamatory song. The surviving masque music of Campion, in contrast, is robust in musical structure, firm in its movement, and

---

[41] See McDonald Emslie, 'Nicholas Lanier's Innovations in English Song', *M&L* 41 (1960), 13–27.

[42] See below, p. 142.   [43] See Emslie, op. cit., pp. 14–17.

[44] I discuss the interrelation of speech and song in *A Maske* in 'Songs and dances in *Comus*', *John Milton: Odes, Pastorals, Masques*, ed. J. B. Broadbent (Cambridge, 1975), pp. 171–80. Lawes's music for *A Maske* is in his autograph MS, ff. 37–9; it is printed in Sabol, *Four Hundred Songs and Dances*, pp. 122–30.

tuneful. Only three masque songs with both verse and setting by him survive, and two are for his masque in celebration of Lord Hay's wedding, in 1607.[45] For it a considerable body of musicians was available, including one consort of ten instrumentalists, another of twelve, and a group of six wind players and six singers; there were forty-two players and singers in all. For the transformation scene, in which nine knights of Apollo who had been turned into trees are restored to their own shape,

the foure Silvans *played on their instruments the first straine of this song following, and at the repetition thereof the voices fell in with the instruments which were thus devided: a treble and a base were placed neere his Majestie, and an other treble and base neere the grove, that the words of the song might be heard of all, because the trees of gould instantly at the first sound of their voices began to move and dance according to the measure of the time which the musitians kept in singing, and the nature of the wordes which they delivered.*

> *Song.* Move now with measured sound,
>   You charmed grove of gould,
>   Trace forth the sacred ground
>   That shall your formes unfold . . .[46]

The free and subtle rhythms appropriate in lutenist ayres would not only fail to make their effect here, but would be too wayward for dancing to; Campion secures a firm movement in the verse by aligning speech rhythms and metrical pattern, closely but flexibly, in a stanza form that provides variety by following four short alternately rhymed lines by four longer ones with couplet rhyme. The music matches the verse pattern, although not in the strict ratios of *musique mesurée*, providing both bold declamation of the words, and

---

[45] The third is 'Wooe her, and win her, he that can', from *The Lords' Masque*, of 1613. Another song for this masque may be probably reassembled by using the setting of 'Come away, arm'd with loves delights', second book of ayres, for 'Come away; bring thy golden theft', as Davis suggests (*Works of Thomas Campion*, p. 108, note 38). Campion's masque songs, and songs and dances by other composers for his masques, are printed in Sabol, op. cit., including two dance tunes by Thomas Lupo and one by Thomas Giles, used in the *Lord Hayes' Masque*, to which Campion wrote lyrics for printing with it: they were not sung in it ('Shewes and nightly revels, signes of joy and peace' and 'Time that leads the fatall round' to Lupo's music, and 'Triumph now with Joy and mirth' to Giles's).

[46] *Works*, pp. 220–1.

a clear musical pattern for dancing.[47] His style here shows affinity with the French method of setting words to music, with the principles applied with some freedom, and it serves the conditions and musical forces of the occasion well.

Although Campion did not practise the declamatory style himself, he made provision for it when writing a text for which others composed the music. For the festivities celebrating the wedding of the Earl of Somerset and Lady Frances Howard in 1613, he wrote the masque known as *The Masque of Squires*, for which Coperario and Lanier made song settings.[48] Coperario was strongly influenced by Italian music, and his interest was passed on to his pupils, who included William and probably also Henry Lawes, as well as the royal princes.[49] After the death of Prince Henry, he composed a group of songs of mourning, setting words by Campion, that combine a highly declamatory vocal line with firm musical control; in ''Tis now dead night', the second song, for instance, the voice declaims the words in melodic phrases of widely varying length, expressive of the outpouring of grief, while a splendidly mobile bass line outlines the harmonic structure. (Both these *Songs of Mourning*, of 1613, and his earlier *Funeral Teares*, of 1606, for the Earl of Devonshire, deserve to be more frequently heard.) His songs for the Somerset masque are musically far less adventurous and subtle, probably partly because of their less serious subject and forthright nature—two celebratory songs and a sailors' song—and partly because they are composed for performing in the banqueting room of Whitehall, not for singing in the private chamber. In their balanced construction and patterned movement they are not far from Campion's own masque ayres. Lanier's contribution to *The Masque of Squires*, sung by himself in the role of Eternity, is different not just in degree, but in kind. Campion's verse invites rhetorical setting, its lines apt for treatment as individual rhythmical units, and Lanier's setting (Ex. 22) goes beyond the use of declamatory idioms (such as the deferring of the voice's entry by an initial rest to evade bar-ictus, or the repetition of quavers on the same note for two or three syllables at the start of a phrase, followed by a long note), to a kind of ayre wholly declamatory in conception. The setting, for voice

[47] In his second book of ayres, Campion used the same music for the lyric 'The peacefull westerne winde'.

[48] Printed in Sabol, op. cit., pp. 76–81.

[49] Ferrabosco also taught music to Prince Henry and Prince Charles.

Ex. 22

accompanied by lute and bass viol, is framed to produce the effective delivery of these particular words, phrase by phrase; it is not designed to have a free-standing musical life of its own.[50]

There is considerable diversity in both form and style too in the settings, by George Mason and John Earsdon, for the song-lyrics probably by Campion in another entertainment: that presented by the Earl of Cumberland to the king at Brougham Castle, in 1617; they include a 'ballad', a dance-song, and two dialogues, and vary from tuneful strophic ayre to recitative in musical style.[51]

A composer would take into account several considerations, besides his own preference, in his choice of style for the songs in an entertainment or masque: the requirements of the author's invention; the linking of some of the songs with dances; and the number of musicians involved, whether the sizeable groups of Campion's *Lord Hayes' Masque*, held together in tuneful and 'measured sound', or a single voice, supported by one or few instruments, as in Milton's *A Maske*, making its impact by means of declamatory monody. He would be aware both of the practical factors, and of the range of styles available. As practical musicians, many playing the lute or viol, or singing or dancing in entertainments and masques, composers were well aware of the conditions for dramatic success and the audience's acclaim. They also, those in the royal service especially, found themselves working together in several contexts. Some served both in the Chapel Royal and in various consorts made up from the King's Musick as occasion required. In 1612, for example, the composers Robert Johnson, Philip Rosseter, John Dowland, and perhaps John Coperario were all lutenists in King James's Musick, and Ferrabosco was one of the 'viols and violins', whilst Ferrabosco, Johnson, John Bull, and Thomas Ford were among the musicians expert on various instruments appointed to Prince Henry; by 1616 Nicholas Lanier had joined the lutes. There was no lack of opportunity for interchange of ideas and experience.[52]

---

[50] Yet other words were fitted to it: in John Gamble's Commonplace Book (New York Public Library, Drexel MS 4257) and elsewhere, it appears with words beginning 'Weep no more, weep no more my wearied eyes'. (Printed in *English Songs 1625–1660*, ed. Spink (*Musica Britannica*, vol. 33, 1971).)

[51] See above, p. 137; and Campion's *Works*, pp. 463–71; Ian Spink, 'Campion's Entertainment at Brougham Castle, 1617', in *Music in English Renaissance Drama*, pp. 57–74; and Mason and Earsdon, *Ayres*, 1618 (*ELS* 2nd series, vol. 18).

[52] See Walter L. Woodfill, *Musicians in English Society* (Princeton, 1953), pp. 161–97 and 296–306.

As a poet, Campion was the last for whom Sidney's concept of a lyric poet as one whose verses are actually made with aptness for some kind of musical partnership in mind fully and generally holds true. For him, a lyric was essentially a short poem for singing, whether as part of an entertainment or masque or as a single ayre: that it should be framed aptly for setting to music was basic to his conception. For other poets who began writing lyric poetry about the same time, at the start of the 1590s, the connection was often occasional, as with Jonson, or notional rather than practical, as with Donne.

Jonson indeed was skilled at preparing verse for music; he wrote many lyrics to be sung in his masques and plays, and most are patterned appropriately for strophic setting, or, later, given stronger non-repeating rhythms that lend themselves to declamatory setting. Some of these lyrics can well stand without their context, and invite being chosen by composers in search of song-texts, but only a few are known to have been made into separate songs in this way. In the two plays he was commissioned to write for the Children of the Chapel, *Cynthia's Revels* and *Poetaster*, Jonson appropriately gave scope for the children's musical talents and training to be displayed, and the six songs in *Cynthia's Revels* are particularly and variously well-made for setting. One of his most famous lyrics is among them, 'Slow, slow, fresh fount, keepe time with my salt teares'. It is a true madrigal in structure, one of the few consummately beautiful English lyrics to use the form. The lines, with their varying lengths, are uninsistent in their rhyming, and by their heavy beats and pauses measure their own grave pace; the lyric carries its own sufficient music but also prepares a composer's way. Only one setting of it survives, by Henry Youll, in his *Canzonets To Three Voyces*, of 1608, and since he is not known to have been concerned with composing for plays, this may well be an instance of a lyric chosen for setting for its own sake. His music is madrigalian in style, with many verbal repetitions that leave intact much of the lyric's phrasing and heighten its plangency but obscure its form.[53]

'Queene, and Huntresse, chaste, and faire' invites lute-song setting as clearly as 'Slow, slow, fresh fount' invites madrigal setting, but none is known. The only other song in the play found with an early

[53] Chan conjectures that the setting may originally have been for solo treble, the two lower voice parts being adaptations from instrumental parts (*Music in the Theatre of Ben Jonson*, p. 54). See *EM* vol. 28.

setting is 'O, That ioy so soone should waste';[54] the music was probably made for its stage performance, for the 'long *die*-note' the courtier Amorphus comments upon is only one of the witty excesses which make the song its own parody. It is anonymous, but Sabol's suggestion of Nathaniel Giles is apt; he was Master of the Children of the Chapel from 1597 until his death in 1633, and collaborated with Henry Evans and Edward Kirkham to reinstate them in the Black-friars Theatre in 1600. Of the five songs in *Poetaster*, only one survives with what may be its original, appropriately trite, setting, 'If I freely may discouer'.[55] Both of these were later chosen for setting by Henry Lawes,[56] a prolific song-composer—his autograph collection of his own songs contains three hundred and twenty-five—who also made into a song one of the First Grace's enquiries after Cupid in the Haddington masque, 'Beauties, haue yee seene this toy'.[57] The Graces' descriptions of Cupid, in nine sixains of seven-syllabled lines, are eminently suited for setting, but it seems from the text that they were to be spoken (the same would be supposed of the masque's marriage song too but for Jonson's description of the manner of its performance).

Jonson again made provision for boys' voices in writing a text for a May Day entertainment, given in 1604 at the house of Sir William Cornwallis for King James and Queen Anne, and Martin Peerson, who became master of the singing boys of St Paul's, preserved his setting of one of its songs, 'See, see, ô see, who here is come a Maying:', by printing it in his *Priuate Musicke* years later, in 1620. *Epicœne*, like *Cynthia's Revels* and *Poetaster*, was written for the children's company (which in 1604 had become the Children of the Queen's Revels), but it contains only one song, 'Still to be neat, still to be drest'. Two settings of it are known, but neither is early enough to be the original one.[58]

---

[54] In Christ Church, Oxford, MS Mus. 439 (pp. 38–9), a collection of late sixteenth-and early seventeenth-century songs, for treble and bass, which may represent the repertoire of a choir-school. (It includes versions of six of Ferrabosco's settings of songs in Jonson's masques.)

[55] In BL Add. MS 24665, ff. 59ᵛ–60. Only the first stanza appears with the music. The song is printed in *Songs from Manuscript Sources*, 2 (1979), ed. D. Greer.

[56] Autograph MS, f. 5 and f. 7 respectively.

[57] Ibid., f. 36ᵛ.

[58] One setting, probably by William Lawes and perhaps made for the revival of the play in 1636, was published in Playford's *Select Ayres and Dialogues*, 1669; the other appears in two manuscripts, New York Public Library, Drexel MS 4257 (no. 179) and Drexel MS 4041 (no. 64).

From the plays for adult actors, one other song, besides 'Come my Celia', stands out with a beauty that is startling against the surrounding grotesquerie: 'Haue you seene but a bright Lilly grow', from Act II of *The Devil is an Ass*. Heard as a separate song, it is a praise of the loved one that makes its effect as a straight love-song; but heard in dramatic context, with the lover, Wittipol, at one window earnestly addressing himself to Mrs Fitz-dottrell at her opposite window, it is undercut by the ludicrous situation. Like 'Come my Celia' it has a kind of double identity; and the anonymous setting found in several manuscripts, for this stanza alone,[59] preserves the ambivalence, with a melodic line closely moulded to the words and heightening them with an affecting eloquence that approaches the verge of mockery without toppling into it: by a hair's breadth the song's fragile but true beauty is affirmed. In two sources the vocal line is florid: if the setting was made for the play, these probably represent later, embellished versions of the song.[60] The extent to which the ornamentation of vocal lines was practised in England in the first two decades of the seventeenth century is difficult to ascertain, since skilful singers might apply it according to their own judgement without indication or notation in the musical text; some surviving written examples were made for lady amateurs.[61] In Italy, it was discussed and practised as soon as the 'new music' developed, but in England there is little evidence for it before about 1625. From the unfinished play *The Sad Shepherd* both Nicholas Lanier and John Wilson set its only song, 'Though I am young, and cannot tell', presumably choosing it simply

[59] In the play there is one preceding stanza, beginning 'Doe but looke, on her eyes: They doe light—'. Jonson used the lyric again in a non-dramatic context, in 'A Celebration of Charis in ten Lyrick Peeces' in *Under-woods*, with another stanza preceding both: 'See the Chariot at hand here of Love'.

[60] The earliest source of the setting is in BL Add. MS 15117, and this may well be the version originally used in the play, if Mary Joiner is right in suggesting that the compiler of this manuscript was collecting music associated with the theatre ('BM Add. MS 15117: a Commentary, Index and Bibliography', *passim*'); she uses this source for the musical text in her book (Chan, *Music in the Theatre of Ben Jonson*, pp. 106–8). Spink uses the plain version of New York Public Library, Drexel MS 4175 in editing Robert Johnson's *Ayres, Songs and Dialogues* (*ELS* 2nd series, vol. 17) and cites support for ascribing the setting to Johnson; it has also been attributed to Ferrabosco.

[61] In Elizabeth Davenant's book (Christ Church, Oxford, MS 87), Elizabeth Roger's Virginal Book (BL Add. MS 10337), Lady Ann Blount's Book (Lambeth Palace Library, London, MS 1041), and Ann Twice's Book (New York Public Library, Drexel MS 4175). See Vincent Duckles, 'Florid Embellishment in English Song of the late Sixteenth and early Seventeenth Centuries', *AM* v (1957), 329–45.

as a suitable text for a song, since their settings are earlier in date than the earliest, post-Restoration, recorded performance of the play.

The association of Jonson's 'A Hymne to God the Father' with music by Ferrabosco is of a different kind. Ferrabosco's Four-Note Pavan was one of his most celebrated compositions for viols, and in all probability Jonson patterned his hymn, 'Heare mee, O God:', to go to its recurring motif. The words are found with the music in several manuscript versions, usually with the five-part music but also arranged for voice and lute.[62] Proof that Jonson, or Jonson and Ferrabosco, intended the partnership is lacking; a reference in Jonson's *Conversations with William Drummond of Hawthornden* is sometimes adduced, but 'Feraboscos Pauane with his letter' is an unwarranted emendation for 'Parabostes Pariane with his letter'.[63] Their known friendship, however, strengthens the probability; and if it is true that the motif itself was 'associated with the idea of God'[64] the pairing has added point, but I have not so far found evidence of awareness of such an association at the time.

With Jonson the lyric is most often inset in a larger whole, to be sung in a masque or entertainment or play, and it is usually shaped with care to fit it for setting and singing. Donne in effect if not by intent led the lyric away from music, for in his hands it is not set within a drama, but is often itself a whole brief implicit drama, and its mode is not that of song but of impassioned speech. It was not his way of handling rhythm to rein it in to recurrent strophic patterns, but to let it ride free to respond to the promptings of speech stress, breaking or overrunning the lines with the sense. Yet he showed some interest in writing verse for singing. His proclamation that when he has fettered his grief in verse,

> Some man, his art and voice to show,
> Doth set and sing my paine,

so making the lover a 'triple fool', might be discounted; in serving wit, it perhaps need not also serve truth, though its point is weak unless in the circle amongst whom Donne's poems passed, at least

[62] Spink prints a version for solo voice and lute from BL Egerton MS 2013 in *Songs from Manuscript Sources*; a consort version, for voice or treble viol, alto viol, two tenor viols, and bass viol, is printed in *Jacobean Consort Music*, ed. T. Dart and W. Coates (*Musica Britannica*, vol. 9, 1955).

[63] Made by R. F. Patterson in his edition of 1923; rejected by Herford and Simpson, *Ben Jonson*, iii. 131.

[64] Grove's *Dictionary of Music and Musicians*, 5th ed., vol. iii, p. 68, states that Arnold Dolmetsch affirmed this.

one or two lyrics were current as songs.[65] A more specific lead is given by the fact that in one manuscript six of his lyrics appear under the heading 'Songs which were made to certaine Aires that were made before', and four other manuscripts give the same indication for three of the six.[66] In several of these, the degree of strophic correspondence of rhythmical patterns is high, either throughout, or in part, as if a tune had furnished at least a partial pattern. Not one, unfortunately, is found together with what can be vouched to be its originating tune.

'The Baite', of course, provides its own clue, and its air should be the one Marlowe's passionate shepherd sang to. Corkine arranged as one of the pieces for lyra viol in his second book of ayres a tune with the incipit 'Come liue with me, and be my Loue', and Donne's lyric can be made to jog along to it, but it seems likelier that the passionate shepherd's lines, not his notes, were in his mind. The two lyrics that show the most care for strophic correspondence are 'Goe, and catche a falling starre', and 'Send home my long strayd eyes to mee'; in the first the rhythms reinforce the trochaic metre throughout, with the extra syllable of the last line producing the only awkwardness, and in the second the iambic pattern is similarly sustained, except in the last line of each of the first two stanzas. But the tunes they went to have not been identified, and the manuscript settings for voice and lute that do survive with them and appear to have been made for them, an anonymous one for 'Goe, and catche a falling starre', and one by Coperario for 'The Message', take no advantage of their aptness for strophic setting: in each case, only the poem's first stanza appears with the music.[67] Donne's poems were not published in Coperario's lifetime, so the composer would probably have written out as much of the lyric as he intended his setting to serve.

In 'Sweetest love, I do not goe' the only stanza Donne seems to

---

[65] It was as songs that the wider contemporary public gained their only chance to encounter any of Donne's lyrics: 'The Expiration', in Ferrabosco's *Ayres* of 1609, and 'Breake of Day', in Corkine's *The Second Booke of Ayres*, 1612, were the only ones published in his lifetime.

[66] The six lyrics are 'Send home my long strayd eyes to mee', 'Sweetest love, I do not goe', 'Come live with mee, and bee my love', 'Goe, and catche a falling starre', 'Good wee must love, and must hate ill', and 'Some man unworthy to be possessor'. For details of manuscripts, and a list of settings, see *John Donne. The Elegies and the Songs and Sonnets*, ed. Helen Gardner (Oxford, 1965), Appendix B, 'Musical Settings of Donne's Poems'. My quotations from Donne are from this edition.

[67] See Souris, *Poèmes de Donne, Herbert et Crashaw*, for the music of these and other settings of Donne, and the prefatory 'Notes Critiques' in it, by Jean Jacquot, for details of sources.

have written with a tune in mind throughout is the first; in succeeding ones he lets the sixth and seventh lines acquire an extra, initial, strongly stressed syllable that turns them into trochaic metre. The music that survives for it in two manuscripts, the same melody appearing once plain and once in ornamented form, was probably made for the words, not the words for it, and the anonymous composer's partial solution has been to alter the line-division of the sixth and seventh lines in the first stanza, ending the sixth after only four syllables, and to shorten the sixth line of the second stanza from

> But believe that I shall make

to

> Since I doe make.

At this point, although with the plain setting all stanzas appear, later ones cannot be accommodated to the music's pattern; and in the ornate version, only the first stanza is given.

For the other two of the six lyrics described as having been written to tunes, no settings are known. The versification of 'Confined Love' suggests that only the three short concluding lines of the stanzas sprang from a tune, the rest being independent; whilst in 'Communitie' the attempt to write to a tune may have left its mark in the uncertain rhythmic handling of the third line in the first two stanzas, before Donne threw off its constraint.

The evidence of these lyrics suggests an absence of aptitude in Donne for writing words to or for music. 'Sweet stay a while, why will you rise?' offers itself to music as 'Breake of Day' does not, carrying a tender, uncomplicated plea in lilting lines, using closely similar rhythms in both its stanzas; on such grounds alone one would question the attribution of it to him.[68] It is not surprising that composers preferred the anonymous lyric; Corkine, in undertaking to set Donne's poem, was faced with lines that embody the urgencies of speech, disregarding the need of strophic setting for repetition of rhythmic grouping. Each of the opening four questions takes up the length of a line: the third and fourth lines of the first stanza run:

> Why should we rise, because 'tis light?
> Did we lie downe, because 'twas night?

but as this stage of the last stanza short phrases pile up and overspill the line:

[68] See above, pp. 121–2.

The poore, the foule, the false, love can
Admit, but not the busied man.

Corkine makes a brave shot at reconciling these divergent needs by
the use of declamatory phrasing, repeating the first phrase of the third
line to a sequential melodic figure that breaks the line with rests, and
proceeding to the fourth line without pause (Ex. 23). There are no
infelicities as striking as in Ferrabosco's music for 'The Expiration',[69]
but the text's recalcitrance to strophic setting is clear.[70]

Ex. 23

What will you rise,   what will you rise   be - cause tis light? Did we lye downe

Only one poem of Donne's, in fact, is found with a strophic setting
in which words and music complement each other throughout; and
that is not one of the *Songs and Sonnets* but one of the *Divine Poems*,
'A Hymne to God the Father', probably written many years later.
Walton states that Donne wrote it at the time of his severe illness in
1623, and 'caus'd it to be set to a most grave and solemn Tune, and to
be often sung to the *Organ*, by the *Choristers* of St. *Pauls* Church, in
his own hearing',[71] and that it gave him great pleasure. John Hilton's
setting, for voice and bass, may well be the original one sung by the
choirboys to the organ; it has a grave beauty that finely conveys the
penitence and supplication of the words.[72]

In his hymn, Donne observed a strophic discipline that both served
to express its chastened spirit and opened the way for musical setting.
More often, his poems are astir with turbulence, and their shifts of
stance or emotion or thought throw up complex and non-recurring
rhythms. He was well-disposed to the concept of lyrics as songs, but
his own strong lines were rarely subdued to the strophic account-
ability needed for the practical partnership of the ayre.

[69] See above, pp. 128–30.
[70] Corkine's setting is in his *Second Booke of Ayres*, 1612; *ELS* 2nd series, vol. 13.
[71] *The Life of Dr. John Donne*, in *Lives* (4th ed., 1675), p. 54.
[72] Hilton's setting is in BL Egerton MS 2013 (f. 13ᵛ); it is printed in *English Songs 1625–1660*, ed. Spink (*Musica Britannica*, vol. 33, 1971). Later, Pelham Humfrey also made a successful setting for this hymn (published in *Harmonia Sacra*, 1688), choosing to use through-setting except for the refrain line of the first two stanzas, for which the melody is the same; the contrasting affirmation of the last stanza has its own melodic phrasing, triumphant and serene. Helen Gardner prints the melody (ed. cit., p. 247), and notes a modern edition.

5

Ballads, Songs, and Masques in the Plays of Shakespeare

To a dramatist, song is a rich resource, and to Shakespeare and his contemporaries, the whole range of kinds of song so far discussed was available: ballad, dance-song, part-song, consort song, madrigal, ayre, and masque song. Of all dramatists writing plays for an adult company, Shakespeare most fully explored and exploited the dramatic potentialities of song, making both traditional and innovatory uses of it. Sometimes he used, or adapted, existing ballads; occasionally he wrote his own counterfeit ballads; he shaped many lyrics in refrain-song, lute-song, or madrigal form; and the matching of text and dramatic context, song-style and function, is an aspect of his dramatic mastery that has long seemed to me to invite closer study. The chief aim of this chapter is to make possible a fuller appreciation of it, through investigation of Shakespeare's techniques and practice in such matching in all his plays containing song.[1]

[1] There are of course other aspects of Shakespeare's use of music and song, and other dramatists whose usage rewards study. F. W. Sternfeld's bibliography in *Music in Shakespearean Tragedy* (1963) includes general studies of music in Elizabethan and Jacobean drama, and studies relating to individual authors, and his Chapter X, 'A Retrospect of Scholarship on Shakespeare and Music', is a useful *catalogue raisonnée*. In his book he discusses the use and place of both vocal and instrumental music in the tragedies, and in *Songs from Shakespeare's Tragedies* (1964) he edits twenty songs for performance. John Stevens, in his essay 'Shakespeare and the Music of the Elizabethan Stage' in *Shakespeare in Music*, ed. Phyllis Hartnoll (1964), sketches in the uses of instrumental music, as well as song, in Shakespeare's plays, with some wider discussion of earlier and contemporary dramatic practice. The most informative single work on Shakespeare's songs is Peter J. Seng's *The Vocal Songs in the Plays of Shakespeare* (Cambridge, Mass., 1967), which gives detailed comment on every song, ballad texts, information on surviving musical sources and modern transcriptions, and excerpts from comments by other scholars. I make footnote reference to it in this chapter when the further information it gives is especially relevant, but it should be referred to for full documentation of all the songs; I give references only to one or two accessible printings of music, where known, for each song. Seng prints the song-texts from the earliest authoritative edition of each play; in view of this, I use a modern edition, Peter Alexander's *William Shakespeare: The Complete Works* (1951; repr. 1985), for all quotations and line references, for the reader's ease of reference, discussing variant readings where necessary.

The degree to which he made use of song in individual plays was influenced by various factors, among them the genre of the play, the resources of personnel and finance available, contemporary taste, and his own sense of fitness. At all stages of his career, and in each major kind, there are plays that make little or no use of song, and plays making extensive and subtle use of it; but a trend is discernible towards increasingly integrated use. Within each kind, chronologically viewed, this pattern may be seen to emerge.

The scope for song, and for music of other kinds, is fullest and most various in the comedies, and in them Shakespeare moves from relatively simple and external introductions of song in early plays towards the permeation of the whole atmosphere and dramatic texture that characterizes the late romances. The tragedies, most of which were written within a single decade, show more restricted but potent use, early perfected: in *Hamlet*, Shakespeare's handling of song is as profound as it was ever to be.

In the history plays, song and, except in *King Henry the Eighth*, music, play a smaller part, but their use becomes more diversified. Only *King Henry the Fourth* and *King Henry the Eighth* contain any songs at all; in the rest, trumpets sound alarms and parleys, drums indicate marches, and so on, but song, and music *per se*, do not occur. For sound effects, and the setting of scene, even of atmosphere, martial noises and instrumental music will suffice; or song can be used for such purposes, as it is in the first part of *King Henry the Fourth*, in the first scene of Act III, when Lady Mortimer sings. The scene takes place in Glendower's castle: Mortimer and Hotspur are about to leave their wives and set out to encounter the king at Shrewsbury, and Mortimer's wife, who speaks no English, tries to stay her husband. Glendower, her father, translates her speech:

> She bids you on the wanton rushes lay you down,
> And rest your gentle head upon her lap,
> And she will sing the song that pleaseth you,
> And on your eyelids crown the god of sleep . . .   (lines 213–16.)

and, after Hotspur's mischievous repartee with his own wife, Lady Mortimer 'sings a Welsh song'. The episode glows with the light of domestic love against the dark background of civil strife, and the song contributes to the contrast. This is one of the rare occurrences of 'blank song' (where song is called for but no text or name is supplied) in Shakespeare's plays—and an understandable one, since the words were Welsh. One of the company's apprentices at this time, a player of tender women's roles, was Robert Goffe; the surname is glossed by Camden in his *Remains of a Greater Work concerning Britain*, 1605: 'Goff, *id est*, Smith in Welsh.'[2] So Lady Mortimer may well have sung an authentic Welsh song. But another consideration, besides its language, makes the absence of a text acceptable here: it is not the song's substance, but its mere presence, that carries significance in this context. Elsewhere in the play, only trumpets are called for, to sound a parley or a retreat, and their tongues speak of war; the song belongs to the life of peace, and any Welsh song of gentle mood may serve.

Only snatches of song are sung in Part Two, but they are specified. In Act II, scene iv, Falstaff enters The Boar's Head tavern singing 'When Arthur first in court . . . And was a worthy king'; and in Act V, scene iii, in Justice Shallow's orchard, Justice Silence has six bouts of singing snippets of song before he is carried off to bed: every remark calls some ditty to his mind. Falstaff's entry in Act II, scene iv, guarantees an uproarious response from an audience that recognizes the broadside ballad 'Sir Launcelot du Lake'; the bathetic command to Francis, 'Empty the jordan', which he interjects between phrases of the song emphasizes that Sir John of Eastcheap is a knight of a different order from Sir Launcelot. Despite the hilarity, the shift of focus on Falstaff that began in the battle scenes at the end of Part One, and that casts an increasingly hard light on him throughout Part Two, is perceptible. In Act V, scene iii, it is Silence who sings scraps of two Shrovetide carols, three drinking-songs, and a Robin Hood ballad, in a scene that provides a sharp contrast to the preceding one in which the new King Henry V is reconciled to the Lord Chief Justice, but Falstaff is there, roistering with the fuddled country justices, and reaching the apogee of misplaced exaltation when Pistol brings the news of Hal's accession—'Blessed are they that have been my friends; and woe to my Lord Chief Justice!'

The last of the history plays, *King Henry the Eighth*, shows a great increase in the use of music, for in it, as in the other late plays, the romances, masque and ceremonial are major elements; and it contains the only song actually given in any of the history plays; but there is a complication here, for the scene is generally thought to be

---

[2] Noted by T. W. Baldwin, *The Organization and Personnel of the Shakespearean Company* (Princeton, 1927), pp. 416–18.

not by Shakespeare but by Fletcher.[3] The song comes at the opening of Act III: the trial of Queen Katharine has been adjourned, but she knows the outcome is not in doubt. She and her women are at their needlework; she says to one of them

> Take thy lute, wench. My soul grows sad with troubles;
> Sing and disperse 'em, if thou canst. Leave working.

and the waiting woman sings,

> Orpheus with his lute made trees . . .[4]

It is a lovely lyric, well framed for a lute-song, the two six-line stanzas (printed continuously in the First Folio) having such close replication of rhythms that a strophic setting can easily match both, so long as the divergent phrasing of the last two lines of each is provided for. But the song glosses, rather than answers, the queen's request, by recalling the effects of the music of Orpheus, and commenting on the Orphic powers of music in general; and we hear nothing of the song's success in assuaging the killing care and grief of the queen. With the gentleman's entry, it is done with; it does not reverberate. By contrast with other occasions in Shakespeare's plays when a song is called for in a special situation—the serenade to Silvia, for instance, in *The Two Gentlemen of Verona*,[5] or, more closely analogous, the song sung by a boy to the forsaken Mariana in *Measure for Measure*[6]— 'Orpheus with his lute' has the separateness of appliqué. Perhaps the Orphic theme itself assures us that the queen's sadness will be allayed by the music; but for Shakespeare, song was a strand to be woven into the dramatic fabric, and the isolation and unsubtlety here support the view that the song and the scene are not his.

The histories, then, probably contain not a single song of Shakespeare's own making; but *King Henry the Fourth*, Part Two, shows him exploring a usage of borrowed song that he developed further in both comedies and tragedies. For drinking-songs and ballads can be used, not only to throw comic or ironic light on

---

[3] For brief discussion of problems of the play's authorship, and further references, see the New Arden ed., Intro., pp. xv–xxvi.

[4] The syntax, and hence the sense, of the first lines is open to misreading: the New Arden editor, for example, annotating III. i. 5, asks, '. . . did the compositor misread MS *bowd* as *bowe*, and hence print the present tense?' No: the song does not say that Orpheus made trees, and that mountain tops bowed, but that Orpheus made trees and mountain tops bow.

[5] See below, pp. 174–6.   [6] See below, pp. 207–9.

character and situation, in plays of all kinds—Petruchio's snippets of song in *The Taming of the Shrew* and Mercutio's bawdy snatch in *Romeo and Juliet* are early examples in comedy and tragedy—but also to move a plot onwards towards its tragic or comic end.

In two of the tragedies, drinking-songs form part of scenes in which disgrace or downfall is foreshadowed or actually engineered. It is not the spontaneous exuberance of conviviality that prompts Iago to sing: in Act I, scene iii he had cogitated:

> Cassio's a proper man. Let me see now:
> To get his place, and to plume up my will
> In double knavery. How, how? Let's see: (lines 386–8.)

and his songs in Act II, scene iii are part of his answer. Cassio, in charge of the guard on the night of revelry proclaimed by Othello to celebrate both the defeat of the Turkish fleet and his marriage, is well aware he has 'very poor and unhappy brains for drinking'; but he yields to Iago's persuasion, and as Iago strikes up 'And let me the canakin clink, clink' and then 'King Stephen was and a worthy peer', the wine and the apparent camaraderie both work upon him. So the brawl that leads to his disgrace can be provoked; and Iago can use that in turn to work Othello's misery too, by leading Cassio to ask Desdemona to plead for him. Iago's songs would have the more impact on an audience if they were familiar ones, and it seems probable that Shakespeare was borrowing from popular song, but there is no evidence for this: no contemporary association with a tune is known for either of them.[7]

The drinking scene in *Antony and Cleopatra*, Act II, scene vii, is more ambiguously presented. It is Enobarbus who proposes to Antony,

> Ha, my brave emperor!
> Shall we dance now the Egyptian Bacchanals
> And celebrate our drink?

and who places hand in hand the newly reconciled Pompey, Antony, Caesar, and Lepidus. As music plays and a boy sings 'Come, thou monarch of the vine', they all dance and bear the chorus,

---

[7] A version of 'King Stephen was and a worthy peer' appears in the Percy Folio MS and another in Ramsay's *Tea-Table Miscellany*, and several eighteenth- and nineteenth-century folk-song collections include a traditional Scots tune for 'Tak your auld cloak about ye', but no sources earlier than the play are known.

> Cup us till the world go round,
> Cup us till the world go round!   (lines 111–16.)

Lepidus has already been carried off, but the remaining two of the triple pillars of the world, with Pompey and others, drunkenly swaying, themselves go round. Enobarbus has a shrewd recognition of the fragility of the new pacts, and a sardonic humour; but he does not, as Iago does, engineer disaster: he foresees it, and the audience is led to share his foresight. The singing and dancing contribute to this, as the boy sings an invocation to Bacchus, and the revellers take it up as if familiar with it. Here a song that seems to belong to the Roman stock, not the English, is appropriate, and Shakespeare provides one that suggests this, although it is probably his own; the tune for it is not known.

The song in *Antony and Cleopatra* best fulfils its purpose by seeming to be known to its Roman participants; the audience need not know it too. But the Roman plays preserve an awareness of distance in place and time as many of the other plays do not: in the tragedies and comedies, life in other times and places may be almost imperceptibly assimilated to life in Elizabethan England. In *Othello*, Iago does explain that he learned 'And let me the canakin clink, clink' in England; but how Desdemona's mother's maid came to know the Willow song, the audience is not told and is very unlikely to ask. Shakespeare often drew on existing popular songs and broadside ballads, rather than writing songs of his own in these veins, tapping the power their familiarity gave them to elicit rapport with an audience, to communicate a mood, to awaken associations.

The subtlest and most complex use of this kind is in *Hamlet*, in Ophelia's mad scene, Act IV, scene v:

Enter OPHELIA distracted.

Oph.   Where is the beauteous Majesty of Denmark?
Queen.   How now, Ophelia!
Oph.   [*Sings*]
> How should I your true love know
>   From another one?
> By his cockle hat and staff,
>   And his sandal shoon.

Queen.   Alas, sweet lady, what imports this song?

Oph. Say you? Nay, pray you mark.

[*Sings*] He is dead and gone, lady,
  He is dead and gone;
  At his head a grass-green turf,
  At his heels a stone.

O, ho!

Queen. Nay, but, Ophelia—
Oph. Pray you mark.

[*Sings*] White his shroud as the mountain snow—

Enter KING.

Queen. Alas, look here, my lord.
Oph. Larded with sweet flowers;
  Which bewept to the grave did not go
  With true-love showers.

King. How do you, pretty lady?

Oph. Well, God dild you! They say the owl was a baker's daughter. Lord, we know what we are, but know not what we may be. God be at your table!

King. Conceit upon her father.

Oph. Pray let's have no words of this; but when they ask you what it means, say you this:

[*Sings*] To-morrow is Saint Valentine's day,
  All in the morning betime,
  And I a maid at your window,
  To be your Valentine.

  Then up he rose, and donn'd his clothes,
  And dupp'd the chamber-door;
  Let in the maid, that out a maid
  Never departed more.

King. Pretty Ophelia!

Oph. Indeed, la, without an oath, I'll make an end on't.

[*Sings*] By Gis, and by Saint Charity,
  Alack, and fie for shame!
  Young men will do't, if they come to't;
  By Cock, they are to blame.

> Quoth she 'Before you tumbled me,
>   You promis'd me to wed'.

He answers

>   'So would I 'a done, by yonder sun,
>   An thou hadst not come to my bed'.   (lines 21–64.)

After Ophelia has gone out, Claudius says,

> O, this is the poison of deep grief; it springs
> All from her father's death.

Does it all? The death of her father is of course in her mind, in part prompting these songs, and others that follow, to the surface: 'They bore him barefac'd on the bier' and 'And will 'a not come again?' No, her father will not come again; but neither will Hamlet, her love. In the maze of her distraught mind the two griefs are merging, suffusing the songs she sings. The first line she sings concerns a 'true love', and the song on St Valentine's Day is about love betrayed. The love between her and Hamlet has been betrayed, not by themselves but by the suspicions and evil acts of others; she is unhinged by the loss and death of love as well as by the loss and death of her father. And they are inextricably interconnected: the deaths of their fathers have blighted the love of their children. Hamlet, obsessed with the need for revenge and with distrust of all sexual love because of his father's death and his mother's remarriage, spurns Ophelia and cares little about killing her father. The body of Polonius is bundled away and interred 'in hugger-mugger'; and Ophelia sings of a dead loved one

> Which bewept to the grave did not go
> With true-love showers.

The lines run awkwardly, the negative jarring against the consolation and the rhythm of the song: it arrests attention as an intrusion. If the listening queen has taken the song's opening question to herself,

> How shall I your true love know
> From another one?

she is reminded that if her first husband was her true love, as her hasty remarriage casts in doubt, he too has been deprived of the decency of due mourning.

The source-text of Ophelia's song is lost, but enough analogues and references exist to indicate that Shakespeare had in mind an existing ballad;[8] and such ancestry gives the song extra power. If it shares a common parentage with the ballad 'As ye came from the holy land of Walsingham', it probably went to the highly popular tune 'Walsingham', which survives in many early manuscript lute books and virginal books[9] (the Fitzwilliam Book contains sets of variations on it by both Byrd and Bull). As the play's audience listened to Ophelia, some version of the ballad would sing itself in the minds of many of them. The one ascribed to 'Sir W.R.' in one manuscript, and now generally accepted as Ralegh's, begins:

> As you came from the holy land
>   Of Walsinghame
> Mett you not with my true loue
>   By the way as you came?
>
> How shall I know your trew loue
>   That haue mett many one
> As I went to the holy lande
>   That haue come, that haue gone?
>
> She is neyther whyte nor browne
>   But as the heauens fayre
> There is none hathe a forme so diuine
>   In the earth or the ayre.[10]

The deserted lover, here a man, becomes Ophelia; the lost one (herself a pilgrim, disguised as a man, in another version) suggests Hamlet, who 'weeps for what is done' (Act IV, scene i, line 27) and is voyaging to England, perhaps never to return. Long trains of thought are for readers, not spectators, and few in the audience might formulate such reflections; but far more responses and associations would be aroused in them by a song at once familiar and poignantly different than by a wholly new song. Moreover, it is both more natural and more pathetic that Ophelia's songs are old, widely known ballads. The mere fact that she, a court lady, sings in the presence of the queen, and the king, shows that the controls of reason

---

[8] Shakespeare seems to have recast a lost version of the Walsingham ballad; the surviving manuscript sources, and the earliest printed version, have variants suggesting a common original, which he may have known. See Seng, op. cit., pp. 131–56.

[9] John Ward, in 'Apropos *The British Broadside Ballad and Its Music*', *JAMS* xx (1967), 79–82, added further sources to those previously known, bringing the total to thirty manuscript and five printed sources.

[10] *The Poems of Sir Walter Ralegh*, ed. Agnes Latham (1962), pp. 22–3; from Bodleian MS Rawlinson Poet. 85, f. 123.

and social propriety have snapped; and as she becomes simple and childish, it is entirely credible that songs heard in childhood, from servants or nurse, should float up in her mind and become vents for her double distress. Her father and brother have seen to it that love is linked with seduction in her mind: it is their warnings, not anything that has passed between her and Hamlet—her thoughts are all for him, not for herself, when he spurns her—that bring the song on St Valentines Day to her recollection. The tune that survives for this song in theatre tradition has been thought to lack authentication, but the presence of its opening bars in a song-setting printed in 1606 suggests an early provenance.[11]

When Ophelia re-enters, after Laertes's arrival, it is her father she is lamenting:

> They bore him barefac'd on the bier;

But she is bereft of both father and lover, and her thoughts are of both:

> There's rosemary, that's for remembrance; pray you, love, remember.

She strews herbs for her father's bier; she will remember him: will Hamlet remember her? A nonsense refrain, one sometimes used in place of bawdy rhyme-words, has already intruded into her dirge:

> Hey non nonny, nonny, hey nonny;

now another refrain that could carry a *double entendre* comes into her head:

> For bonny sweet Robin is all my joy.

Hamlet, as well as Polonius, is surely in her mind as she sings

> And will 'a not come again?

and perhaps King Hamlet too, for if 'Go to thy death-bed' is her change from something like 'Gone to his death-bed', as the context suggests, the injunction may be for both herself and the queen.[12]

---

[11] Vincent Duckles has pointed out that its first two bars are used in the instrumental preludes in Coperario's setting of 'In darknesse let me dwell' in his *Funeral Teares*, 1606. ('The English Musical Elegy of the Late Renaissance', in *Aspects of Medieval and Renaissance Music*, ed. Jan La Rue (1966), pp. 134–53.)

[12] For 'Bonny Sweet Robin' a tune survives in many early manuscript and printed sources (Sternfeld lists thirty, and gives the tune, *Music in Shakespearean Tragedy*, pp. 68–77). For the other two of this group of songs, the original music is not known.

The scene of Ophelia's madness shows more powerfully than perhaps any other scene of Shakespeare's his genius in the usage of song, in his choice of kind in respect both of its emotional effects and its appropriateness to the dramatic texture. The tissue of consequence and inconsequence in what Ophelia sings and says is subtly woven, and the subtleties have the greater chance of appreciation because of the familiarity of the ballads, their tunes, their words, their associations; but the interweaving of speech and song that is exploited to multiple effect is itself facilitated by the use of popular song. Whereas new-made songs would stand apart, lessening the credibility of the scene, these old ballads seem part of the eddy and surge of Ophelia's consciousness, and make juxtapositions of association that shock and convince, moving the hearers in the play's audience, but also the hearers within the play, and so affecting the action: Ophelia's deranged singing moves Laertes to a passionate grief and rage that will use honourable or dishonourable means alike to achieve revenge:

Hadst thou thy wits, and didst persuade revenge,
It could not move thus.   (lines 165–6.)

Desdemona *has* her wits, so for her to sing would be even more unexpected than for Ophelia, if it occurred in the presence of other noble persons. Men and women of high rank would rarely be heard to sing in real life, and it was not expected of such characters in drama, especially tragic drama. In the willow-song scene in *Othello*, as in the scene of Ophelia's madness in *Hamlet*, Shakespeare makes what is in fact an innovative use of song with the utmost skill, giving it to a heroine in tragedy with arresting effect, but without letting either Ophelia or Desdemona behave with deliberate indecorum, for neither is wittingly giving a public performance. Ophelia is no longer in control of herself; and Desdemona is in her chamber preparing to go to bed, and only her maid hears her sing. In both cases, the circumstances give credibility to the occurrence, and the songs are made part of the whole verbal tissue. Ophelia's songs are glossed by her own comments and those of her hearers; Desdemona introduces her song herself, explaining how she came to know it:

Des. My mother had a maid call'd Barbary:
She was in love; and he she lov'd prov'd mad,
And did forsake her. She had a song of 'willow';
An old thing 'twas, but it express'd her fortune,

And she died singing it. That song to-night
Will not go from my mind; I have much to do
But to go hang my head all at one side
And sing it like poor Barbary. Prithee dispatch.

    Emil. Shall I go fetch your night-gown?

    Des. No, unpin me here.
This Lodovico is a proper man.

    Emil. A very handsome man.

    Des. He speaks well.

    Emil. I know a lady in Venice would have walk'd barefoot to
Palestine for a touch of his nether lip.

    Des.
[*Sings*]   The poor soul sat sighing by a sycamore tree,
          Sing all a green willow;
       Her hand on her bosom, her head on her knee.
          Sing willow, willow, willow.
       The fresh streams ran by her, and murmur'd her moans;
          Sing willow, willow, willow;
       Her salt tears fell from her and soft'ned the stones;
          Sing willow—
Lay by these—
                willow, willow.—
Prithee, hie thee; he'll come anon,—
       Sing all a green willow must be my garland.
       Let nobody blame him; his scorn I approve—
Nay, that's not next. Hark! Who is't that knocks?

    Emil. It is the wind.

    Des.
[*Sings*]   I call'd my love false love; but what said he then?
          Sing willow, willow, willow:
       If I court moe women; you'll couch with moe men—
So, get thee gone; good night. Mine eyes do itch;
Doth that bode weeping?

    Emil. 'Tis neither here nor there.

    Des. I have heard it said so. O, these men, these men!
Dost thou in conscience think—tell me, Emilia—

That there be women do abuse their husbands
In such gross kind?   (Act IV, scene iii, lines 25–61.)

The integration of the song into the scene is total, effected by means of the reminiscence that leads into it; of the likeness of Barbary's plight to her own, her lord in the grip of a jealous rage akin to madness; and of her question to Emilia arising out of it. (The song is also referred back to in Act V, scene iii, lines 249–51, when Emilia recalls it and sings a few words of the refrain as she is dying.)

An early manuscript music setting, for voice with lute accompaniment, gives eight stanzas of song-text which are clearly close to the version Shakespeare knew, and comparison with it makes the significances of Desdemona's misordering and altering of some such source more apparent.[13] Shakespeare gives Desdemona only three and a half stanzas; her first is the opening one, changed to fit her sex: the verse lines in the manuscript run:

> The poore soule sate sighinge by a Sickamore tree,
> with his hand in his bosom & his heade vpon his knee.

A much later stanza starts next to her mind—a naturalistic touch in portraying someone calling a lengthy ballad to mind, but also apt, for it foreshadows her dying attempt to avert blame from Othello:

> Let nobody blame him; his scorn I approve

corresponds to the manuscript version's

> Let nobody chyde her, her scornes I approue

—but she checks herself and takes up an earlier stanza. For her last, Shakespeare provides one related to one in the ballad, but differing significantly from it: into the lament

---

[13] The manuscript, BL Add MS 15117, contains settings with a span of at least forty years, up to about 1616; its music for the Willow Song may preserve the melody Desdemona sang. But another willow song, of which vocal fragments survive, probably from the 1530s or 1540s, may preserve an older melody; it is related to lute pieces in the Lodge and Dallis books, which have no texts but are headed, respectively, 'All of grene willowe' and 'All a greene willowe'. For facsimiles and adaptations, see Sternfeld's book, pp. 25–52, and Ward, '*Joan qd John* and Other Fragments at Western Reserve University', in *Aspects of Medieval and Renaissance Music*, pp. 832–55. Sternfeld also reviews arguments and evidence for considering the Folio text of the play, which includes the Willow Song, to be more reliable than the Quarto, which does not.

> Com all you forsaken & mourne you with mee
> who speakes of a false loue, mynes falser then shee

reported dialogue intrudes:

> I call'd my love false love; but what said he then?
> If I court moe women, you'll couch with moe men—

and at this Desdemona breaks off, choked with horror at the faithlessness that she sings of and that she stands accused of, to demand of Emilia if she believes there are any women so wicked.

The popularity of the willow song in the late sixteenth and early seventeenth centuries is evidenced by the number of versions and analogues that survive (and it has been kept alive by many other sets of verse that take up its metrical pattern, its theme and refrain). Shakespeare handled the old song consummately for his own purpose, altering it to underline the gross error of the accusations against Desdemona and her appalled innocence, using its cadences of plangent lament, and the added power born of familiarity, to evoke resonances of response in the hearers. This is his most unsparingly tragic use of old song, for whereas Ophelia no longer feels her own suffering with the acuteness of sane awareness, and her condition calls forth a slightly distanced pity, Desdemona suffers the full pain of what is happening to her, and as she sings the audience empathizes with her in her distress.

The songs given to Ophelia and Desdemona effect a lyric softening in dramatic tone, but they sustain the tragic mood. Within *Hamlet* itself, and still more in *King Lear*, Shakespeare risked more ambivalent effects. In *Hamlet*, song is used again after Ophelia's death, in Act V, scene i, but this time the effect is to inlay a bizarre streak of comedy into a tragic context. An early anticipation of this kind of use occurred in *Romeo and Juliet*, in the encounter between the nurse's servant Peter and the musicians who arrived to play for Juliet's wedding, to find her apparently dead (Act IV, scene v). In this episode Peter puns and plays on the names of songs and quizzes the musicians on the text of the song 'When griping grief the heart doth wound', of which he recites or sings a few lines. Many in the play's first audiences would know the lyric of Richard Edwards's song from its inclusion in his miscellany, *The Paradyse of daynty deuises*, and perhaps the tune too;[14] and for some of them any scene that gave

---

[14] See above, p. 25.

scope to Will Kemp, who played Peter, would need no further justification. But, although Juliet is indeed not truly dead, already the build-up towards tragic tone is in progress, and this passage of repartee imperils it.

There is no such uncertainty of handling in the last act of *Hamlet*, where a comic element arises from the actual singing of a song, and from its macabre relation to the situation. The act opens with the two grave-diggers digging a grave for Ophelia and arguing, comically but pertinently, whether it is right for her to receive Christian burial or whether, like suicides of lowlier rank, she should lie in unhallowed ground. As the second grave-digger goes off to fetch beer, and as Hamlet and Horatio are approaching, the first grave-digger gives a jumbled rendering of some stanzas of a song:

> *1 Clo.* [*Digs and sings*]
>> In youth, when I did love, did love,
>>> Methought it was very sweet,
>> To contract-o-the time for-a my behove,
>>> O, methought there-a-was nothing-a meet.

Ham. Has this fellow no feeling of his business, that 'a sings in grave-making?

Hor. Custom hath made it in him a property of easiness.

Ham. 'Tis e'en so; the hand of little employment hath the daintier sense.

> *1 Clo.* [*Sings*]
>> But age, with his stealing steps,
>>> Hath clawed me in his clutch,
>> And hath shipped me intil the land
>>> As if I had never been such.

> [*Throws up a skull.*

Ham. That skull had a tongue in it, and could sing once. How the knave jowls it to the ground, as if 'twere Cain's jawbone, that did the first murder! This might be the pate of a politician, which this ass now o'erreaches; one that would circumvent God, might it not?

Hor. It might, my lord.

Ham. Or of a courtier; which could say 'Good morrow, sweet lord! How dost thou, sweet lord?' This might be my Lord Such-a-one, that praised my Lord Such-a-one's horse, when 'a meant to beg it—might it not?

Hor. Ay, my lord.

Ham. Why, e'en so; and now my Lady Worm's, chapless, and knock'd about the mazard with a sexton's spade. Here's fine revolution, an we had the trick to see't. Did these bones cost no more the breeding but to play at loggats with them? Mine ache to think on't.

1 Clo. [Sings]

> A pick-axe and a spade, a spade,
> > For and a shrouding sheet:
> O, a pit of clay for to be made
> > For such a guest is meet.

> *[Throws up another skull.*
> (Act V, scene i, lines 61–95.)

Like 'When griping grief the heart doth wound', the song would be familiar to the hearers because of its inclusion in a poetic miscellany, the best-known one of all, Tottel's; two contemporary tunes for it survive.[15] Ex. 24 reproduces the setting found in BL Add. MS 4900 (ff. 62ᵛ–63), and two other songs. Lord Vaux's lyric runs:

> I Lothe that I did loue,
> > In youth that I thought swete:
> As time requires for my behoue
> Me thinkes they are not mete,
> > My lustes they do me leaue,
> My fancies all be fledde:
> And tract of time begins to weaue,
> Gray heares vpon my hedde.
> > For age with stelyng steppes,
> Hath clawed me with his cowche:[16]
> And lusty life away she leapes,
> As there had bene none such.
> > My muse dothe not delight
> Me as she did before:
> My hand and pen are not in plight,
> As they haue bene of yore.
> > For reason me denies,
> This youthly idle rime:
> And day by day to me she cryes,
> Leaue of these toyes in time.

---

[15] See above, p. 11.   [16] Corrected in later editions of Tottel to 'crutch'.

The wrincles in my brow,
The furrowes in my face:
Say limpyng age will hedge him now,
Where youth must geue him place.

    The harbinger of death,
To me I see him ride:
The cough, the colde, the gaspyng breath,
Dothe bid me to prouide.

    A pikaxe and a spade,
And eke a shrowdyng shete,
A house of claye for to be made,
For such a gest most mete.

    Me thinkes I heare the clarke,
That knols the careful knell:
And bids me leaue my wofull worke,
Er nature me compell.

    My kepers knit the knot,
That youth did laugh to scorne:
Of me that clene shalbe forgot,
As I had not ben borne.

    Thus must I youth geue vp,
Whose badge I long did weare:
To them I yelde the wanton cup
That better may it beare.

    Loe here the bared scull,
By whose balde signe I know:
That stoupyng age away shall pull,
Which youthfull yeres did sowe.

    For beauty with her bande
These croked cares hath wrought:
And shipped me into the lande,
From whence I first was brought.

    And ye that bide behinde,
Haue ye none other trust:
As ye of claye were cast by kinde,
So shall ye waste to dust.

It is a song of one once quick with youth and love, but now ready for a house of clay: as Ophelia is, and as Hamlet soon will be: his youthful love for Ophelia has been cankered by disgust at his

Ex. 24 In the manuscript, the voice part is written upside down;

My litell prætie one.

Whatt cause gave I for to reioyce.

I losse that I did love.

singer and lutenist would sit sharing the book across a table.

mother's hasty remarriage, and his suspicion of worse; he is prematurely out of love with both love and life—'What should such fellows as I do crawling between earth and heaven?'—and a 'pit' of clay (the grave-digger's earthy substitution for 'house') will shortly receive him. The pickaxe and spade of the song (the 'bared scull' of a later quatrain might be in a contemporary hearer's mind too) make it an appropriate one for the grave-digger to use as a work-shanty to dig to; and his singing, mangling both words and metre, heightens the macabre effect of the scene, as his quibbling heightens the tension and poignancy, for Hamlet elicits from him that the grave is for a woman, but not for whom, and learns that one of the skulls is that of Yorick, his father's jester, whom he had known in childhood. The scene contains comedy, but it is also a meditation on several aspects of death; it is taut with suspense and irony, and the song contributes to both its comedy and its tension. As the song about an old man wearied by love is sung at the making of a grave for a girl who has died with love unfulfilled, incongruity and comedy slacken one strand of the cord of tragic emotion, while shock and suspense tug another strand tight; the audience is given a breather but also kept catching its breath in a scene that is comic, gruesome, releasing, agonizing.

In *Hamlet* and *Othello*, Shakespeare was making calculated breaches of tragic decorum: in both he allowed his heroine to sing— and to sing popular and even, in Ophelia's case, bawdy, songs; in *Hamlet* he also allowed a clown not only to figure in tragedy but to sing, and at a climactic moment. In *King Lear* he developed further still the use of a singing clown, and the consequent twisting together of comic and tragic, grotesque and grim; yet the tragic tension is not lost. As Felver well said, 'The Fool becomes a tragic interlocutor',[17] and part of that tragic dialogue takes the medium of doggerel song, spliced into the environing texture of blank verse and prose.

On his first entry, in Act I, scene iv, the Fool offers Kent his coxcomb for the folly of loyalty to King Lear, recites two rhyming speeches, the second riddling on a sweet and bitter fool, for whom Lear is made to stand; riddles in prose about crowns, taunting Lear for his folly in giving his golden one away, and presumably sings (there is neither stage direction nor typographical evidence to establish this) two snatches of song, both continuing the alignment of the fool and his betters. Both are in ballad metre, and although no

---

[17] Charles S. Felver, *Robert Armin, Shakespeare's Fool* (Kent, Ohio, 1961), p. 59.

tune has survived for the first, it seems probable that, like the second, it had a ballad source: it runs:

> Fools had ne'er less grace in a year;
>> For wise men are grown foppish,
> And know not how their wits to wear,
>> Their manners are so apish.

The second points directly to Lear:

> Then they for sudden joy did weep,
>> And I for sorrow sung,
> That such a king should play bo-peep
>> And go the fools among.[18]

The tune for this may be preserved in two staves of handwritten music in the British Library copy of Ravenscroft's *Mvsicks Miscellanie* (1609), with underneath them the words

> Late as I waked out of sleepe I harde a pretty thinge
> some men for suddaine ioy do wepe, and some for
>> sorrow singe fa la la.

This entry and the Fool's song probably share a common origin in the popular ballad of 'John Careless', first entered in the Stationers' Register in 1586, which gave rise to many parodies and derivatives. The version in BL MS Sloane 1896 begins:

> Some men for sodayne joye do wepe,
>> and some in sorrowe synge;
> When as they are in daunger depe,
>> to put away mournyng.

The Fool recites two more of his sententious verses in the scene in which Lear finds Kent in the stocks (Act II, scene iv), but does not sing again until Act III, scene ii. There, as Lear cries out to the storm, the Fool, longing for shelter, recites a wry verse, and then, as Kent prevails on Lear to go to the hovel, and the king takes notice of the Fool's shivering state, he sings:

---

[18] Here, as Seng points out (op. cit., p. 203), the Folio reading 'And goe the Foole among', in the adverbial meaning 'betweenwhiles' given in *NED*, makes better sense than the Q1 and Q2 'fooles'.

> He that has and a little tiny wit
> With heigh-ho, the wind and the rain—
> Must make content with his fortunes fit,
> Though the rain it raineth every day.

The stanza has the same pattern as Feste's song at the end of *Twelfth Night*, and the refrain is the same (except that it begins with 'For' in *Twelfth Night*). The tune traditionally associated with the song in the comedy cannot be traced farther back than the eighteenth century, but the stanza form, of two verse lines interspersed with two lines of refrain, all in tetrameter, points to song.

There are many unresolved textual puzzles here, as to whether a lost popular song lies behind Shakespeare's uses, whether Robert Armin, who played both Feste and Lear's Fool, had a hand in these lyrics, and whether the stanza in *King Lear* precedes the longer song in *Twelfth Night*, which must then be presumed to have been added to a revision of the comedy.[19] The dual reference and force of the Fool's solitary stanza are clear; ostensibly it is a philosophical acceptance of his own plight, a fool by occupation, and doubly a fool by worldly-wise standards for his fidelity, as he told Kent:

> That sir which serves and seeks for gain,
> And follows but for form,
> Will pack when it begins to rain,
> And leave thee in the storm.
> But I will tarry; the fool will stay
> And let the wise man fly.
> The knave turns fool that runs away;
> The fool no knave, perdy.
>
> (Act II, scene iv, lines 76–83.)

But the rain and wind beat on the royal fool too, whose folly has brought them both into this plight; and he must abide its consequences.

Probably the Fool sings once more, at his last appearance, in Act III, scene vi, bawdily rounding out a stanza begun by Edgar, as mad Tom, at Lear's imaginary arraignment of Goneril and Regan,

> Come o'er the bourn, Bessy, to me;

---

[19] See Seng, op. cit., pp. 123–30, and Sternfeld's book, pp. 171–3 and, for the tune, pp. 189–91.

the survival of two tunes, and a spiritual parody, points to a long-popular song with words now lost. And Edgar may sing that opening line; and perhaps sings others of his verses and fragments.

The Fool's contribution to *King Lear* is a complex one, and his songs compound the complexity. He is, as Lear says, a bitter fool; both biting, and bitter at the loss of his dear mistress Cordelia, and his privileged status allows him to vent his perception of Lear's folly. His cruelly apposite riddles and snatches must twist in Lear's brain like a knife; yet even this uncomfortable companion is a frail bulwark against total dereliction, and if his taunts prompt Lear to the self-knowledge that leads to madness, his plight awakens in the king the first signs of basic human awareness and compassion. He disorientates the audience, as well as Lear; for we respond with delight and momentary relief to the visual fun of his clowning and his comical, bawdy wit, but with near-simultaneous horror and pity as his taunts strike home to their target. The scenes in which he appears divert us within but not from the tragic action, to which they are integral; and they complicate but do not dissipate tragic emotion: they enhance it.

Not all Shakespeare's tragedies show such remarkable uses of song as *Hamlet*, *Othello*, and *King Lear*; in some it plays little or no part, or fulfils a familiar role. His first and last tragedies, *Titus Andronicus* and *Coriolanus*, contain no song at all; nor, probably, did *Macbeth* in its original form.[20] *Julius Caesar* contains only a blank song: in Act IV, scene iii, when Brutus requests Lucius to play, 'Music and a song' are heard, but they are unspecified; they fulfil a traditional function of music in drama, that of serving as prelude to a supernatural event: as the boy falls asleep and Brutus takes his instrument from him, the ghost of Caesar enters. But in *Hamlet*, *Othello*, and *King Lear*, Shakespeare's designs for the use of song are boldly conceived and embodied. They depend almost wholly on the exploiting of already known songs and ballads, and these tragedies contain his subtlest use of such kinds. In other plays Shakespeare showed that he knew when a song of his own making would best serve his purpose; in these he showed that he knew when to set older strings vibrating.

In the comedies, Shakespeare uses song far more freely and variously, and the range of kinds of song is much wider: refrain-song,

[20] The songs the Folio edition calls for in *Macbeth*, III. v, where Hecate departs to '*Music and a song within*: "Come away, come away, etc." ' and IV. i, where '*Music and a song*: "Black spirits, etc." ' accompany Hecate's departure, are probably interpolations from Middleton's *The Witch*, added for a revival of the play at Blackfriars.

dance-song, lute-song, and masque song all contribute. Ballads and drinking-songs are used where they are appropriate, but these traditional kinds do not predominate, and the subtlest effects are not gained through them but through more sophisticated kinds. Most of these art-songs are new-made for their context, so far as is known, the lyrics written by Shakespeare to be sung, not to existing tunes, but to musical settings specially composed. But the settings were not copied into the prompt books, or included when plays were printed, and given the fragility of unbound sheet music it is not surprising that they have been lost, or may survive apart from the plays embedded in collections of printed or manuscript music. Some surviving contemporary settings may be, or be close to, those used in the plays, but firm musical evidence is lacking. The nature of the setting of a particular song, however, and of its performance, is often made clear by textual evidence: the form of the lyric, comments made on the song or the singer within the play, and stage directions—although some ambiguities and puzzles remain.

The earliest play of Shakespeare's to contain a song of his own making is *The Two Gentlemen of Verona*, and here the lyric proclaims itself as art-song. His first comedy, *The Comedy of Errors*, was close to farce, and in it he used no music at all; and in his next, *The Taming of the Shrew*, Petruchio's snatches of ballads as he swaggers and bullies his way to the domination of Kate heighten the comic effect but offer no musical treat. But in *The Two Gentlemen of Verona* a serenade is to be sung to Silvia, accompanied by instruments, and Shakespeare provides a lyric of three stanzas perfectly shaped for strophic song:

> Who is Silvia? What is she,
>   That all our swains commend her?
> Holy, fair, and wise is she;
>   The heaven such grace did lend her,
> That she might admired be.
>
> Is she kind as she is fair?
>   For beauty lives with kindness.
> Love doth to her eyes repair,
>   To help him of his blindness;
> And, being help'd, inhabits there.
>
> Then to Silvia let us sing
>   That Silvia is excelling;

She excels each mortal thing
Upon the dull earth dwelling.
To her let us garlands bring.

(Act iv, scene ii, lines 38–52.)

The lines have seven syllables, and rhyme alternately, *ababa*, with feminine rhymes in each stanza for the second and fourth lines, which have an iambic, three-beat movement, while the first, third, and fifth lines have a trochaic, four-beat movement. The feminine rhymes, the shortness of the lines, and the use of an odd number of syllables throughout, give the lyric the lightness and delicacy of madrigal verse; but it is cast in the typically English form of a few short stanzas, and with the rhythmic stress-patterns reinforcing the metre throughout (with a slight deviation only in the last line of the second stanza), it is finely designed for singing to a melody repeated for every stanza. The combination of elements is characteristic of Shakespeare's songs: they have the qualities that gave Italian madrigal verse its vogue in England, but Shakespeare preferred the patterns of the native lyrics to madrigal form.

The original music for the song is not known, but a setting for one voice and several instruments is required, and as an offering to Silvia, the serenade must be well-performed: Thurio had resolved 'To sort some gentlemen well skill'd in music'. Some skill in the singer, as well as the players, is called for, and a pleasing voice. The plays of the first half of Shakespeare's career suggest that the company was short of such talent, especially in its adult actors, and the early comedies show several expedients being tried to supply, or disguise, the lack of it. The company employed some instrumentalists, and a singer could be brought in to join them; but to hire one to perform only briefly was an expensive solution; moreover, the use of performers who have no acting parts in the play tends to set the music apart from the action, and make it seem merely decorative addition—an effect hard to avoid with any song that has musical artistry and completeness. In *The Two Gentlemen of Verona* it is dramatically appropriate for the music to form a set piece, as the serenade Proteus advised Thurio to commission, and there is no disjunction of dramatic and musical attention: the audience listens with heightened involvement because it is being heard not only by Silvia but by the disguised Julia too. The dramatist is not only giving the audience a love-song to enjoy, but also evoking their response to Julia's realization of the fickleness of Proteus. But is it Proteus himself who sings the song? Thurio, arriving with the musicians, says,

> How now, Sir Proteus, are you crept before us?

His surprise may be at seeing him there already, or at seeing him there at all; and the mere presence of Proteus could be taken as enough to associate him with the tribute to Silvia.[21] But in Julia's subsequent conversation with the host, whilst instrumental music continues, her sad remark, 'the musician likes me not', clearly refers to Proteus. The episode has most point if the actor playing Proteus is able to sing the serenade, accompanying himself on an instrument, with the hired musicians completing the consort; if he is not, the group of musicians must include the singer; and the wording admits performance in either way.

In *Love's Labour's Lost*, there is more talk of song than actual singing, and it seems likely that if the company's apprentices had included one with a pleasing voice when the play was written, Armado's desire for song would have been gratified. In Act I, scene ii, Armado commands Moth to sing, but Moth evades complying:

> *Arm.* Sing, boy; my spirit grows heavy in love.
> *Moth.* And that's great marvel, loving a light wench.
> *Arm.* I say, sing.
> *Moth.* Forbear till this company be past.   (lines 117–20.)

Act III opens with a similar command:

> *Arm.* Warble, child; make passionate my sense of hearing.

And Moth sings 'Concolinel', which Armado applauds with 'Sweet air!' The one word that stands for the song could signify a popular one that Moth sang, but no further trace of it has been found. Act IV contains only a jingle of popular song, begun by Rosaline and capped by Boyet; its tune is preserved in Ballet's lute book. No more songs are sung until the very end of the play, and there the songs of

---

[21] This is presumably the view taken by Sternfeld, who refers to 'Who is Silvia?' and 'Tell me where is Fancy bred?' as songs 'given to adult characters, it is true, but not to one of the main actors and not to a nobleman' ('*Troilus and Cressida*: Music for the Play', *English Institute Essays 1952* (1954), p. 128). John H. Long, on the other hand, in his conjectural reconstruction of the staging of the scene, gives the direction:

[Proteus alone sings the song accompanied by the instrumental music of the consort.]

(*Shakespeare's Use of Music: Seven Comedies* (Gainesville, Florida, 1955), p. 55.)

the cuckoo and the owl come as strange caudal appendages.[22] The courtier-scholars are strangers to the bucolic world of the songs; their rustication was in a royal park, not in the crude countryside; the hardships and homely comforts of rural winter are unknown to them, and as yet the cuckoo's song holds no threat for them. Ingenuity is probably misapplied in finding abstruse appositeness in 'When daisies pied and violets blue' and 'When icicles hang by the wall'; the audience expected a song or festive dance to conclude a comedy, and clearly they could not have a wedding-dance here. Instead, these refrain-songs, with winter's chill left to prevail at the end, since spring is for love and love's rewards are deferred, offer vivid and comic depiction that lends itself to lively enactment. But who was to sing them? Only Moth has been named as a singer, and he could not present both Ver and Hiems. Since 'All' enter and no one is individually called on to sing, all of these entrants, or several, may sing: it has been suggested that Moth, Nathaniel, and Holofernes sing the song of spring, and Jaquenetta, Costard, and Dull the song of winter.[23]

A boy who is called on to sing, but scarcely does so, and two songs sung by unspecified singers: Shakespeare shows little confidence in his singers in *Love's Labour's Lost*. In his next comedy, *A Midsummer Night's Dream*, he expects comic, not musical, talent from the only adult actor who sings, for the hoarser the voice of Bottom, the funnier the effect; but the fairies' song in Act II, scene ii, gives scope for musical singing by boys:

1 Fairy. You spotted snakes with double tongue,
Thorny hedgehogs, be not seen;
Newts and blind-worms, do no wrong,
Come not near our fairy Queen.

Chorus. Philomel with melody
Sing in our sweet lullaby.
Lulla, lulla, lullaby; lulla, lulla, lullaby.

---

[22] See Seng, op. cit., pp. 12–25, for discussion of textual problems and of the possibility that the songs were added to a posited revision made in 1597, and summary of critical views on the relation of the songs to the play.

[23] By Long, *Shakespeare's Use of Music*, p. 73. But if Ringler is right in thinking that one boy doubled the parts of Jaquenetta and Maria, Jaquenetta cannot appear, because Maria is already on stage with the Princess. (Wm. A. Ringler, Jr., 'The Number of Actors in Shakespeare's Early Plays', in *The Seventeenth-Century Stage*, ed. G. E. Bentley (Chicago, 1968), pp. 128–9.)

> Never harm
> Nor spell nor charm
> Come our lovely lady nigh.
> So good night, with lullaby.

2 Fairy.   Weaving spiders, come not here;
                Hence, you long-legg'd spinners, hence.
                Beetles black, approach not near;
                Worm nor snail do no offence.

Chorus.   Philomel with melody, etc.

                                    [*Titania sleeps.*
                                    (lines 9–24.)

The song has the form chosen most often by Shakespeare for his own songs, that of refrain-song. The two stanzas are simple quatrains rhyming *abab*; except for the eight-syllabled opening line, the lines of stanzas and refrain alike are seven-syllabled, and their trochaic movement is incantatory in effect. The verbal stresses fall on the metrical beats, inviting a strophic setting with strongly marked rhythms for dancing to. No contemporary setting is known.[24] The form suggests that each stanza would be sung by a solo voice, with the refrain sung by all the fairies; the First Quarto however allots the second stanza to '1. Fai.', which gives the first stanza to the whole fairy band, and it is the only authoritative text. The lyric is not a rondel in form; Titania's request for 'a roundel and a fairy song' suggests that the fairies danced a round before their song, or that they accompanied the refrain with dancing.

Fairies who can dance and sing in a scene of delicate beauty imply boy players with some training and skill. It was not only at St Paul's Cathedral or in the royal household that singing-boys were maintained and trained, but also in some noble households, and the presence of this dancing-song, and of opportunity for another, gives force to the possibility that the play was written for first performance at a splendid wedding: that of Lord Carey's daughter Elizabeth to Thomas Berkeley at Blackfriars on 19 February 1596, or that of the

---

[24] Long, op. cit., p. 87, points out that Dowland addressed Lord Carey as his patron in dedicating his first book of ayres to him in 1597, and conjectures that if he was in Lord Carey's employment and the play was written for the wedding of Elizabeth Carey, he may have set the song.

Earl of Derby to Elizabeth Vere at Greenwich on 26 January 1595.[25] It may have been with performance in such a setting, and with such resources, in mind, that the playwright gave opportunity for another fairy song at the end:

> *Obe.* Through the house give glimmering light,
> By the dead and drowsy fire;
> Every elf and fairy sprite
> Hop as light as bird from brier;
> And this ditty, after me,
> Sing and dance it trippingly.
>
> *Tita.* First, rehearse your song by rote,
> To each word a warbling note;
> Hand in hand, with fairy grace,
> Will we sing, and bless this place.
>
> (Act v, scene i, lines 380–9.)

No lyric seems to be provided; but in the Folio the next twenty-two lines, beginning

> Now, until the break of day,

are headed '*The Song*' and italicized: perhaps they were sung at a performance when singing-boys were available, and otherwise Oberon spoke them, but the lines themselves seem written for speaking.

The only adult voice indubitably raised in song in the play is the raucous one of Bottom; ass-headed all unaware, and deserted by his companions, he sings 'that they shall hear I am not afraid':

> The ousel cock, so black of hue,
> With orange-tawny bill,
> The throstle with his note so true,
> The wren with little quill.
>
> *Tita.* What angel wakes me from my flow'ry bed?
>
> *Bot.* [*Sings*]
> The finch, the sparrow, and the lark,
> The plain-song cuckoo grey,

---

[25] E. K. Chambers considers that one or other of these two weddings was more probably the occasion than others that have been suggested. (*William Shakespeare* (Oxford, 1930), vol. i, pp. 358–9.)

Whose note full many a man doth mark,
And dares not answer nay—

(Act III, scene i, lines 114–22.)

The audience would enjoy the much-used cuckoo innuendo,
whether or not Bottom's opening line reminded them of another
lyric about birds, 'A poeme of a Mayde forsaken', which occurs in
The Arbor of amorous Deuises, 1597.[26] Some similar song may have
been in his and their minds; however much or little of the lyric is
Shakespeare's own, he is appropriately giving Bottom a song of popular type and tone, which arises naturally out of his current situation of
finding himself alone in the forest, and precipitates his next situation,
of finding himself the object of Titania's infatuation. The humour
comes largely from incongruity, and it is aural as well as visual:
Bottom's song and his singing are as indelicate as his translated shape.

The Merry Wives of Windsor, written several years later than *A
Midsummer Night's Dream*, about 1600–1, shows interesting
similarities, and dissimilarities, to the earlier play in its uses of song. It
too contains a song sung in fright, this time with words that are
certainly borrowed, and garbled to excellent comic effect; and a fairy
song of a sort, but sung with very different intent. Like Bottom
deserted by his mates in the forest, Sir Hugh Evans is left alone in a
field near Frogmore, while Simple looks about to see if Dr Caius is
coming: he sings in order not to cry with fright at the prospect of
duelling, and in his 'trempling of mind' produces a most unparsonical
mix, with Marlowe's 'Come live with me and be my love' coming far
more readily to his tongue that Psalm 137, of which he manages only
the first phrase:

To shallow rivers, to whose falls
Melodious birds sings madrigals;
There will we make our peds of roses,
And a thousand fragrant posies.
To shallow—

Mercy on me! I have a great dispositions to cry.   [*Sings.*

Melodious birds sing madrigals—
Whenas I sat in Pabylon—
And a thousand vagram posies.
To shallow, etc.

(Act III, scene i, lines 15–24.)

[26] Cited by Seng, op. cit., p. 35.

The audience would respond with delight to this hybrid text; most of them would have sung both contributory sources, but in differing contexts. Marlowe's lyric was one of the most famous Elizabethan invitations to love, and had recently been published, in *The Passionate Pilgrime* in 1599 (an incomplete version, but sufficient for Sir Hugh) and in *Englands Helicon* in 1600. The psalms in the metrical version of Sternhold and Hopkins, from which Sir Hugh's fragment comes, were first published complete in London by John Day in 1562,[27] with eighty-five tunes, and were kept in print for generations; they were sung in church, and sung in the open air too by the thousands of people who gathered to hear the sermons at Paul's Cross. Sir Hugh may have quavered his random recollections to the tune of the love-lyric,[28] perhaps with a snatch of psalm-tune for the words from the psalm, but they would probably be greeted by the audience with extra delight if they were put to the psalm-tune throughout; the provision of sacred parodies, edifying words written to popular tunes 'for auoyding of sin and harlatrie',[29] was a practice much favoured during and after the Reformation, and for a parson spontaneously to invert the process would be a hilarious reversal. We cannot now know whether the joke was given this musical dimension; its essential elements are the conflation and confusion of sacred and profane words by a cleric, and the fact that the latter were uppermost in his mind. Shakespeare mixes together two sets of words not his own and not in themselves comic: the result is surrealistically funny.[30]

The fairy song is a changeling of another sort. In the play's last

[27] The tune given by Day for Psalm 137, and in other early psalm books, such as Thomas East's (1592), is printed by Maurice Frost, *English & Scottish Psalm & Hymn Tunes c.1543–1677* (1953), p. 189; and by Simpson, *The British Broadside Ballad and its Music*, p. 585.

[28] Probably the tune preserved by Corkine as one of his 'diuers new Descants vpon old Grounds, *set to the Lyra-Violl*', in *The Second Booke of Ayres*, 1612; printed by Simpson, op. cit., p. 120.

[29] From the title-page of *Ane Compendious buik of godlie Psalmes and spirituall Sangis collectit furthe of sindrie partis of the Scripture, with diueris vtheris Ballattis changeit out of prophane Sangis in godlie sangis, for auoyding of sin and harlatrie. With augmentation of sindrie gude and godlie Ballatis not contenit in the first editioun* (Edinburgh, 1578). The date of the first edition of the book (usually known as *Gude and godlie Ballatis*) is uncertain; Rollins, *MLN* xxxiv (1919), 349, gives 1567.

[30] The 1602 Bad Quarto has, in place of the opening of the psalm, 'There dwelt a man in Babylon', from one of the ballads on the constancy of Susanna, based on the story in the Book of Daniel, ch. 13. The allusion is less apt, and the musical joke is lost; the line reads like an attempt to supply a partially lost line, with mention of Babylon serving as pivot.

scene Falstaff, disguised as Herne the Hunter, is pinched and tormen-
ted by Mistress Page's daughter Anne, her son William, and others,
disguised as fairies; they trip round him, touching him with their lit
tapers and singing 'a scornful rhyme':

> Fie on sinful fantasy!
> Fie on lust and luxury!
> Lust is but a bloody fire,
> Kindled with unchaste desire,
> Fed in heart, whose flames aspire,
> As thoughts do blow them, higher and higher.
> Pinch him, fairies, mutually;
> Pinch him for his villainy;
> Pinch him and burn him and turn him about,
> Till candles and star-light and moonshine be out.

> (Act v, scene v, lines 91–100.)

Every line of the single ten-line stanza has four stresses, but the triple
measure reserved for the final couplet gives extra emphasis to the
beats and speeds the song to a mocking crescendo. It is part of a serio-
comic rite, the hoax and the fantasy designed to exorcise the demon
of lust from the importunate old knight, but the theatrical effect is
one of broad farce.

The atmosphere of this scene of make-believe fairies is in total
contrast to that of the lullaby scene of 'real' fairies in *A Midsummer
Night's Dream*, in which Titania was lulled to rest with a charm to
protect her from harm. The plays, of course, are comedies of quite
different kinds; but the dramatic climate outside the plays was
different too. For most of the 1590s, the dramatic activities of the
boys' companies were in abeyance. The Children of the Chapel and
the Children of Paul's had been performing together at court and at
the Blackfriars hall, the first Blackfriars Theatre, in the years just
before they lost the lease of the theatre in 1584. From then until 1600,
there is no record of the Children of the Chapel performing at court
or elsewhere in London; the Children of Paul's, with Lyly as their
playwright, fared better, giving performances at court from 1587 to
1590, and commercial performances at their theatre in the cathedral
precincts too.[31] Then they seem to have acted no more in London for
most of the following decade, until late 1596 or early 1597. At the

---

[31] For discussion of its exact location, see Reavley Gair, *The Children of Paul's*
(Cambridge, 1982), pp. 44–55.

turn of the century, both companies were revived on a commercial footing, and with Jonson, Daniel, Marston, Middleton, Chapman, and Beaumont and Fletcher writing plays for them, and the added attraction of their accomplished singing, they were strong competitors for the favour of playgoers for about a decade. The remark of Rosencrantz to Hamlet that

> there is, sir, an eyrie of children, little eyases, that cry out on the top of question, and are most tyrannically clapp'd for't. These are now the fashion . . .
>
> (Act II, scene ii, lines 334–7.)

is well known. In *The Merry Wives of Windsor*, written about the same time as *Hamlet*, some 'little eyases' appear; and Shakespeare's treatment of them is ambivalent. If the story is true that the play was written in response to Queen Elizabeth's expressed desire to see Falstaff in love, at least one court performance seems probable, and for it singing boys of the royal household could be used. But their special skills are not essential; for other performances, the Chamberlain's company could use its own boy actors, employed to play women's and youthful roles. The scene is designed to produce more comic than musical delight; it provides occasion, and cover, for the stealthy abductions of fairies by Dr Caius, Slender, and Fenton, each of the first two deceived in thinking Anne Page is his prize, and these events partly distract the audience's attention from the singing and dancing. The presence of adult sprites such as 'that Welsh fairy' Sir Hugh Evans adds to the number who caper about, and tilts the balance towards burlesque; if Lyly's *Endimion*, in which fairies 'daunce, and with a song pinch' Corsites, had indeed been performed again recently by child actors,[32] this scene could be given an edge of parody.

Probably soon after writing *A Midsummer Night's Dream*, and some years before writing *The Merry Wives of Windsor*, Shakespeare wrote *The Merchant of Venice*. In it there is only one song, clearly made especially for its context, but teasingly ambiguous in its dramatic effect. When, in the casket scene, Act III, scene ii, Bassanio prepares to make his fateful choice, Portia wishes him to wait a while: a day or two, even 'some month or two', rather than rush upon the venture that may part them. When he presses on:

---

[32] W. J. Lawrence, in 'Thomas Ravenscroft's Theatrical Associations', *MLR* 19 (1924), posited a revival in 1600 by the boys of St Paul's, connecting a fairy pinching song by Ravenscroft with it, but without evidence.

> Let me choose;
> For as I am, I live upon the rack

she calls for music. The princes of Morocco and Arragon made their
choices with only a flourish of cornets to herald them, but for
Bassanio she bids

> Let music sound while he doth make his choice;
> Then, if he lose, he makes a swan-like end,
> Fading in music

and a song is sung '*the whilst Bassanio comments on the caskets to
himself*':

> Tell me where is fancy bred,
> Or in the heart or in the head,
> How begot, how nourished?
>   Reply, reply.
> It is engend'red in the eyes,
> With gazing fed; and fancy dies
> In the cradle where it lies.
>   Let us all ring fancy's knell:
>   I'll begin it—Ding, dong, bell.

All.   Ding, dong, bell.   (lines 63–72.)

To have background music at a significant moment, to strike a note of
suspense, was a device already in use by Shakespeare himself and by
others; but the song is far more than this. As the words tell how fancy
begotten in the eye will die, the sound supplies its own gloss on the
sense: the first three lines end with the heavily weighted rhyme-
sound 'éd', and the last ones spell out the missing first consonant,
'ell'.[33] But what ought we to infer from this? Not, surely, that Portia
is cheating, frustrating her father's device in order to fulfil her desire.
The song expresses thoughts she must hope will arise in Bassanio's
mind; but that is not to say that she has it sung to prompt or to guide
his decision. It arises aptly from what has already happened, reflecting on the choices made by the princes. The audience will indeed hear
it as more, and will be on tenterhooks: will Bassanio catch the clues?
If only he would listen! But the First Quarto gives the stage direction:
'A Song the whilst Bassanio comments on the caskets to himselfe',

---

[33] Many commentators have pointed this out; for interpretations of the song's
significance, and also its form, see Seng, op. cit., pp. 36–43.

and the Folio preserves the direction. If that is acted upon, he is not listening: he is absorbed in his own thoughts, and when he remarks,

> So may the outward shows be least themselves;
> The world is still deceiv'd with ornament

he is not commenting on the song, but pursuing his own train of thought as he contemplates the caskets, and he then develops it. The song and the observation are in parallel; they are not signal and sequel. If the song has an effect on Bassanio's mind, it is sub-conscious, the sound and drift of it sinking in to reinforce his line of thought, not to initiate it. For the audience, it has made more tantalizing the suspense of the scene.

The mode of performance implied is hard to determine too. The first verse triplet is followed by the injunction 'Reply, reply', which suggests that a second singer may answer its questions with the second triplet; either singer or both could then introduce the refrain. But 'Reply, reply', and the repeated last line, may indicate that it should be performed as an echo-song, with a chorus taking up softly the last sounds of the lines, which would emphasize the hint they embed; another possibility that has been proposed is that a chorus might sing the last line throughout as a running burden. Without the evidence of the original music, which is not known, we cannot be sure; but the song could be effectively sung by two, or more, boys' or mens' voices,[34] one soloist answering the other, and both or all combining at the end; probably with instrumental accompaniment. It is essential to the full effect of the scene that the song be sung, and audibly sung; it is not specified, and not important, who sings it.

The next three comedies show Shakespeare making increasing use of song, and the songs are of diverse kinds. For *Much Ado about Nothing* he wrote one refrain-song and one with a single complex stanza; he also borrowed a scrap from a ballad. The first song comes early in the episode contrived by Don Pedro, abetted by Leonato and Claudio, to convince Benedick that Beatrice is languishing for love of him, in Act II, scene iii. Don Pedro requests Balthasar to sing; and the song appropriately offers advice to ladies sighing for love of men— the case Benedick is about to hear that Beatrice is in:

---

[34] Sternfeld thinks it 'is by its context an adult song', and assumes that one of Portia's attendants sings it. (*Music in Shakespearean Tragedy*, p. 105.)

> Sigh no more, ladies, sigh no more,
>> Men were deceivers ever,
> One foot in sea and one on shore,
>> To one thing constant never.
> Then sigh not so, but let them go,
>> And be you blithe and bonny;
> Converting all your sounds of woe
>> Into Hey nonny nonny.
>
> Sing no more ditties, sing no moe
>> Of dumps, so dull and heavy;
> The fraud of men was ever so,
>> Since summer first was leavy.
> Then sigh not so, &c.   (lines 57–69.)

The lyric invites a simple strophic setting; its two stanzas run smoothly, the stresses patterned alike in each, and alternate lines of both verse and refrain end with the softened glide of disyllabic rhyme. There is a manuscript setting by Thomas Ford[35] of a lyric that begins with Shakespeare's first stanza, but with an extra line inserted, and two further stanzas in this changed pattern follow, instead of Shakespeare's second stanza; the music is set out for three voices. It could be contemporary: Ford was born about 1580, and his *Musicke of Sundrie Kindes* was published in 1607; but it seems likely to be a separate song, utilizing the lyric but not made for the play, in which a single singer is specified.

Shakespeare achieves many effects of chiaroscuro in this play, and the songs contribute to them. When this first song is sung, with its light-hearted warning not to trust men, the audience has just heard Borachio unfold to Don John his plan to discredit Hero. This example of men's deceitfulness is of a different order from lovers' fickleness and it is unlikely to shadow their hearing of the song, which is part of a merrier, innocent plot, and contributes to a lightening of mood. But not for Claudio: the 'fraud of men' is on his mind, since he believes 'the Prince woos for himself'; and as soon as the song is ended the prince is arranging a serenade to Hero. That serenade is never offered; at the appointed time it is a dirge for Hero that must be performed. For those taking part in the ceremony, who believe Hero is dead, and for the audience, who know she is not, this solemn rite is necessary, and it meets both kinds of need. Within the

---

[35] In a set of part-books, Christ Church MS 736–8.

play, Leonato requires Claudio to do this penance before he receives a bride; and the audience requires it of him too in expiation of the wrong he has done in believing ill of Hero, before they can accept him back into favour. Claudio reads an epitaph from a scroll, then calls for a 'solemn hymn':

> 'Done to death by slanderous tongues
> Was the Hero that here lies;
> Death, in guerdon of her wrongs,
> Gives her fame which never dies.
> So the life that died with shame
> Lives in death with glorious fame.'
>
> Hang thou there upon the tomb,
> Praising her when I am dumb.
> Now, music, sound, and sing your solemn hymn.
>
> *Song.*
> Pardon, goddess of the night,
> Those that slew thy virgin knight;
> For the which, with songs of woe,
> Round about her tomb they go.
>   Midnight, assist our moan;
>   Help us to sigh and groan,
>   Heavily, heavily.
>   Graves, yawn, and yield your dead,
>   Till death be uttered,
>   Heavily, heavily.
>
> *Claud.* Now, unto thy bones good night.
>   Yearly will I do this rite.
>
>   (Act v, scene iii, lines 3–23.)

The Quarto and Folio texts print the hymn in nine lines, having a long fifth line with internal rhyme; the ten-line arrangement shows the verse pattern more clearly. The first four lines are in trochaic metre, the seven syllables of each bearing four stresses; then the movement becomes even weightier, with the first two lines of each triplet opening with a spondee and bearing four stresses in only six syllables. With its deliberate tread, matching the sad pacing 'about her tomb', the stanza is a *tour de force* of embodiment of the heaviness it speaks of;[36] and such stylized presentation of grief is appropriate to the solemnity, yet unreality, of the occasion.

Besides these two songs, the only other singing in the play is the snippet Benedick sings in Leonato's orchard while waiting for Margaret to call Beatrice:

> The god of love,
> That sits above,
> And knows me, and knows me,
> How pitiful I deserve—

I mean in singing; but in loving—

> (Act v, scene ii, lines 23–7.)

Both the words of the ballad, by William Elderton, and the tune it went to, were highly popular; the ballad became known in 1562, and set off a spate of sequels and answers (including the praise of 'The ioy of Virginitie' in *A Handefull of pleasant delites*), and the melody survives as a dance tune in several music books of the middle and late sixteenth century under various names including 'My lord Essex measures' and 'Turkeyloney'.[37] Benedick's translation into a lover is complete; it is a scrap from a languishing lover's plea that comes into his head as he whiles away time, waiting for Beatrice. The first stanza in the Braye Lute Book begins:

> The gods off loue^{yt} sytts a bove
> & knowe me & knowe me
> howe sorroffull I do serue
> Graunt my request y^t at the least
> she showe me she showe me
> somme pytty whan I deserve/[38]

and Benedick's confusion of its third and sixth lines gives rise to a rueful comment on his singing ability, in contrast to his great desert in love.

---

[36] Its pattern may derive from a ballad-tune, now lost; and perhaps its original melody too. Seng, op. cit., p. 68, cites Collier's reference to a tract called *Laugh, and lie down*, 1605, and quotes the relevant passage: 'This poor man . . . fell to sing the song of *Oken Leaues* began to wither: to the tune of Heauilie, heauilie.'

[37] For transcriptions of the tune see Ward, 'Music for *A Handefull of pleasant delites*', p. 164, and his edition of *The Dublin Virginal Manuscript* (Wellesley, Mass., 1954), pp. 25–6 and 55–6; also Simpson, *The British Broadside Ballad and its Music*, pp. 261–2.

[38] Quoted from Seng, op. cit., p. 63.

Benedick, as a young lord, is not required to be able to sing well; Balthasar too is a gentleman, nephew of Leonato, and disclaims having a good voice, quibbling with Don Pedro before singing 'Sigh no more, ladies, sigh no more', and apologizing after it. The half-hearted reassurances given him by Claudio may result from preoccupation with a train of thoughts started by the song's theme, but the verdict of Benedick, who thinks himself unseen and unheard, is unequivocal:

> *D. Pedro.* By my troth, a good song.
> *Balth.* And an ill singer, my lord.
> *Claud.* Ha, no; no, faith; thou sing'st well enough for a shift.
> *Bene.* An he had been a dog that should have howl'd thus, they would have hang'd him; and I pray God his bad voice bode no mischief. I had as lief have heard the night-raven, come what plague could have come after it.
>
> (Act II, scene iii, lines 70–7.)

Balthasar goes out a moment later, and is not named as appearing again; there is no indication of who sings the dirge for Hero. The fact that in the First Folio, the stage direction for the entry of the prince and his companions is

Enter Prince, Leonato, Claudio, and Iacke Wilson

indicates that the actor and singer Jack Wilson played Balthasar at some time;[39] but the comments within the play may mean that the first Balthasar was a barely adequate singer, pressed into service because Shakespeare wanted the song to be sung by someone involved in the play's action, and given a gentleman's rank to excuse his shortcomings.

There is a similar part, within the range of one who excels neither as actor nor as singer, but can serve as both, in *As You Like It*, that of Amiens, who sings two of the play's five songs. The increased

---

[39] T. W. Baldwin, *The Organization and Personnel of the Shakespearean Company*, pp. 420–1, favours Collier's proposed identification of this Jack Wilson with a John Wilson baptized on 24 April 1585, who could have joined the company as an apprentice, at the age of ten, in 1595. (Other roles Baldwin conjecturally assigns to him include Ophelia, summer 1603, and Desdemona, summer 1604.) Another identification often suggested is with the composer Dr John Wilson; if the date of birth given on his tombstone, 5 April 1595, is correct, it is necessary to posit that he played the role in a revival of the play.

number of songs in this play, the relatively simple ways in which they are used, and the attention focused upon them, combine to suggest that Shakespeare was keen to fit more musical strings to his bow to compete with the boys' companies, many of whose plays included four or five songs. In *As You Like It* the sheer presence and enjoyableness of the songs, with their variety in kind and mood and mode of performance, constitute their chief *raison d'être*; they add vividness to the portrayal of life in the forest, and they serve practical functions, such as indicating the passage of time, or covering the narration of events already known to the audience, but they are less integral, and less integrated, than is usual in Shakespeare's plays.

The first two songs both draw on long traditions: the first is a song of the greenwood tree, a kind with an ancestry medieval at least, and with many sixteenth- and seventeenth-century collaterals. Its generalized sentiment, and the presence of a refrain, fit it for corporate, convivial singing, and its performance, with some talk about it, takes up the whole of Act II, scene v. Probably Amiens sings the first verse alone, and others join him in the refrain, since when Jaques demands more, Amiens protests that his 'voice is ragged', and Jaques ends his persuasion by saying 'Come, sing; and you that will not, hold your tongues.' It seems from the Folio direction '*Altogether heere*' that several voices sing both the next verse and the refrain. Jaques then caps the song with a verse of his own making; whether he reads it himself or passes it to Amiens to sing is not clear,[40] but the jolt in tone is the same: from celebration of the simplicity of forest life to deflation of the bubble of pastoral idyll by a reminder to these sequestered lords of the amenities they have left behind. Both notes have already been struck: the greenwood one in the answer given by Charles the wrestler to Oliver's question as to where the banished duke will live:

> They say he is already in the Forest of Arden, and a many merry men with him; and there they live like the old Robin Hood of England. They say many young gentlemen flock to him every day, and fleet the time carelessly, as they did in the golden world.
>
> (Act I, scene i, lines 105–9.)

And Jaques's cynical rider reinforces Touchstone's laconic remarks:

---

[40] Amiens says 'And I'll sing it', and the Folio allocates it to him, but in doing so names him as speaker three times successively, which suggests a possible error.

Ros. Well, this is the Forest of Arden.

Touch. Ay, now am I in Arden; the more fool I; when I was at home I was in a better place; but travellers must be content.

(Act II, scene iv, lines 12–15.)

The second song, at the close of Act II, also underlines ideas that have already been expressed, and it too has a long lineage. The act opens with Duke Senior preferring

the icy fang
And churlish chiding of the winter's wind

to the envy and flattery of the court, and the refrain of the first song takes up the theme:

Here shall he see
No enemy
But winter and rough weather.

The second song expands it further:

Blow, blow, thou winter wind,
Thou art not so unkind
    As man's ingratitude;
Thy tooth is not so keen,
Because thou art not seen,
    Although thy breath be rude.
Heigh-ho! sing heigh-ho! unto the green holly.
Most friendship is feigning, most loving mere folly.
    Then, heigh-ho, the holly!
    This life is most jolly.

Freeze, freeze, thou bitter sky,
That dost not bite so nigh
    As benefits forgot;
Though thou the waters warp,
Thy sting is not so sharp
    As friend rememb'red not.
Heigh-ho! sing, &c.

(Act II, scene vii, lines 174–90.)

The refrain links it to medieval festive songs of holly, or holly and ivy, but the verses replace the usual contrast between holly and ivy with the contrast between the harshness of winter and the callousness of man. This holly-song has nothing to celebrate but the bleak consolation of having only the lesser evils of winter to bear; and it is sung while Adam and Orlando eat, Orlando in exile because of a brother's persecution, an offence against both kinship and kindness, and Adam unfeelingly turned off after a lifetime of service. The duke's request, 'good cousin, sing', is presumably made to Amiens; there is no indication that other lords take up the refrain.

　　The original settings of these two songs are not known; for the next one, again a refrain-song, a seventeenth-century one survives, and it may embody the original tune. John Hilton's *Catch that Catch can, or A Choice Collection of Catches, Rovnds, & Canons for 3 or 4 Voyces*, published in 1652, contains the words of the forester-song, set as a round for four voices, with the third line omitted. The Folio sets out the song as follows:

> What shall he haue that kild the Deare?
> His Leather skin, and hornes to weare:
> Then sing him home, the rest shall beare this burthen;
> Take thou no scorne to weare the horne,
> It was a crest ere thou wast borne,
> Thy fathers father wore it
> And thy father bore it,
> The horne, the horne, the lusty horne,
> Is not a thing to laugh to scorne.

Editorial emendations of the third line are various: Alexander arranges the opening lines thus:

> What shall he have that kill'd the deer?
> His leather skin and horns to wear.
> 　　　　　　　　*[The rest shall bear this burden*:
> Then sing him home.
> 　　　　　　　　　　　　(Act IV, scene ii, lines 10–12.)

In Hilton's song-book, the omission of the third line, reducing the lyric to four rhyming couplets, fits it for singing as a round, with a couplet for each voice before the next voice joins in; but it does not solve the question of whether the Folio's third line, or the latter part of it, crept in from dialogue or stage direction. In the play, the song was probably sung as solo and chorus, one lord singing the first two lines (or possibly three, ending with 'Then sing him home') and the others then joining in the refrain. In the strict musical sense, the refrain is not a burden, which is an undersong accompanying a verse throughout; either *double entendre* or etymological nicety must be given up, and the layout in the Folio suggests the latter, presenting the whole third line as text to be heard (whether sung or, as Seng has suggested,[41] perhaps interjected by Jaques): the burden of horns is to be borne by all. The scene allows Jaques to press home his scorn at the pastime of these noble huntsmen; his views on the killing of deer by interlopers into their native dwelling-place have been related earlier by one of the lords (in Act II, scene i); now, sardonically, he urges the foresters on to bear home the killer in triumph, wearing the traditional trophy of this honour, which is also a universal badge of shame.

The scene is a triumph in brief of making a whole that is more than the sum of its parts. Again Shakespeare has patterned a song upon a known tradition, this time the forester-song, with its well-worn pun. Again he has worked up a song to provide a whole short scene—less than twenty lines long—and again the scene develops a view that has been expressed before. The rollicking bawdy song comes as an earthy relief after the high romanticizing of Rosalind and Orlando, but it is sung at Jaques's ironic request, which turns the joke upon the huntsmen's own heads; by his attitude to their 'victory', the episode is made part of the play's debate about the innocence of the simple life.

The last act also contains a short scene, scene iii, made to frame a song, and this one is more delicate than the forester's in both thematic bearing and musical pleasure, a joyous song about springtime, love, and marriage. A scene of love and lovers has just gone before, and Rosalind has promised to bring contentment to all the lovers. She herself has been dallying with love as well as probing it, by keeping up her disguise when the need for it is past; she is now ready to 'take the present time'. 'It was a lover and his lass' serves as a light-hearted but true bidding, not only to Touchstone and Audrey, to whom it is sung, but to all the play's lovers; and in telling of spring, in contrast to the first two songs' reflections on winter, it mirrors a change in the play's inner weather. The forest's seasons are not shown to change, but the cold in man's heart is thawing. Already Oliver's change of heart has occurred, brought about by Orlando's noble kindness in saving his life, and at the end of the play Duke Frederick's conversion

---

[41] Seng cites his own views on this line, and those of others, op. cit., pp. 82–5.

is reported. The song expresses the new mood, of faith in both friendship and loving; and in Morley's setting it is also a piece of sheer musical delight. It occurs in his *The First Booke of Ayres*, printed in 1600: the date is close to that of the play's first performance, and leaves open the possibilities that the setting was made for the play, or that the whole song, words and music, was borrowed from Morley. Whether or not Shakespeare and Morley collaborated personally in making the song, as has been argued on rather slender grounds,[42] Morley's book preserves what seems a better text than that available to the Folio editors. The Folio's opening line for one stanza,

> And therefore take the present time,

sounds like an ill-remembered attempt at Morley's

> Then prettie louers take the time,

and it places this stanza second, perhaps reflecting a custom of singing only two stanzas in performances of the play; the song-book follows the sense of the lyric in placing it last, and most editors of the play use this order.[43]

In form, the lyric is a roundelay, and this provides a clue to how the pages would sing it. In a roundelay, one singer advances the story a line at a time, and the other interpolates a running commentary on it. *Englands Helicon* contains a song beginning

> Fie on the sleights that men deuise,
>   Heigh hoe sillie sleights:
> When simple Maydes they would entice,
>   Maides are yong mens chief delights

with the heading 'A *Pastorall Song betweene* Phillis *and* Amarillis, *two Nimphes, each aunswering other line for line*'. In the August eclogue of Spenser's *The Shepheards Calender*, the alternation of the singers is clearly set out:

> *Perigot.*   It fell vpon a holly eue,
> *Willye.*   hey ho hollidaye,

---

[42] By Ernest Brennecke, in 'Shakespeare's Musical Collaboration with Morley', *PMLA* liv (1939), 139–49; his and other views are summarized by Seng, op. cit., pp. 89–90 and 97–100.

[43] Other minor differences include 'countrie fooles' in the song-book, for 'country folks', and the plural 'corne fields'. Fellowes argues in favour of Morley's text in *Memoirs of an Amateur Musician* (1946), pp. 134–5.

Per.	When holly fathers wont to shrieue:
Wil.	now gynneth this roundelay . . .

and Cuddy's appraisal distinguishes their roles:

> Sicker sike a roundle neuer heard I none.
> Little lacketh *Perigot* of the best.
> And Willye is not greatly ouergone,
> So weren his vndersongs well addrest.
>
> (lines 53–6 and 125–8.)

In 'It was a lover and his lass' there are four lines of 'undersong' to every two that advance the narrative, and as they remain constant, they form a refrain; part of this may have been sung by both pages together, but it seems clear they should take alternate lines at the start of each verse—with Touchstone sitting between them, turning from one to the other as they sing 'both in a tune, like two gipsies on a horse': that is, sharing the tune.[44] Despite Touchstone's disparagement, they would be good singers; probably two of the company's own apprentices, with voices 'tuneable' enough for the scene to give musical delight.

The final song has a ritual function: to solemnize the wedding of the four couples. The scene is in the nature of a transformation scene, as Rosalind appears once more as herself, and the god Hymen is with her. To still music, Hymen presents her to her father and, when the amazement subsides, joins each couple's hands; then a short, jubilant 'wedlock-hymn' is sung, probably by most of those present: the singers are not specified, and the original music for it has not survived. A few loose strands are tidied up, by the entrance of Sir Rowland's second son, and the leave-taking of Jaques, and then a dance concludes the play. Hymen's appearance and ceremonial blessing, the song, and the dance, combine to give a masque-like effect to the close.

As the songs in this play are not involved in the action, and the themes they touch on would still be present without them; and, further, as three of them occur in short free-standing scenes, it is not impossible that some of them were added after composition of the

---

[44] Felver, *Robert Armin*, p. 45, notes the view of Roffe, *New Variorum Shakespeare*, vol. viii, p. 262, that the second page's reply to Touchstone, 'We are for you; sit i' the middle' (v. iii. 8), suggests that the song would be sung as a trio. But Touchstone's comments after the song are those of a critical listener, not of a participant. (Morley's setting is for one voice, with lute and bass viol.)

play was complete. But Shakespeare was unlikely to plan a comedy at this time without including several songs, and the way most of these are used, to comment upon or to generalize a theme seen elsewhere in the play in terms of personal experience, is characteristic. Many of his songs fall into a situation with a certain detachment, putting a particular plight into a wider perspective:

Men were deceivers ever,

sings Balthasar, in *Much Ado about Nothing*; and

Most friendship is feigning, most loving mere folly

sings Amiens. Each of the songs in *As You Like It* adds its contribution of comedy or comment, celebration or sheer musical pleasure, to the play, and no other justification is needed. Yet the number of them, and the inclusion of songs for both adult and boy singers, may owe something to factors outside the play itself: to competition from the Children of Paul's, or to the personnel of his own company, or both.

The Children of Paul's were already playing again when the play was written, in late 1599 or early 1600, and the Children of the Chapel began acting again in 1600. One possible way of meeting the challenge of their musical attractions was to compete with them in their own kind, using boy singers, and 'It was a lover and his lass' shows Shakespeare providing a delightful song for the two pages to sing. But the fact that they make their sole appearance to sing it points to the limited usefulness of boys as singers in a company of adult actors. In a boys' company, they of course played adult roles of both sexes; in an adult company, they played only women and boys and girls. Even if one or two of the Chamberlain's Men's own boys sang well enough to give musical pleasure—and they were not likely to have such skill or talent as the trained, at times forcibly enlisted, cathedral and chapel boys—they could not be used to make songs a natural part of the whole dramatic texture. Only an adult singing-actor would serve for that. The absence of roles for such a character in the early comedies suggests that the company lacked such a man; *Twelfth Night* shows that the gap has been filled.

In between come two ambiguous cases: in *Much Ado about Nothing* and *As You Like It*. The role of Balthasar has already been discussed; it shows Shakespeare beginning to develop a far more dramatically versatile use of song than was possible so long as the singer was an extraneous figure, brought in only to sing, or even remaining unseen. Even on these terms, a song could serve a dramatic as well as decorative purpose, and have a bearing upon both atmosphere and action: the song in the casket-scene of *The Merchant of Venice* is a case in point. But when a singer is written into the cast, or an actor can make an acceptable shift to sing, songs can be called for, and sung, with far greater naturalness.

In *As You Like It*, the songs which are sung wholly or partly by one adult arise easily from the pastime or occupation in hand, or as background to it. The hunting lord clearly need not sing well (and so need not necessarily have been Amiens): Jaques says,

Sing it; 'tis no matter how it be in tune, so it make noise enough.

Amiens himself is a lord, and so, like Balthasar, makes no claims as a singer; and it is noticeable that he is like Balthasar also in having only a slight acting part. At his first entry, in Act II, scene i, the stage direction reads:

Enter Duke Senior, Amiens, *and two or three* Lords, *like foresters*

but Amiens speaks only two and a half lines, whereas the First Lord has nearly forty describing the reflections of Jaques on the wounded deer, which he and Amiens together heard. Is Amiens named only to establish that the singer is one of the dramatis personae? On his next appearance, in Act II, scene v, a brief scene in which he enters with Jaques and others, he sings 'Under the greenwood tree' with no preamble at all. When Jaques requests more, he protests about his voice, in the customary way, and *all* sing the next verse: so Amiens has sung only one verse alone, and spoken only a few words; and the audience is helped to recognize him by the First Lord's naming him: 'Today my Lord of Amiens and myself . . .'. The next time he appears, in the eighth scene of the same act, the scene is dominated by Jaques crowing at his encounter with Touchstone, until Orlando enters with sword drawn. Amiens does not speak at all: when Duke Senior requests a song, 'Blow, blow thou winter wind' follows at once. In the remaining three acts of the play Amiens never speaks again, and perhaps never sings again either, unless he is the unnamed forester in Act IV, scene ii; he is not named as appearing in any scene in these acts except the last: and this raises an intriguing possibility. The chief musical attractions offered by *As You Like It* are the greenwood and holly songs, with some solo singing by Amiens, and the pages' ballett. The chief comic attraction and novelty is the new-style witty clown, as the fanfare of Jaques for him proclaims:

> O noble fool!
> A worthy fool!   Motley's the only wear.
>
> (Act II, scene vii, lines 33–4.)

With the creation of Touchstone Shakespeare exultantly presents the company's new clown, the jester Robert Armin who joined the Chamberlain's Men after Will Kemp's departure in 1599. But Armin was also a singer: could he have played Amiens too?[45] Technically, he could: Amiens and Touchstone never appear together, except that Amiens is named in the final scene when the whole cast is assembled, which could easily be an oversight; also, the play has an unusually large cast of men, and some doubling would certainly be necessary. But this particular doubling does not commend itself. The similarity of the roles of Balthasar and Amiens suggests rather that both were devised for the same person, someone who excelled neither as singer nor actor, but who was pressed into the double service because in both plays Shakespeare felt the need of a singing adult actor. With the acquisition of Armin, in 1599 or 1600, he had one: but Armin was first and foremost a jester, and it is probably as jester only that his gifts are displayed in *As You Like It*. 'Good my lord, like this fellow', says Jaques to Duke Senior in the play's last scene, and 'Good my lords, like this fellow', Shakespeare is saying to his audience. That they did like him is clear from the parts Shakespeare went on to provide for him: notably, in comedy, that of Feste in *Twelfth Night*, with the witty fool now the chief singer too, and later probably that of Autolycus in *The Winter's Tale*; and in tragedy, the roles of the first grave-digger in *Hamlet*, and Lear's fool.

Each of these parts shows Shakespeare exploiting this ideal answer to the company's need for a singing actor: a singing jester; and of them all, the part of Feste turns his dramatic potential to fullest use. A lord cannot be displayed as a singer, and one of lowly occupation cannot mix with noble company; but a fool, especially a witty fool,

---

[45] Felver, *Robert Armin*, pp. 20 and 45, thinks Armin may have played Amiens as well as Touchstone, and distinguishes between Amiens, whom he classes with Feste as a skilled singer, and Balthasar, who apologizes for his voice; but so in fact does Amiens, II. v. 14. Long, *Seven Comedies*, pp. 182–5, surmises that Armin played both Balthasar and Amiens; but Armin joined the company after Kemp left, and Kemp is known to have played Dogberry in the winter of 1598. Baldwin gives March or April 1600 as the date when Armin joined (*Organization and Personnel*, p. 84).

has a privileged place, and can interact with groups of all kinds. The naturalness with which songs spring up from their contexts in *Twelfth Night* is largely due to the presence of Feste, for whom song is as natural a mode of expression as nimble speech.

At his first appearance, towards the end of Act I, when Feste is chided for his absence, it is his witty fooling that restores him to Olivia's favour. At his next entry, in Act II, scene iii, Sir Toby greets him with a request for a catch, Sir Andrew demands a song—a love-song, not 'a song of good life', and Feste sings:

Clown sings.

O mistress mine, where are you roaming?
O, stay and hear; your true love's coming,
    That can sing both high and low.
    Trip no further, pretty sweeting;
    Journeys end in lovers meeting,
    Every wise man's son doth know.

Sir And. Excellent good, i' faith!
Sir To. Good, good!

Clown sings.

What is love? 'Tis not hereafter;
Present mirth hath present laughter;
    What's to come is still unsure.
    In delay there lies no plenty,
    Then come kiss me, sweet and twenty;
    Youth's a stuff will not endure.   (lines 38–51.)

It is a solo song intended to provide real musical pleasure, and asking some artistry of the singer, and in giving the clown such a song for his musical début, Shakespeare presents him as a singer worth hearing. Dramatically, the song plays a part in the scene's dynamics, providing a moment of stillness before the action accelerates: there is a lull in the fooling as Feste sings of youth and love to listeners desiring love but themselves unlovely, and a hint of poignancy hovers until Sir Toby routs it. The song itself lingers in the mind, and its further resonance is recognized later, when true love does come to Feste's mistress, whose youth was in danger of being sacrificed to the memory of her brother. The song presents complex problems of authorship both of words and music; its well-known tune antedates the play, already called 'O mistress mine', and Shakespeare may have written these words to it, or he may have adapted or borrowed an existing lyric that went to it. Both Morley and Byrd used the tune in instrumental pieces; one of them may have composed it, but quite probably both were using an already popular tune.[46]

After Feste's 'mellifluous voice' has been praised, the clown is drawn in to 'make the welkin dance' with the two knights, and the three of them sing a catch, 'Hold thy peace, thou knave',[47] until Maria comes in to protest at the noise. Sir Toby responds with a farrago of snippets of ballads; the convivial commotion brings in Malvolio, and his chiding, ending with

> and it would please you to take leave of her, she is very willing to bid you farewell

reminds Sir Toby of a song of a very different sort from his others, which he can address to Maria, and Feste takes it up after her protest:

Sir To. [*Sings*]
   Farewell, dear heart, since I must needs be gone.
Mar. Nay, good Sir Toby.
Clo. [*Sings*]
   His eyes do show his days are almost done.
Mal. Is't even so?
Sir To. [*Sings*] But I will never die.   [*Falls down*
Clo. [*Sings*]   Sir Toby, there you lie.
Mal. This is much credit to you.
Sir To. [*Sings*] Shall I bid him go?
Clo. [*Sings*]   What an if you do?

---

[46] An instrumental arrangement of the tune is found in Morley's *The First Booke of Consort Lessons* of 1599; the Fitzwilliam Virginal Book contains a set of variations on it by Byrd; and it is partnered with a lyric, probably Campion's, 'Long have mine eies gaz'd with delight' (which occurs with a different tune in Rosseter's *A Booke of Ayres*, 1601), in John Gamble's Commonplace Book (New York Public Library, Drexel MS 4257, no. 118). Morley's version and Byrd's will both accommodate the words quite well; but Shakespeare may have known another variant of the tune, and written his verses for that. For views on authorship of the music, see Seng, op. cit., pp. 97–100. Chappell, *Popular Music of the Olden Time*, vol. 1, p. 209, prints Byrd's version; Sydney Beck, in 'The Case of "O Mistresse mine" ', *RN* 6 (1953), 19–23, gives Morley's, and his transcription is reproduced in the New Penguin edition of *Twelfth Night*, which also gives versions of the tunes known for other songs in the play.

[47] The tune may be the one preserved in Ravenscroft's *Deuteromelia* (1609), or the different one in a collection in King's College, Cambridge, MS KC I, *c.*1580.

Sir To. [*Sings*]	Shall I bid him go, and spare not?
Clo. [*Sings*]	O, no, no, no, no, you dare not.

(lines 97–107.)

The song was a lute-song of Robert Jones's, newly published in his *The First Booke of Songes or Ayres*, 1600. It begins:

> Farewel dear loue since thou wilt needs be gon,
> mine eies do shew my life is almost done,
>   nay I will neuer die,
>   so long as I can spie . . .

After Feste's improvised riposte in place of the fourth line, Malvolio butts in again, and Sir Toby switches to the second half of the next stanza, which needs only changes of pronoun to direct it at the steward: in the song-book it runs:

> Shall I bid her goe,
> What and if I doe?
> Shall I bid her go and spare not,
> O no no no no I dare not.

The lute-song has turned into a comic antiphon, and the scene has taken off in a hilarious crescendo of song and comic action that also serves as a trigger to set off further events: the uproar leads to Malvolio's intervention, and his officiousness provokes Maria to unfold to the revellers a plot to deflate his pomposity. Feste's presence has made this a drinking-scene with a difference, piquant and various in its ingredients and multiple in its effects.

Feste is heard singing again in the next scene, but this time his presence seems strangely contrived. Music was sounding as the play began, and Orsino was feeding his love-languor upon it; in the scene that follows the knights' carousal he expresses a desire to hear again a song that had charmed him, and Feste is fetched, and sings

> Come away, come away, death;
> And in sad cypress let me be laid;
>   Fly away, fly away, breath,
> I am slain by a fair cruel maid.
> My shroud of white, stuck all with yew,
>   O, prepare it!
> My part of death no one so true
>   Did share it.

> Not a flower, not a flower sweet,
> On my black coffin let there be strown;
> Not a friend, not a friend greet
> My poor corpse where my bones shall be thrown;
> A thousand thousand sighs to save,
> Lay me, O, where
> Sad true lover never find my grave,
> To weep there!
>
> (Act II, scene iv, lines 50–65.)

The song does not answer to the duke's description of it, which suggests something like a spinning-song:

> it is old and plain;
> The spinsters and the knitters in the sun,
> And the free maids that weave their thread with bones,
> Do use to chant it; it is silly sooth,
> And dallies with the innocence of love,
> Like the old age.   (lines 42–7.)

But what Feste sings is not a traditional song of innocent love, but a highly mannered lament of a lover pining to death. Moreover, it is odd that he, who is not of the duke's household but of Olivia's, is fetched to sing it; and that Viola, who in urging the Sea Captain to present her to serve Orsino had claimed

> I can sing
> And speak to him in many sorts of music

is never heard to sing. Conjectures that the text embodies revision made for later performance, when Viola was supposedly played by a boy whose voice was breaking, are less attractive than the view that the replacing of 'Cesario' by Feste as singer reflects second thoughts in the course of composition.[48] The affected lyric invites a rendering that combines the answering of Orsino's request with a tinge of mockery of his luxurious melancholy: more clichés and trappings of self-pitying lovesickness could scarcely be couched in two stanzas, and the cadences ask to be set to dying falls. If the original setting, now unknown, took up the cues for music of slightly over-languishing beauty, no one could achieve more deftly than Feste a performance combining musical pleasure and hinted parodic effect.

---

[48] Suggested by M. M. Mahood in her Introduction, *Twelfth Night*, New Penguin edition, pp. 18–20.

When next Feste sings, in Act IV, scene ii, the trick played on Malvolio has caused the deluded steward to be shut up in a dark room, where the clown is sent to visit him. He first pretends to be the curate Sir Topas, then in his own person sings part of a song that is unkindly apt: the words, as Wyatt wrote them and almost as Cornysh set them, begin

> A Robyn
> Joly Robyn
> tell me how thy leman doeth
> and thou shall knowe of myn
> My lady is vnkynd perde
> alack whi is she so
> she loveth an othr better then me
> and yet she will say no.[49]

The farcical pitch heightens as Feste converses with himself and Malvolio, speaking now in his own voice and now as Sir Topas, until he goes off to fetch Malvolio light and paper and ink, appropriately both promising to return and likening himself to the Vice, the comic minor devil of a morality play:

> I am gone, sir,
> And anon, sir,
> I'll be with you again,
> In a trice,
> Like to the old Vice,
> Your need to sustain;
>
> Who with dagger of lath,
> In his rage and his wrath,
> Cries, Ah, ha! to the devil;
> Like a mad lad,
> pare thy nails, dad.
> Adieu, goodman devil.   (lines 116–27.)

Whether he recites or sings the doggerel verse is not made clear in the Folio, which does not say he sings, or italicize the text, here or at 'Hey, Robin, jolly Robin', as it does for Feste's other songs; no tune for it is known.

---

[49] From BL MS Egerton 2711, f. 37ᵛ. The music survives in BL Add. MS 31922, ff. 53ᵛ–54, and is printed in *Music at the Court of Henry VIII*, ed. John Stevens, pp. 38–9.

Feste's last song, 'When that I was and a little tiny boy', has provoked many critics to try to disown it on Shakespeare's behalf, as being for the most part too poor in quality and tenuous in bearing to be his work, but there is no external evidence disproving his hand. The song is of a popular kind, two verse lines alternating with two refrain lines in each stanza. Its pattern is one that invites extemporization or the writing of new lines to slot into the refrain; the Fool in *King Lear* is given his own single-stanza version, and the effectiveness of that in its context is clear. At the least, Feste's song serves to round off the play with music, as was customary in comedy, and to return the audience from its brief make-believe to the chill continuities of everyday life.[50]

Many kinds of song are turned to serve the dramatist's ends in *Twelfth Night*, and the ends are various too; the virtuosity of Shakespeare's handling of song in this play is striking. A love-song brings incongruous beauty into a drinking-scene; an old song of Wyatt's serves a new turn; a fashionable lute-song is comically bandied between knight and clown; a love-lament humours the duke's melancholy: all these are art-songs, two of them giving real musical delight, all of them reflecting upon, and reflected on by, their contexts. And besides these there are songs of more popular kinds: the drinkers 'rouse the night-owl in a catch' and sing scraps of ballads that most of the audience would know, and Feste's farewell has a proverbial refrain. If, as seems likely, the play was written with indoor performance in mind—it was performed at the Middle Temple on 2 February 1602, and possibly at court before that [51]— both the taste of a more sophisticated audience and the better acoustics would invite its richer provision of song (and of instrumental music); but it offers not only an increase in the number of songs, but an advance in their integration with action and dialogue, and it is the availability of a skilled adult singer–jester, making possible the creation of the role of Feste, that brings this bonus.

After *Twelfth Night*, such a life-affirming note is not heard again in Shakespeare's plays for most of a decade; his company now had several members whose bent was for tragic roles, and his plays

---

[50] The song's moresca-like rhythm, suggestive of a rounding-off dance, gives it an effect analogous to that of the customary jig.

[51] Chan, *Music in the Theatre of Ben Jonson*, p. 34, notes that L. Hotson, in *The First Night of 'Twelfth Night'* (1954), argues for performance at court in 1601, and that G. P. V. Akrigg, in '*Twelfth Night* at the Middle Temple', *SQ* ix (1958), argues for first performance in 1602.

confront harsher aspects of life. Tragedies predominate; and the plays classed as comedies are ambiguous in mood and kind: *Troilus and Cressida*, *All's Well that Ends Well*, and *Measure for Measure*. Gaiety is lacking, wit is scurrilous, love is tainted; it is not surprising that music and song are almost absent, each of these plays containing, at most, only one song.

The song in *Troilus and Cressida* occurs near the start of Act III. Pandarus comes to Priam's palace with a message from Troilus to Paris; when Paris and Helen enter, he can scarcely deliver it for their insistent demands that he must sing, in recompense for drawing them from the consort music they were listening to. He acquiesces and asks for an instrument, and Helen, after a bawdy exchange with him, asks for a song of love, and Paris seconds her wish:

Ay, good now, love, love, nothing but love.

Pandarus replies

In good troth, it begins so

and sings a lewd song, punning and playing on the progression of sensual experiences in the sexual act, which begins

Love, love, nothing but love, still love, still more!

Although 'it begins so', neither the Quarto, of 1609, nor the Folio uses italics for Paris's request (as the Folio does for Sir Andrew's in *Twelfth Night*: 'Let our Catch be, *Thou Knaue*'), and editors who supply them weaken the point. Paris and Helen want 'nothing but love', and are given a song that lays bare the nature of their insatiable desire. The absence of an early setting for it is more than usually tantalizing; if the instrument handed to Pandarus was a lute, this is a highly unusual lute-song: the lyrics of ayres span a wide spectrum of love, from the languishing to the frankly enticing, but they do not gloat on the sensation of gratified lust. The content asks for a bawdy ballad, but the verse-form invites a more sophisticated musical match. (Madrigalian treatment could both take advantage of the shape, and take the sting from the sense, at once lightening the tone and obfuscating the obscenity, but even the versatile Pandarus could not perform a madrigal alone.) The song is a *tour de force*, a deliberately shocking conjunction of sentiments fit for a brothel ballad with verse that asks for artistic setting, for a lord who is also a 'broker-lackey', as Troilus later calls him, to sing to a royal abductor and his wanton mistress. It gives scope for vivid rendering, with its exclamations of successive passions (the role of Pandarus was probably another of Armin's); and it epitomizes the voluptuousness that saps the Trojan court. The unseemliness of Pandarus singing at all, as a lord, and an old one, is nothing to the unseemliness of the song, and of the desire of the 'noble' Paris and Helen for such entertainment.

The song in *All's Well that Ends Well* concerns Helen of Troy too. In Act I, scene iii, the clown has just spoken four lines of a ballad when he is told to tell Helena the Countess wishes to speak with her, and a song about the other Helen comes into his mind, ' "Was this fair face the cause", quoth she'. The ballad entitled 'The Lamentation of Hecuba and the Ladyes of Troy', entered in the Stationers' Register on 1 August 1586, is a possible source, but both words and music are now lost.[52] The clown's version does not suggest ballad verse at first sight; nor, I think, does it suggest that he is singing, except perhaps the opening lines: he is reciting it, altering it as he goes to build up to his final gibe. 'You corrupt the song, sirrah', protests the Countess. In his rendering the reference is to women instead of men, and the odds are one good in ten; the inference is that the original reference is to sons of Priam with Paris being one *bad* in ten. The clown is probably corrupting the song's form as well as its import, stressing his reversed proportions of bad to good by repeating that line, having prepared the way by doubling the earlier line it rhymes with. Without these repeats, his ditty would fall into two ballad stanzas, regular in form except for a missing rhyme in line three of the first, which reads like one imperfectly remembered or, in this context, lamely changed to suit his purpose. Set out in the common pattern of lines of four and three stresses alternating, it would appear:

> 'Was this fair face the cause' quoth she
>   'Why the Grecians sacked Troy?
> Fond done, done fond,
>   Was this King Priam's joy?'

---

[52] It is no. 1464 in Rollins's 'Analytical Index to the Ballad-Entries in the Registers of the Company of Stationers of London', *Studies in Philology*, xxi (1924).

With that she sighed as she stood,
And gave this sentence then:
'Among nine bad if one be good,
There's yet one good in ten'.[53]

The Folio gives no indication of whether or not the clown sings; if he does, his repetitions of the fifth and seventh lines are likely to mar the tune unless he drops into speech after the first four lines; but if he is reciting, his repetition of the punch line

'Among nine bad if one be good,
Among nine bad if one be good,
There's yet one good in ten'   (lines 73–5.)

both drives home his point, and makes it natural that the Countess should swallow his bait and take it up.

Ironically, it is the woman who is faithful and virtuous, the man who deserts and disowns, in *All's Well that Ends Well* and also in *Measure for Measure*. The two plays have this strand of their stories in common, and both plots are resolved by means of a substitution, the wronged wife or fiancée taking the place of someone else at an assignation. The third act of *Measure for Measure* ends with the Duke, in his disguise as a friar, on stage alone, revealing his plan to trick Angelo by this device. Act IV opens at the moated grange, and Mariana, who has previously been only referred to, not seen, comes in attended by a boy singing. He has sung only one stanza when the disguised duke enters, and Mariana at once dismisses him and apologizes to the duke for being found 'so musical', saying,

My mirth it much displeas'd, but pleas'd my woe.

Her love melancholy, like that of Orsino in *Twelfth Night*, has been ministered to by music, but unlike him she has good cause for sadness, rejected by Angelo to whom she is betrothed.

[53] Following the cues given as to content and form, one might expect the lost ballad to run something like this:

'Was this fair face the cause', quoth she
'Why the Grecians sacked Troy?
Fond done, for Paris he
Was Priam's only joy.'
With that she sighed as she stood,
And gave this sentence then:
'If one be bad among ten good,
There's yet nine good in ten.'

The song voices the lament of a forsaken lover in a single stanza finely expressive of sorrow:

> Take, O, take those lips away,
>   That so sweetly were forsworn;
> And those eyes, the break of day,
>   Lights that do mislead the morn;
> But my kisses bring again, bring again;
> Seals of love, but seal'd in vain, seal'd in vain.

It achieves perfection as verse for singing: the content is simple, and statement, imagery, and rhythms combine to convey the emotion. The translucent imagery becomes more luminous as it expands in the mind: the metaphor linking eyes and daybreak arouses connotations that are congruent—light, brightness, softness—making the change to a false dawn carry the shock of betrayal. The verse is skilfully framed for a solo voice to sing, with open vowels that can be dwelt on, and repeated phrases at the end of the last two lines that invite, or imply, a sequential musical 'dying fall'. A setting for voice and lute would be appropriate, so that if the singer had skill enough, he could accompany himself. The song seems completed as it stands; Mariana's command

> Break off thy song, and haste thee quick away

implies other stanzas to follow, but they need exist only as dramatic fiction, not in fact. The dramatist has provided, and his audience has heard, all that is needed—a stanza that hints a whole ayre, with a pattern that could well be repeated if more was to follow; but no more is dramatically required. It seems more probable that the invitation of the pattern was taken up by another writer, who added the second stanza that appears with this one in Fletcher's *The Bloody Brother* (printed in 1639 but probably written about fifteen years earlier), than that Shakespeare was borrowing part of an existing song. The second stanza is different in tone and tenor, dwelling more on sensuous delights denied than on broken faith, besides being a plaint that can only be made by a man.

The setting now known, an eloquent one in the style of declamatory ayre, is too late to be the one the play's first audiences heard. It appears in John Wilson's collection of his own songs (Bodleian MS Mus. b.i.), and is attributed to him in other early sources; he would have been only nine or ten when the play was first produced. Conjectures that he may have composed his setting for a later revival of the play, before the First Folio was compiled, and that the song may first have been introduced then, are unconvincing; the setting does not use or accommodate the repeated phrases of Shakespeare's stanza, and in all early manuscript and printed sources it is found with the two stanzas, as in Fletcher's play. If it was composed to be sung in a play, the likelier one is Fletcher's.[54]

In *Pericles*, as in *Measure for Measure*, one song is sung, but for Marina's song no text is known. In Act V, scene i, she is sent for to try to arouse Pericles from his torpor; after she and her attendant have been left alone with him, Lysimachus asks:

> Mark'd he your music?
> *Mar.*   No, nor look'd on us.

(Marina's reply, linking her maid with herself in the music, perhaps implies that the girl accompanied her on the lute.) 'She sings like one immortal', Gower has just said, and the fact that Marina sings in the presence of Pericles, and sings beautifully, is of more importance than what she sings, for although Pericles does not respond to the song, the healing power of music may be assumed to be at work, initiating his cure, just as the music called for by Cerimon as he ministers to Thaisa, in Act III, scene ii, is felt to be an agent of her recovery, not a mere accompaniment to it. Nevertheless, it is unlikely that Shakespeare, who rarely called for a song without supplying a lyric or quoting a ballad, passed over the opportunity of providing one for Marina; the absence of a lyric here is probably due to the lack of a good text of the play: the earliest text extant is the Quarto of 1609, which gives the barest possible indications of music, and the play was not included in the first two editions of the Folio.[55]

In *Cymbeline* too only one song is sung, although in this play texts for two are provided; and for this song a singer is specially brought in—appropriately since, as in *The Two Gentlemen of Verona*, a

---

[54] Wilson's setting was first printed in Playford's *Select Musicall Ayres and Dialogues* in 1652; Sternfeld gives this version in *Music in Shakespearean Tragedy*, pp. 94–5, and in *Songs from Shakespeare's Tragedies*, p. 17.

[55] J. H. Long, *Shakespeare's Use of Music: The Final Comedies* (Gainesville, Florida, 1961), pp. 44–5, suggests that the lyric occurring at the parallel point in one of Shakespeare's sources for the play, Lawrence Twyne's *The patterne of Painfull Adventures*, 1576, which had been reprinted in 1607, may have been used. It tells of the singer's situation, and of her royal parentage. There is no evidence for this, and the faulty nature of the only substantive text for *Pericles* is a more probable explanation.

wooer is presenting a song as a gift in hope of furthering his suit. In both cases, the context complicates the effect. Here, the wooer is Cloten, the lady is Imogen, and before music is heard, in Act II, scene iii, the conceited stupidity of Cloten and the fiendish trickery of Iachimo that will destroy Imogen's happiness have both been displayed. Now, in an antechamber to Imogen's apartments, Cloten instructs the musicians to perform an instrumental piece and then a song (which would be accompanied by one or more instruments), and his gross comments both preface and follow the delicate, aureate lyric:

> Hark, hark! the lark at heaven's gate sings,
> And Phoebus 'gins arise,
> His steeds to water at those springs
>   On chalic'd flow'rs that lies;
> And winking Mary-buds begin
>   To ope their golden eyes.
> With everything that pretty bin,
>   My lady sweet, arise;
>   Arise, arise!   (lines 19–27.)

Brief as it is, the song is shortened by the omission of the third and fourth lines in the earliest known setting of it, which is found in a manuscript collection that includes songs by Robert Johnson, John Wilson, and John Hilton.[56] Spink considers that this song may be by Johnson, and appends it to his edition of Johnson's *Ayres, Songs and Dialogues*.[57] The omitted lines can be accommodated by positing a repeat of part of the melody,[58] but it is not certain that the setting was made for the play's first production—or for dramatic performance at all: the composer may have chosen, and changed, the lyric simply as an attractive text for a song.

[56] Bodleian MS Don. c.57 (p. 78).

[57] Ward's witty compendium of occupations and attributes, some mutually exclusive, with which Johnson has been credited ('*Joan qd John* and Other Fragments at Western Reserve University', p. 840) invites caution concerning attributions to him. Ian Spink, in the Preface to his edition of Johnson's *Ayres, Songs and Dialogues* for *The English Lute-Songs* Second Series (vol. 17: 2nd rev. ed. 1974) presents a less shadowy figure, composing instrumental music for masques, and vocal music for plays performed by the King's Men. He was one of the earliest English composers to write declamatory song. (See also above, p. 145, note 60.)

[58] Cutts (*La Musique de scène de la troupe de Shakespeare*, Paris 1959, p. 121) suggests that these lines might be sung to a repeat of the music for the next part of the text; Sternfeld (*Songs from Shakespeare's Tragedies*, p. 29) more appropriately repeats all but the opening two bars of the setting of the first two lines.

The other song in *Cymbeline* is not sung but spoken by Arviragus and Guiderius as they prepare to bury the apparently dead Fidele, and their conversation probably embodies the real reason: Arviragus says:

> And let us, Polydore, though now our voices
> Have got the mannish crack, sing him to th' ground,

but Guiderius replies:

> Cadwal,
> I cannot sing. I'll weep, and word it with thee;
> For notes of sorrow out of tune are worse
> Than priests and fanes that lie.

(Act iv, scene ii, lines 236–7 and 240–3.)

It is a pity, because the lyric asks to become an ayre, with three stanzas patterned with enough similarity to permit strophic setting, four falling stresses to each line. There are six lines to a stanza, the first four rhyming alternately, and the last two making a couplet that forms a semi-refrain, having the same rhyme, and the same final phrase, in all three stanzas. A fourth stanza forms a contrast, with its change of pattern to three stresses in each of the first four lines, and couplet rhyme throughout; it would require different music if the song were set, but would be effective as an antiphonally spoken coda. Here is the '*Song*':

> *Gui.*   Fear no more the heat o' th' sun
>   Nor the furious winter's rages;
>   Thou thy worldly task hast done,
>   Home art gone, and ta'en thy wages.
>   Golden lads and girls all must,
>   As chimney-sweepers, come to dust.
>
> *Arv.*   Fear no more the frown o' th' great;
>   Thou art past the tyrant's stroke.
>   Care no more to clothe and eat;
>   To thee the reed is as the oak.
>   The sceptre, learning, physic, must
>   All follow this and come to dust.
>
> *Gui.*   Fear no more the lightning flash,
> *Arv.*   Nor th'all-dreaded thunder-stone;
> *Gui.*   Fear not slander, censure rash;

Arv.	Thou hast finish'd joy and moan.
Both.	All lovers young, all lovers must
	Consign to thee and come to dust.

Gui.	No exorciser harm thee!
Arv.	Nor no witchcraft charm thee!
Gui.	Ghost unlaid forbear thee!
Arv.	Nothing ill come near thee!
Both.	Quiet consummation have,
	And renowned be thy grave!

(lines 259–82.)

If the structure of the dirge suggests that it was framed with the expectation that three stanzas would be sung, the dialogue form indicates that this plan was abandoned: the Folio sets out both the third and fourth stanzas antiphonally, Guiderius and Arviragus speaking the first four lines of each alternately, and saying the closing couplets together. Several writers have criticized the final couplets of each stanza as inferior to the rest of the dirge, and argued, on this ground alone, that they must be non-Shakespearean additions. A more objective aspect of the obsequies is worth bearing in mind: they are being performed for someone who, in contrast to what the mourners believe, is neither dead nor Fidele, but alive and Imogen; what would be jarring in a truly tragic situation may serve to mark mourning that will later give way to rejoicing.

The Winter's Tale contains no music at all until the fourth act, but that is full of singing and dancing. The play presents with terrifying speed the wild jealousy of Leontes and its fearful consequences; until the very end of Act III, when the old shepherd and his son appear, the atmosphere is that of tragedy. But with the first sight of Bohemia and its inhabitants, the mood begins to change: Perdita is found by the kind shepherd as soon as she is abandoned, and the impact of events dire in themselves, shipwreck and the gory death of Antigonus, is softened by the clown's comically confused narration of them. The fourth act effects a distancing both in space and time from all that suffering: sixteen years have elapsed and the action takes place wholly in 'fair Bohemia', where all seems fresh and free. Unlike Sicilia, it is a place where it is natural to sing, and its typical season is not winter but spring; when Autolycus makes his first entry, in scene iii, he is singing of spring. With him, Shakespeare reintroduces ballads, which have so far been absent from the romances; but some, like their singer, are counterfeit coin. His first song is a ballad, and a spring-song, with a difference from others: 'When daffodils begin to peer' celebrates spring—as the season when lusty desire revives, when sheets laid out to dry tempt a light-fingered thief, when hay offers a soft illicit bed. The daffodils, the white sheet bleaching, the singing lark, belong to the world of rustic innocence; but Autolycus and his doxies and 'aunts' do not, and his underworld slang lets the audience know that here is a wolf among the sheep. He describes himself as a one-time servant of Prince Florizel who has been 'whipt out of the court', and his next song describes his present life of cheerful, unscrupulous vagabondage: 'But shall I go mourn for that, my dear?' These songs are not found in contemporary ballad collections, nor entered in the Stationers' Register: most probably Shakespeare is not using old ballads, but making new ones to measure for this novel rogue, and they share his genuine gaiety and his spurious innocence. No contemporary melody is known for either of these songs, but the one that Autolycus goes off singing after robbing the clown, 'Jog on, jog on, the footpath way', has left its name on a tune. It is possible that Shakespeare borrowed the words, but more probable that he wrote them either for singing to any appropriate tune, or with a well-known tune called 'Hanskin' in mind: it became known as 'Jog on'. The Fitzwilliam Virginal Book includes a set of variations on it by Richard Farnaby, and Playford's *The English Dancing Master* kept it in circulation, with the title 'Jog on', from 1651 until 1698; other Restoration collections contain the song (with two other stanzas that are probably later additions) arranged as a catch for three voices by John Hilton.[59]

The comedy of this scene preludes the perilous beauty of the sheep-shearing feast in scene iv, when Perdita, as queen of the feast, is admired not only by Florizel, but by the disguised Polixenes and Camillo; then a servant excitedly tells of the pedlar and his wonderful songs and wares, and again Autolycus comes in singing, and three songs later goes off singing still. This time he makes his entry with a pedlar's catalogue-song, 'Lawn as white as driven snow', extolling his wares in five rhyming couplets and a two-line cry. John Wilson published a setting of it in his *Cheerfull Ayres or Ballads First composed for one single Voice and since set for three Voices*, of 1660. He offers two ways of singing the songs in his book: the Cantus Primus provides tune and through bass, the Cantus Secundus and

---

[59] The tune is given by Chappell, *Popular Music of the Olden Time*, vol. i, p. 212.

Bassus make provision for additional voices. Most of the tunes are his own, but some, as he said, were composed by others and only arranged by himself. As Wilson was born in 1595, he could scarcely have composed songs for the play's first performance in 1611, but the setting he gives may possibly embody the original tune.[60]

Autolycus describes some of the ballads he has in stock to the clown and the shepherdesses (the happenings in many 'true ballads' of the time are scarcely less fantastic), and meets Mopsa's request for 'some merry ones' with one that 'goes to the tune of "Two maids wooing a man" ', and has words for both the maids and the man to sing. Mopsa and Dorcas know the tune already, so they sing 'Get you hence, for I must go' with Autolycus until the clown leads them off. No tune called 'Two maids wooing a man' is now known, but the words have been found in a setting made for one voice with lyra-viol accompaniment in a manuscript collection[61] that includes some songs composed by Robert Johnson for plays the King's Men are known to have performed; this too may be his. But as sung by Mopsa, Dorcas, and Autolycus, ' 'tis in three parts', a 'three-men's song', in the term then commonly used for songs for three voices to sing. As Autolycus goes off, he sings a stanza of another pedlar's song, not found elsewhere, 'Will you buy any tape?'

The songs of Autolycus show Shakespeare using several popular kinds, ballad and pedlar's song and dialogue-song, but writing his own examples of them, taking advantage of the familiarity of the genre but slanting it to his own particular purposes, which are wider than simply to give scope for Autolycus to display samples of his various musical wares. The vagabond's racy gusto and unscrupulous wit bring to vivid and comic life the earthy side of bucolic life; his first two appearances also form a contrasting frame for the beauty and grace of the sheep-shearing scene.

The sheep-shearing scene itself comes close to masque. Perdita is dressed as Mistress of the Feast, and Florizel as 'a poor humble swain'; Polixenes and Camillo, disguised, appear as unexpected guests; and contrasting kinds of dancing are interspersed with songs and dialogue. The chief dancers are Florizel and Perdita themselves;

---

[60] The music, for one voice, is given by Cutts, *La Musique de scène*, pp. 20–1.

[61] New York Public Library, Drexel MS 4175. Spink gives the music in his edition of Johnson's songs. Another, incomplete, setting of the same melody, in Drexel 4041, gives a second stanza, which aptly continues the theme but is not so apt throughout for the tune; it is probably a non-Shakespearean addition.

the dance of shepherds and shepherdesses will be a graceful one, and when Perdita and Florizel dance it together, 'for as moche as by the association of a man and a woman in daunsinge may be signified matrimonie', as Elyot had said in *The Gouernour*,[62] the act is seen as significant by Polixenes within the play, and by all educated people in its audience too. (The same symbolism is drawn on in *Pericles*, in Act II, scene iii: when at the feast that follows the tilting, King Simonides calls on the knights to dance, and then bids Pericles to lead out Thaisa to dance, he is prefiguring his blessing and consent.) Later, after the appearance of Autolycus disguised as a pedlar, and his patter-songs and dialogue-song, there is a dance by twelve carters and herdsmen dressed as satyrs, and theirs will be a vigorous, uncouth dance, with the grotesquerie of an antimasque.[63]

Shakespeare is drawing on the obvious attractions of songs and dances, but on the symbolic dimension implied by masque too. The view that he 'gives pause to the action of the play here for the sake of music, dance and spectacle'[64] leaves these overtones out of account. 'The hiatus in the action seems a deliberate device on Shakespeare's part to provide song, dance and spectacle for an audience who loved those things', Seng continues. But the romances are less concerned with the action than with its significance, and we miss much of the enrichment masque brought to Shakespeare's last plays if we treat it as a merely external feature added to cater for fashionable taste. Shakespeare certainly made use of the increased resources of place and personnel available to the King's Men. With the Blackfriars Theatre leased to them in August 1608, they could play there as well as at the Globe from then on, plague permitting; from time to time they were commanded to give court performances at the Whitehall banqueting house, which had been designed with theatrical productions and the taste for elaborate devices in mind; and Shakespeare responded to these opportunities, and to the desire of theatre audiences to share some of the delights the court masques lavished upon the privileged few. But the response he made was fully

---

[62] XXI; ed. cit., p. 94.

[63] It may be, or may be directly indebted to, the dance of satyrs in Jonson's *Masque of Oberon*, first performed at court on New Year's Day, 1611: *The Winter's Tale* is known to have been performed at the Globe on 15 May of that year. The dance called 'Satyres Masque' in the masque music collection BL Add. MS 10444 (ff. 31,82b) has been shown by J. P. Cutts to be Johnson's music for *Oberon*, and to be associated also with *The Winter's Tale* ('Robert Johnson: King's Musician in His Majesty's Public Entertainment', *M&L* 36 (1955), 110–25).   [64] Seng, op. cit., p. 247.

dramatic: masque episodes, ceremonies, and dances in the last plays do not arrest the matter, they form part of the communication of the matter.

To some extent, this is true of much earlier plays. In its simplest form, a masque was an entry of noble persons in disguise, and a dance; in *Love's Labour's Lost*, Act V, scene iii, the king and his lords enter disguised as Russians, with blackamoors to play music, but their device is frustrated by the caprice of the princess: the ladies refuse to dance. The first act of *Timon of Athens* contains a similar masque-entry, when Timon's banquet is followed by the entrance of Cupid *'with a* Masque of Ladies as Amazons, *with lutes in their hands, dancing and playing'*, and the lords rise from table and dance with them. Betrothals and weddings were favourite occasions for masques in real life, and so also in drama: some years before he wrote *The Tempest*, Shakespeare presented a masque of this kind in *As You Like It*, ending the play with a scene in which Hymen appears to present Rosalind to her father and to pair all the couples: a 'wedlock-hymn' is sung, and Duke Senior calls for dancing, which closes the play:

> Play, music; and you brides and bridegrooms all,
> With measure heap'd in joy, to th' measures fall.

In each of these plays, the masque episode is integrated with the action and arises aptly from it; but in the last plays the use of masque goes beyond this. In *The Winter's Tale*, *The Tempest*, and *King Henry the Eighth*, masque is an element of the play's essential medium, its presence is functional and organic as well as spectacular. To the often supreme poetry of the words, masque adds spectacle, vocal and instrumental music, and dancing, each with its own symbolic dimension. As poetry can suggest more than prose can state, dance can adumbrate meaning through movement alone. In *King Henry the Eighth*, Act IV, scene ii, symbolic dance expresses promise and shows Katharine her blessed future with no need of words: white-robed spirits dance a formally patterned dance, doing reverence to the queen and holding a garland over her head; and she knows she is invited to a banquet in heaven, and that eternal happiness awaits her. The vision is in a sense a dumb-show, although subtler in mode.[65]

[65] This play's unparalleled use of ceremony and spectacle may owe much to contemporary events as well as contemporary taste: it was still 'new' when at a

Not all members of any theatre audience would respond at all fully to such symbolic modes of expression; nor did Jonson's court masques meet with the learned attentiveness they invited; but both dramatists chose to avail themselves of the richness of many kinds and sources of meaning. In *The Tempest*, not only do masque and dancing figure largely, they are intrinsic to the mode of the play and convey much of its meaning. The associations of dancing give Ariel's first song its resonance:

> Come unto these yellow sands,
>   And then take hands;
> Curtsied when you have and kiss'd,
>   The wild waves whist,
> Foot it featly here and there,
> And, sweet sprites, the burden bear . . .
>
> (Act I, scene ii, lines 375–80.)

It is a burden-song, and presumably invisible 'sprites' offstage provide the imitation of barking, and perhaps of cock-crowing too, that the burden calls for.[66] But its 'burden' in another sense is more important by far, although more elusive. For the song is a bidding to a dance: a dance of grace and mutual reverence, preluded by taking hands, by curtseying and kissing. It may be thought of as calling others than Ferdinand to dance—sprites, whose dancing is the means of charming the waves to peace after the storm; but it calls and charms him too: it soothes and draws him and leads him to Miranda; and it conveys, more subtly than Prospero's later injunctions, what the manner of his courtship must be. The mystical concept of the whole universe as a dance, the dance of the stars in their courses, the dance of the seas to the moon, gives the pattern for the highest form of human dancing: as the dance of the spheres expresses the perfection of regular movement, of order, so the dancing of men and women can express, or inculcate, design and control. Prospero's desires and designs for a noble, chaste love between Ferdinand and his daughter

performance of it on 29 June 1613, the firing of cannons for the king's masqued entry to Wolsey's house caused the Globe Theatre to be burnt to the ground, so it may well have been written during or just after the months of spectacular celebrations for Princess Elizabeth's wedding to the Elector Palatine.

[66] A burden or burthen is normally a refrain that initiates a song or carol as well as following each stanza; or a continuous undersong. Here, as in relation to the forester's song in *As You Like It*, it seems to be used simply to indicate an element of the song that several voices take up. No contemporary setting is known.

are set in motion by the drawing of Ferdinand into her presence by Ariel in a song which is ceremonial, orderly, restrained: symbolically he is called to a wooing in which impulse is controlled and courtesy and reverence prevail; and the love between him and Miranda will establish concord between their parents.

Ariel's second song too is to be symbolically understood. He sings another burden-song, and this time the burden is sung by sea-nymphs:

> Full fathom five thy father lies;
> 　　Of his bones are coral made;
> Those are pearls that were his eyes;
> 　　Nothing of him that doth fade
> But doth suffer a sea-change
> Into something rich and strange.
> Sea-nymphs hourly ring his knell:
> 　　　　*Burden*. Ding-dong.
> Hark! now I hear them—Ding-dong bell.
> 　　　　　　　　(Act I, scene ii, lines 396–404.)

Ferdinand, hearing this gentle elegy, says, 'The ditty does remember my drown'd father'. But Alonso is not drowned, although for a while Ferdinand must think so; Ariel is speaking a mystery which we do not understand until, in Act III, scene iii, he denounces the 'three men of sin' who ousted Prospero from his dukedom, and Alonso's guilt comes home to him, and with guilt, remorse:

> Methought the billows spoke, and told me of it;
> The winds did sing it to me; and the thunder,
> That deep and dreadful organ-pipe, pronounc'd
> The name of Prosper; it did bass my trespass.
> Therefore my son i' th' ooze is bedded; and
> I'll seek him deeper than e'er plummet sounded,
> And with him there lie mudded.　　　　　(lines 96–102.)

All that was Alonso is to be buried full fathom five; the very fact that he thinks now of the storm in terms of music—of the winds as singing, the thunder as an organ-pipe—signifies that chaos is being subdued to order, discord resolved to harmony, and heralds his repentance: truly

> Nothing of him that doth fade
> But doth suffer a sea-change
> Into something rich and strange.

Through suffering, estrangement, and understanding Alonso is made anew. Robert Johnson's music for this song,[67] probably made for the play, sets the words smoothly to a melody that moves soberly, without wide vocal leaps, and preserves the verse pattern; the 'burden' becomes a thrice-repeated final phrase, 'Ding, dong, ding, dong, bell', set to falling sequences.

All but one of Ariel's songs open up long perspectives. His next, 'While you here do snoring lie', is the exception; it has an immediate relation to the play's action, serving as a way of doing something that has to be done, and it is no more than that. In Act II, scene i, when all but Antonio and Sebastian have been charmed into restorative sleep by solemn music played by Ariel, and the two plot to kill Alonso and Gonzalo, the intended victims must be aroused, and Ariel effects this by singing in Gonzalo's ear. One six-line stanza of warning (for which no contemporary setting is known) suffices: they awake.

By contrast, his last song, 'Where the bee sucks, there suck I', in Act V, scene i, has no dramatic function beyond diversifying the interest of a static moment, as Prospero puts off his magic robe and is dressed again as Duke of Milan, but its note of pure rejoicing at the prospect of freedom is part of the final and lasting concord of the play. It too is short, but its apparent simplicity is that of consummate metrical dexterity; it is one of the most perfect lyrics, and the gayest, that Shakespeare wrote. Each of its seven lines has four stresses, but the first five have seven syllables each and the last two have ten; the odd-syllabled length gives a hovering effect to the rhythm of the first part, and its last word, 'merrily', is taken up and repeated twice to give a dactylic lilt to the longer lines. The couplet sounds like a

---

[67] It survives in two manuscripts, Birmingham City Reference Library MS 57316 and Folger Library MS 747.1, and John Wilson included an arrangement of it in *Cheerfull Ayres or Ballads*. The same early sources also contain Johnson's music for 'Where the bee sucks, there suck I', which is found additionally in Bod. MS Don. c. 57 and in two of Playford's printed collections. It is probable that Johnson wrote other music, vocal and instrumental, for the play: Sir Nicholas L'Estrange's collection of music contains a number of pieces by Johnson for various masques and plays, including one entitled 'The Tempest', and this may have been for the nymphs' and reapers' dance. The songs are included in Johnson's *Ayres, Songs and Dialogues*, ed. cit., pp. 24–7; the New Arden edition of *The Tempest* prints the songs and the instrumental piece, pp. 157–9.

refrain; with only one stanza, Shakespeare has suggested that Ariel has more to sing than Prospero's imperious haste gives time for. Robert Johnson's setting is spirited, and responsive to the verse in its vocal phrasing and its rhythmic implications; the change from trochaic to dactylic movement at the couplet is matched by a shift from duple to triple time, and the couplet is heard twice, swinging along to sequences that echo and exultantly answer each other.

Between Ariel's last two songs come some very different ones: the 'scurvy tunes' of the drunken butler Stephano; the 'howling' of Caliban, his neophyte in drunkenness; and the blessing-song of Juno and Ceres. In Act II, scene ii, Stephano enters singing a fragment that would probably be sung to part of an appropriate existing tune, as his next outburst almost certainly would. This latter consists of a whole nine-line stanza, beginning

> The master, the swabber, the boatswain, and I;

its rollicking rhythms and ribald sentiments give it the ring of a seaman's song, which the landlubber butler could have picked up in the course of the voyage to Tunis. The stanza has an unusual structure, with a marked change of rhythm for lines five and six, followed by a return of the first line's pattern; it goes with a swing that makes it easy to catch and sing. The strength of the beats is characteristic of shanties, and suggests that the words were made with a particular shanty-tune in mind; but there is no record of what tunes Stephano and Caliban sang in early performances of the play. The scene ends with Caliban's song or 'howl', and his ' 'Ban 'Ban, Ca—Caliban' combines the effects of a drunken hiccup and a battle-cry of defiance, its braggart rhythm suggestive of tabor and pipe. These revellers 'troll' for the last time in Act III, scene ii, in an episode that is rich in comic device if not in musical pleasure; Stephano and Trinculo sing the catch Caliban asks for,

> Flout 'em and scout 'em,
> And scout 'em and flout 'em;
> Thought is free,

but he protests 'That's not the tune', so Ariel, invisible, plays the tune on a tabor and pipe and leads them after him; Shakespeare is enjoying himself in employing his versatile spirit.

Act IV has only one song, but it combines with dance and spectacle to make up what is in effect a masque. In the vision that Prospero conjures up to celebrate the betrothal of Miranda and Ferdinand, Juno and Ceres sing their blessings on the couple, probably in turn, Juno singing the first four lines and Ceres the remainder. The verse is incantatory; its trochaic tetrameter couplets, with feminine rhymes, lend themselves to solemn ritual delivery. A chant-like melody seems called for, but no early setting is known. Iris then summons nymphs and reapers to perform a graceful dance. Ferdinand was first drawn into Miranda's presence by a song that called him to a courtly dance; now that bidding has been obeyed, and the association of graceful dancing with concord and marriage makes it fitting that nymphs and reapers should by such dancing

> help to celebrate
> A contract of true love. . . .

These are faery dancers, who may well be given a dance less rustic than the morris, and may foot it more featly than country folk, but this is not a mere *divertissement*; in the manner of masque, it inculcates what it presents and symbolizes, furthering Prospero's 'fancies', his designs for a high and holy love between Ferdinand and Miranda, the beholders for whom the vision is devised.

The whole ambience of *The Tempest* leads the mind still further: beyond the kinds of dancing it actually contains to that celestial dancing it can only faintly foreshadow: the dance of the cosmos, the dance that expresses the harmony, concord, and order that motivate the universe and sustain it, its music the music of the spheres. That ever-fascinating concept hovers behind all the last plays. It is most explicitly embodied in *Pericles*, in Act V, scene i, when Pericles, and he alone, hears the music of the spheres at the moment of overpowering joy and ecstasy when he realizes that Marina is indeed his lost daughter. That music might only be heard, if by human ears at all, by one of unusual purity. Purified by suffering after trials of virtue and fortitude of the highest order, Pericles, if any mortal, might hear it when the gods at last show their favour towards him and begin to recompense him with abundant blessings, and when, too, he is restored to himself. To humour and soothe Pericles in his excess of joy, Lysimachus says he hears the music, but it is not for his ears. In the Quarto the line reads

> Musicke my lord? I heare;

so, if the line incorporates a stage direction, 'Musicke', and should read simply

My lord, I hear   (line 230.)

it is clear that music was to sound at this moment. The Quarto leaves unresolved the question of whether the audience was allowed to hear the harmony; it would give a rare enhancement to the moment if they were. English dramatic practice was more reserved than French or Italian in representing the music of the spheres, but celestial music was sometimes presented; for instance, in Jonson's *Cynthias Reuells*, Mercury grants Eccho's request to sing a mourning strain for Narcissus, saying,

> Begin, and (more to grace thy cunning voice)
> The humorous aire shall mixe her solemne tunes,
> With thy sad words: strike musique from the spheares,
> And with your golden raptures swell our eares.
>
> (Act i, scene ii, lines 61–4.)

Since the play was acted at court, on 6 January 1601, by the Children of Queen Elizabeth's Chapel, there would be musical resources available to give effect to Mercury's command.[68]

Sphere-music is not called for at any specific moment in *The Tempest*, but in this play the concept of the *musica humana*, the human harmony, and its relation to the *musica mundana*, the universal harmony, is pervasively implicit. The play's symbolism is grounded in music, which provides the very dimension in which the play exists. It is as if Shakespeare has created his own sphere within which to seek to sound the proper harmony of humanity: as if he has thought, 'Let us look at life in some frame that lifts it right out of its mundane setting and yet leaves it still obeying its own laws' (for the

---

[68] Campion's *Lords' Masque* also presents celestial music; on the night of the wedding of Princess Elizabeth and the Elector Palatine, 14 February 1613, it was performed with, according to Frances Yates, 'a wondrous presentation of the harmony of the spheres, alluding to the harmony to be established by their wedding' (*Shakespeare's Last Plays: A New Approach*, 1975, p. 34). But although eight stars descended and danced in a spectacular device, while a song, 'Advance your Chorall motions now', was sung, there is no suggestion that a representation of the dancing or music of the spheres was intended: these are stars, or 'lights', that Prometheus stole from heaven, and they dance to the music of Orpheus. Music not of earthly origin is heard in a number of plays and masques, but not all unearthly music is heavenly, and not all heavenly music is to be apprehended as that of the spheres themselves. In *The Tempest*, in the last magic act that Prospero performs he requires 'Some heavenly music' to restore the spell-bound conspirators, but it does not carry this meaning.

magic only creates situations and opportunities, it does not wrest people's natures out of their true course); as if he has projected human life, not into space, but into a realm of sound. There the discord of man with himself and man with his fellows, the clash of passions and conflicts of self-interest, are resolved into concord. The discord in the older generation is resolved by Prospero's choice of forgiveness in place of revenge, and the discord within himself is resolved when he renounces his magic powers: he has learnt that to be fully human is also to be only human, accepting man's proper place in the scale of being, and he has learnt that the obligations of his own social place as ruler of a dukedom are to be accepted too. The holy and joyful love of Ferdinand and Miranda assures the continuance of concord.

The Tempest has thoughts, visions, 'fancies' about human life to offer that need ampler resources than even the supreme poetry of the last plays provides. Dancing and song may help to convey them, because they are part of the harmony at the core of creation that Shakespeare is trying to catch and impart. By their means the play may be seen to be patterned in a series of circles of meaning, a pattern of concentric spheres like that of the Ptolemaic concept of the universe itself. The innermost is the betrothal masque presented by Prospero; his speech to Ferdinand when, remembering he has Caliban's plot to deal with, he dismisses the dancers and the masque-vision vanishes (Act IV, scene i, lines 148–58) leads our thoughts beyond these 'revels' to the whole play, itself a scarcely less 'insubstantial pageant' and imbued with symbolic meaning that asks to be interpreted in the manner of masque. Beyond the play is the containing masque of actual human life; and 'our little life' too is played out in a larger perspective, that of eternity.

In his last plays Shakespeare was asking searching questions about human life and love and finding intimations of answers that are to be reached towards rather than grasped, and so can more fitly be suggested than stated. The significances that music and song and dancing carried, not locked up as in treatises of speculative music but released through dramatic embodiment and enactment, made possible the communication of his insights in a mode that combined dramatic delight with conceptual depth. Shakespeare's use of song was at all times proportioned to his dramatic means and purpose; in the last plays, richer in theatrical resources, unparalleled in their imaginative span, it reached its consummation.

SELECT BIBLIOGRAPHY

For books of lute-songs and madrigals, the first edition title (sometimes shortened) is given, followed by the volume number in the revised editions of *ELS* and *EM*.

(The place of publication is given if other than London.)

Alexander, Peter, ed. See Shakespeare.

Alison, Richard, *An Howres Recreation in Musicke*, 1606; *EM* 33.

Andrews, H. K., *The Technique of Byrd's Vocal Polyphony*, 1966.

Arbeau, Thoinot, *Orchésographie*, 1588, tr. Beaumont, Cyril W., 1925.

Arber, Edward, ed., *A Transcript of the Registers of the Company of Stationers of London; 1554–1640*, 5 vols., 1875–94.

Arbor of Amorous Devices, The, 1597, facs. ed. Rollins, H. E., Camb., Mass., 1936.

Attridge, Derek, *Well-weighed Syllables*, Cambridge, 1974.

Baldwin, T. W., *The Organization and Personnel of the Shakespearean Company*, Princeton, 1927.

Barley, William, *A new Booke of Tabliture*, 1596. See also Newcomb, W. W.

Bateson, Thomas, *The first set of English Madrigales*, 1604; *EM* 21.

Beaumont, Cyril W., tr. See Arbeau, Thoinot.

Beck, Sydney, 'The Case of "O Mistresse mine" ', *RN* 6, 1953.

Bentley, G. E., 'Shakespeare and the Blackfriars Theatre', *SS* 1, 1948.

Bergeron, David M., *English Civic Pageantry 1558–1642*, 1971.

Bowden, W. R., *The English Dramatic Lyric, 1603–42*, New Haven, 1951.

Brennecke, Ernest, 'Shakespeare's Musical Collaboration with Morley', *PMLA* liv, 1939.

—— 'The Entertainment at Elvetham, 1591', *Music in English Renaissance Drama*, ed. Long, J. H., Lexington, 1968.

Brett, Philip, 'The English Consort Song, 1570–1625', *PRMA* 88, 1961.

—— ed., *Consort Songs*, *MB* 22, 1967.

—— See Byrd.

Brittons Bowre of Delights, 1591, facs. ed. Rollins, H. E., Camb., Mass., 1933.

Brown, Howard Mayer, *Embellishing Sixteenth Century Music*, 1976.

Byrd, William, *Psalmes, Sonets, & songs of sadnes and pietie*, 1588; *EM* 14.

—— *Songs of sundrie natures*, 1589; *EM* 15.

—— *Psalmes, Songs, and Sonnets*, 1611; *EM* 16.

—— *The Collected Works*, ed. Fellowes, E. H., rev. Dart, T., and Brett, P., vols. 12–14, 1962–5, as above; vol. 15, *Consort Songs for Voice and Viols*, ed. Brett, P., 1970.

—— *The Byrd Edition*, ed. Brett, P., vol. 16, *Madrigals, Songs and Canons*, 1976.

Byrne, M. St. Clare, ed., *The Elizabethan Home Discovered in 2 Dialogues by Claudius Hollyband and Peter Erondell*, 1925.

Caccini, Giulio, *Le nuove musiche*, Florence, 1602, facs. ed. Vatielli, Francesco, Rome, 1934.

Campion, Thomas, songs in Rosseter's *A Booke of Ayres*, 1601; *ELS* 1st series, 4 and 13.

—— *The Discription of a Maske . . . in honour of the Lord Hayes, and his Bride . . .*, 1607; facs. ed. Greer, D., Menston, 1970.

—— *Two Bookes of Ayres*, c.1613; *ELS* 2nd series, 1 and 2.

—— *The Third Booke of Ayres*, c.1617; *ELS* 2nd series, 10.

—— *The Fourth Booke of Ayres*, c.1617; *ELS* 2nd series, 11.

—— *The Works of Thomas Campion*, ed. Davis, W. R., 1969.

Carlton, Richard, *Madrigals to Five voyces*, 1601; *EM* 27.

Case, A. E., *Bibliography of English Miscellanies 1521–1750*, Oxford, 1935.

Cavendish, Michael, *14. Ayres in Tabletorie to the Lute . . . 6. more to 4. voyces and in Tabletorie. And 8. Madrigalles to 5. voyces*, 1598; *ELS* 2nd series, 7, and *EM* 36.

Chambers, E. K., *William Shakespeare*, 2 vols., Oxford, 1930.

Chan, Mary (née Joiner), '*Cynthia's Revels* and Music for a Choir School: Christ Church Manuscript Mus 439', *SR* xviii, 1971.

—— *Music in the Theatre of Ben Jonson*, Oxford, 1980.

Chappell, William, *Popular Music of the Olden Time*, 2 vols., 1855–9, repr. New York, 1965.

Coperario, John, *Funeral Teares*, 1606; *ELS* 1st series, 17.

—— *Songs of Mourning*, 1613; *ELS* 1st series, 17.

—— *The Masque of Squires*, 1614; *ELS* 1st series, 17.

Corkine, William, *Ayres, To Sing and Play to the Lvte And Basse Violl*, 1610; *ELS* 2nd series, 12.

—— *The Second Booke of Ayres*, 1612; *ELS* 2nd series, 13.

Court of Venus, The, ed. Fraser, Russell A., Durham, NC, 1955.

Cunningham, Dolora, 'The Jonsonian Masque as a Literary Form', *ELH* xxii, 1955.

Cutts, J. P., 'Jacobean Masque and Stage Music', *M&L* 35, 1954.

—— 'Robert Johnson: King's Musician in His Majesty's Public Entertainment', *M&L* 36, 1955.

—— 'Le Rôle de la Musique dans les Masques de Ben Jonson', *Les Fêtes de la Renaissance*, ed. Jacquot, J., Paris, 1956.

—— *La Musique de scène de la troupe de Shakespeare*, Paris, 1959, rev. 1971.

—— 'Robert Johnson and the Court Masque', *M&L* 41, 1960.

Dart, Thurston, ed. See Byrd; Dowland; *The English Lute-Songs*; *The English Madrigalists*.

Davis, Walter R., ed. See Campion.

Demaray, J. G., *Milton and the Masque Tradition*, Camb., Mass., 1968.

Donne, John, *The Elegies and the Songs and Sonnets*, ed. Gardner, Helen, Oxford, 1965.

Dorsten, J. A. van, *Poets, Patrons, and Professors*, Leiden, 1962.

Doughtie, Edward, *Lyrics from English Airs 1596–1622*, Camb., Mass., 1970.

Dowland, John, *The First Booke of Songes or Ayres*, 1597; *ELS* 1st series, 1 and 2.

——*The Second Booke of Songs or Ayres*, 1600; *ELS* 1st series, 5 and 6.

—— *The Third and Last Booke of Songs or Aires*, 1603; *ELS* 1st series, 10 and 11.

—— *A Pilgrimes Solace*, 1612; *ELS* 1st series, 12 and 14.

——*John Dowland: Ayres for four voices*, ed. Dart, Thurston, and Fortune, Nigel, *MB* 6, 1953.

Dowland, Robert, ed., *A Mvsicall Banqvet*, 1610; *ELS* 2nd series, 20.

Duckles, Vincent, 'The Gamble Manuscript as a Source of *Continuo* Song in England', *JAMS* 1, 1948.

—— 'New Light on "O Mistresse mine" ', *RN* 7, 1954.

—— 'Florid Embellishment in English Song of the late 16th and early 17th Centuries', *AM* v, 1957.

—— 'English Song and the Challenge of Italian Monody', *Words to Music*, ed. Duckles, V., and Zimmerman, Franklin B., Los Angeles, 1967.

—— 'The Music for the Lyrics in Early Seventeenth-Century English Drama: a Bibliography of the Primary Sources', *Music in English Renaissance Drama*, ed. Long, J. H., Lexington, 1968.

Earsdon, John, and Mason, George, *Ayres*, 1618; *ELS* 2nd series, 18.

East, Michael, *Madrigales To 3.4. and 5. parts*, 1604; *EM* 29.

Einstein, Alfred, *The Italian Madrigal*, 3 vols., Princeton, 1949.

Elyot, Thomas, *The Governour*, 1531; Everyman ed., 1907.

Englands Helicon, 1600, ed. Rollins, H. E., 2 vols., Camb., Mass., 1935.

—— ed. Macdonald, Hugh, 1962.

—— facs. ed., Menston, 1973.

English Lute-Songs, The (formerly *The English School of Lutenist Song Writers*, ed. Fellowes, E. H.), rev. ed. Dart, Thurston, *et al.* First series, 17 vols., 1959–. Second series, 21 vols., 1961–.

English Lute Songs 1597–1632, in facsimile, gen. ed. Sternfeld, F. W., 9 vols., Menston, 1967–71.

English Madrigalists, The (formerly *The English Madrigal School*, ed. Fellowes, E. H.), rev. ed. Dart, Thurston, *et al.* 37 vols. so far, 1958–.

English Madrigal Verse 1588–1632, ed. Fellowes, E. H., 3rd ed. rev. Sternfeld, F. W., and Greer, D., Oxford, 1967.

Evans, Willa McClung, *Ben Jonson and Elizabethan Music*, Lancaster, Pa., 1929, reissued New York, 1965.

—— *Henry Lawes: Musician and Friend of Poets*, New York, 1941.

Fabry, Frank J., 'Sidney's Verse Adaptations to Two Sixteenth-Century Italian Art Songs', *RQ* xxiii, 1970.

—— 'Sidney's Poetry and Italian Song-Form', *ELR* 3, 1973.

Fellowes, E. H., ed. See Byrd; *English Lute-Songs*; *English Madrigalists*; *English Madrigal Verse 1588–1632*.

Felver, Charles S., *Robert Armin, Shakespeare's Fool*, Kent, Ohio, 1961.

Ferrabosco, Alfonso, II, *Ayres*, 1609; *ELS* 2nd series, 16.

—— *Songs from Manuscript Sources*, *ELS* 2nd series, 19.

Feuillerat, A., ed. See Sidney.

Fitzwilliam Virginal Book, The, ed. Fuller-Maitland, J. A., and Squire, W. Barclay, 2 vols., Leipzig, 1894–9, repr. Ann Arbor, Michigan, 1949.

Forbes, John, *Songs and Fancies*, Aberdeen, 1662, 1666, 1682.

Ford, Thomas, *Mvsicke of Svndrie Kindes*, 1607; *ELS* 1st series, 3.

Fortune, Nigel, 'Italian secular monody from 1600 to 1635', *MQ* 39, 1953.

—— See Dowland, John.

Fraser, Russell A., ed. See *Court of Venus*.

Frost, Maurice, *English and Scottish Psalm and Hymn Tunes c.1547–1677*, 1953.

Fuller, David, 'The Jonsonian Masque and its Music', *M&L* 54, 1973.

—— 'Ben Jonson's Plays and their Contemporary Music', *M&L* 58, 1977.

Fuller, Thomas, *The History of the Worthies of England*, 1662.

Fuller-Maitland, J. A. See *Fitzwilliam Virginal Book*.

Gair, Reavley, *The Children of Paul's: The Story of a Theatre Company, 1553–1608*, Cambridge, 1982.

Gardner, Helen. See Donne.

Gascoigne, George, *A Hundreth sundrie Flowres*, 1573, ed. Prouty, C. T., Columbia, 1942.

—— *A Hundreth sundrie Flowres*, facs. ed., Menston, 1970.

Gibbons, Orlando, *The First Set of Madrigals And Mottets of 5. Parts*, 1612; *EM* 5.

Gombosi, Otto, 'Some Musical Aspects of the English Court Masque', *JAMS* 1, 1948.

Gordon, D. J., ed. Orgel, S., *The Renaissance Imagination*, Berkeley, 1975.

Gorgeous Gallery of Gallant Inventions, A, 1578, ed. Rollins, H. E., Camb., Mass., 1926.

Gorgious Gallery, of gallant Inuentions, A, 1578; facs. ed., Menston, 1972.

Greaves, Thomas, *Songes of sundrie kindes*, 1604; *ELS* 2nd series, 18, and *EM* 36.

Greer, David, 'The Lute Songs of Thomas Morley', *LSJ* viii, 1966.

—— 'The Part-Songs of the English Lutenists', *PRMA* 94, 1968.

—— ed., *Twenty Songs from Printed Sources*, *ELS* 2nd series, 21.

—— ed., *Songs from Manuscript Sources*, 1 and 2, 1979.

—— See Campion.

Gurr, Andrew, *The Shakespearean Stage 1574–1642*, Cambridge, 1970, rev. ed. 1980.

Handefull of pleasant delites, A, 1584; facs. ed., Ilkley, 1973.

Handful of Pleasant Delights, A, 1584, ed. Rollins, H. E., Camb., Mass., 1924.

Harbage, Alfred, *Shakespeare and the Rival Traditions*, New York, 1952.

Harding, D. W., 'The Rhythmical Intention of Wyatt's Poetry', *Scrutiny*, xiv, 1946.

Harman, R. A. See Morley.

Heartz, Daniel, *Pierre Attaingnant, Royal Printer of Music*, Berkeley, 1969.

Herford, C. H. See Jonson.

Hollander, John, *The Untuning of the Sky: Ideas of Music in English Poetry, 1500–1700*, Princeton, 1961.

—— *Vision and Resonance: Two Senses of Poetic Form*, New York, 1975.

Hollybande, Claudius. See Sainliens, Claude de.

Howard, Henry, Earl of Surrey. See *Songes and Sonettes*.

Hughey, Ruth, 'The Harington Manuscript at Arundel Castle and Related Documents', *The Library*, xv, 1935.

Hundreth sundrie Flowres, A. See Gascoigne.

Ing, Catherine, *Elizabethan Lyrics*, 1951.

Jacquot, Jean, ed., *Musique et Poésie au XVIᵉ Siècle* (Colloques Internationaux du Centre National de la Recherche Scïentifique), Paris, 1954.

Johnson, Robert, *Ayres, Songs and Dialogues*, *ELS* 2nd series, 17.

Joiner, Mary, 'BM Add. MS 15117: A Commentary, Index and Bibliography', *RMA Research Chronicle* 7, 1969. See Chan.

Jones, Robert, *The First Booke of Songes or Ayres*, 1600; *ELS* 2nd series, 4.

—— *The Second Booke of Songs and Ayres*, 1601; *ELS* 2nd series, 5.

—— *Vltimvm Vale*, 1605; *ELS* 2nd series, 6.

—— *The First Set of Madrigals*, 1607; *EM* 35 A.

—— *A Mvsicall Dreame*, 1609; *ELS* 2nd series, 14.

—— *The Muses Gardin for Delights*, 1610; *ELS* 2nd series, 15.

Jonson, Ben, *The Complete Masques*, ed. Orgel, S., 1969.

—— *Works*, ed. Herford, C. H., and Simpson, P. and E. M., 11 vols., Oxford, 1925–52.

Kerman, Joseph, *The Elizabethan Madrigal*, New York, 1962.

Kirbye, George, *The first set Of English Madrigalls*, 1597; *EM* 24.

Krummel, D. W., *English Music Printing 1553–1700*, 1975.

Lawes, Henry. See Manuscripts; Milton.

Lewis, C. S., 'The Fifteenth Century Heroic Line', *E&S* xxiv, 1939.

—— *English Literature in the Sixteenth Century, excluding Drama*, Oxford, 1954.

Long, John H., *Shakespeare's Use of Music: Seven Comedies*, Gainesville, Florida, 1955; repr. New York, 1977.

—— *Shakespeare's Use of Music: The Final Comedies*, Gainesville, Florida, 1961; repr. New York, 1977.

—— ed., *Music in English Renaissance Drama*, Lexington, 1968.

Manuscripts:
  BL Add. MS 4900.
  BL Add. MS 5465 (the Fayrfax book).
  BL Add. MS 10444 (Sir Nicholas L'Estrange's collection of masque dances).
  BL Add. MS 15117.
  BL Add. MS 17492 (the Devonshire book).
  BL Add. MS 30513 (the Mulliner book).
  BL Add. MS 31922 ('Henry VIII's Song-book').
  BL Add. MS 53723 (Henry Lawes's autograph song-book).
  BL Add. MS Royal Appendix 58.
  BL MS Stowe 389.
  Bod. MS Don. c. 57.
  Bod. MS Mus. b. 1 (John Wilson's song-book).
  Bod. MS Rawl. Poet. 85.
  Bod. MS Rawl. Poet. 148.
  Christ Church, Oxford, MS 87 (Elizabeth Davenant's book).
  Christ Church, Oxford, MS Mus. 439.
  Christ Church, Oxford, MS 736–8.

Mason, George. See Earsdon.

Maynard, Winifred A., 'The Lyrics of Wyatt: Poems or Songs?' and 'The Lyrics of Wyatt: Poems or Songs? II', *RES* xvi, 1965.

—— 'Songs and dances in *Comus*', *John Milton: Odes, Pastorals, Masques*, ed. Broadbent, J. B., Cambridge, 1975.

Meagher, John C., *Method and Meaning in Jonson's Masques*, 1966.

Milton, John, *A Maske: the earlier versions*, ed. Sprott, S. E., Toronto, 1973.

—— and Lawes, Henry, *The Mask of Comus*, ed. Visiak, E. H., and Foss, H. J., 1937.

Monson, Craig A., *Voices and Viols in England, 1600–1650. The Sources and the Music*, Ann Arbor, Michigan, 1982.

Morley, Thomas, *Madrigalls to Fovre Voyces*, 1594; *EM* 2.

—— *A Plaine and easie introduction to practicall musicke*, 1597.

—— *A Plain and Easy Introduction to Practical Music*, ed. R. A. Harman, 1952.

—— *The First Booke of Ayres*, 1600; *ELS* 1st series, 16.

—— ed., *Madrigales The Triumphes of Oriana*, 1601; *EM* 32.

Mumford, Ivy L., 'Musical Settings to the Poems of Henry Howard Earl of Surrey', *English Miscellany* 8, 1957.

Mundy, John, *Songs And Psalmes*, 1594; *EM* 35 B.

Newcomb, W. W., ed., *Lute Music of Shakespeare's Time*, Pennsylvania, 1966 (Barley's *A new Booke of Tabliture*, 1596).

Nichols, John, *The Progresses and Public Processions of Queen Elizabeth*, 3 vols., 1788–1805, 1823.

—— *The Progresses, Processions and Magnificent Festivities of King James I*, 4 vols., 1828.

Noble, Richmond, *Shakespeare's Use of Song with the Text of the Principal Songs*, 1923.

Nosworthy, J. M., 'Music and its Function in the Romances of Shakespeare', *SS* xi, 1958.

Nott, G. F., ed., *The Works of Henry Howard, Earl of Surrey and of Sir Thomas Wyatt the Elder*, 2 vols., 1816.

Obertello, Alfredo, *Madrigali italiani in Inghilterra*, Milan, 1949.

Orgel, Stephen K., *The Jonsonian Masque*, Camb., Mass., 1965.

—— ed. See Gordon; Jonson.

—— and Strong, Roy C., *Inigo Jones: The Theatre of the Stuart Court*, 1973.

Pafford, J. H. P., 'Music, and the Songs in *The Winter's Tale*', *SQ* x, 1959.

Paradyse of daynty deuises, The, 1576; facs. ed., Menston, 1972.

Paradise of Dainty Devices, The, 1576–1606, ed. Rollins, H. E., Camb., Mass., 1927.

Passionate Pilgrim, The, 1599; facs. ed., Oxford, 1905.

Pattison, Bruce, *Music and Poetry of the English Renaissance*, 1948, 2nd ed. 1970.

Phoenix Nest, The, 1593, ed. Rollins, H. E., Camb., Mass., 1931.

Phoenix Nest, The, 1593, facs. ed., Menston, 1973.

Pilkington, Francis, *The First Booke of Songs or Ayres of 4. parts*, 1605; *ELS* 2nd series, 7 and 15.

—— *The Second Set of Madrigals and Pastorals*, 1624; *EM* 26.

Poetical rapsody, A, 1602; facs. ed., Menston, 1972.

Poetical Rhapsody, A, ed. Rollins, H. E., 2 vols., Camb., Mass., 1931.

Pomeroy, Elizabeth W., *The Elizabethan Miscellanies: Their Development and Conventions*, Berkeley, 1973.

Poulton, Diana, *John Dowland*, 1972; rev. ed. 1982.

Price, David C., *Patrons and Musicians of the English Renaissance*, Cambridge, 1981.

Prouty, C. T., ed. See Gascoigne; Shakespeare.

Ralegh, Sir Walter, *The Poems of Sir Walter Ralegh*, ed. Latham, Agnes, 1951, 1962.

Ringler, Wm. A., 'The Number of Actors in Shakespeare's Early Plays', *The Seventeenth-Century Stage*, ed. Bentley, G. E., Chicago, 1968.

—— See Sidney.

Rollins, Hyder Edward, 'The Black-Letter Ballad', *PMLA* 34, 1919.

—— 'A Handful of Pleasant Delights', *MLN* xli, 1926.

—— ed. See *Arbor of Amorous Devices, Brittons Bowre of Delights, Englands Helicon, Gorgeous Gallery of Gallant Inventions, Handful of Pleasant Delights, Paradise of Dainty Devices, Phoenix Nest, Poetical Rhapsody, Tottel's Miscellany.*

Rosseter, Philip, and Campion, Thomas, *A Booke of Ayres*, 1601; *ELS* 1st series, 8 and 9.

Sabol, Andrew J., 'A newly discovered contemporary song setting for Jonson's *Cynthia's Revels*', *N&Q* New Series 9, 1958.

—— *Four Hundred Songs and Dances from the Stuart Masque*, Providence, Rhode Island, 1978.

Sainliens, Claude de ('Claudius Hollybande'), *The French Schoolemayster*, 1573, 1598.

Seng, Peter J., *The Vocal Songs in the Plays of Shakespeare*, Camb., Mass., 1967.

Shakespeare, William, *Comedies, Histories and Tragedies*, 1623; facs. ed. Kökeritz, Helge, and Prouty, C. T., New Haven, 1955.

—— *William Shakespeare: The Complete Works*, ed. Alexander, Peter, 1951; repr. 1985.

Shapiro, Michael, *Children of the Revels*, New York, 1977.

Sidney, Sir Philip, *The Complete Works of Sir Philip Sidney*, ed. Feuillerat, A., 4 vols., Cambridge, 1912–26.

—— *The Countess of Pembroke's Arcadia*, ed. Evans, Maurice, 1977.

—— *The Countess of Pembroke's Arcadia*, ed. Robertson, Jean, 1973.

—— *The Poems of Sir Philip Sidney*, ed. Ringler, W. A., Oxford, 1962.

Simpson, Claude M., *The British Broadside Ballad and its Music*, New Brunswick, 1966.

Simpson, E. M. and P. See Jonson.

Smith, G. Gregory, ed., *Elizabethan Critical Essays*, 2 vols., 1904.

Songes and Sonettes, written by the ryght honorable Lorde Henry Haward late Earle of Surrey, and other, 1557; facs. ed., Menston, 1967.

—— See *Tottel's Miscellany*.

Souris, André, ed., *Poèmes de Donne, Herbert et Crashaw mis en musique par leurs contemporains*, Paris, 1961.

Spink, Ian, 'Campion's Entertainment at Brougham Castle, 1617', *Music in English Renaissance Drama*, ed. Long, J. H., Lexington, 1968.

—— *English Song Dowland to Purcell*, 1974.

—— ed., *English Songs 1625–1660*, MB 33, 1971.

Sprott, S. E. See Milton.

Squire, W. Barclay, ed. See *Fitzwilliam Virginal Book*.

Steele, Robert, *The Earliest English Music Printing*, 1903, 1965.

Sternfeld, F. W., 'Shakespeare's Use of Popular Song', *Elizabethan and Jacobean Studies*, ed. Davis, H., Oxford, 1959.

—— 'Song in Jonson's Comedy', *Studies in the English Renaissance Drama*, ed. Bennett, J. W., 1959.

—— *Music in Shakespearean Tragedy*, 1963.

—— 'Ophelia's Version of the Walsingham Song', *M&L* 45, 1964.

—— ed., *Songs from Shakespeare's Tragedies*, 1964.

—— ed., *English Lute Songs, 1597–1632; A Collection of Facsimile Reprints*, 9 vols., Menston, 1967–71.

Stevens, Denis, *The Mulliner Book. A Commentary*, 1952.

—— ed., *The Mulliner Book*, MB 1, 1951, rev. ed. 1954.

Stevens, John, *Music and Poetry in the Early Tudor Court*, 1961, 1978.

—— 'Shakespeare and the Music of the Elizabethan Stage', *Shakespeare in Music*, ed. Hartnoll, Phyllis, 1964.

—— *The Old Sound and the New*, Cambridge, 1982.

—— ed., *Music at the Court of Henry VIII*, MB 18, 1961, rev. ed. 1969.

—— ed., *Early Tudor Songs and Carols*, MB 36, 1975.

Strong, Roy C., 'Queen Elizabeth I as Oriana', *SR* vi, 1959.

—— See Orgel.

Swanekamp, Joan, comp., *English Ayres: A Selectively Annotated Bibliography and Discography*, Connecticut, 1984.

Thompson, John, *The Founding of English Metre*, 1961.

Thomson, George, *Greek Lyric Metre*, Cambridge, 1929, 2nd ed. 1961.

Tottel's Miscellany 1557–1587, ed. Rollins, H. E., 2 vols., Camb., Mass., rev. ed. 1965.

—— See *Songes and Sonettes*.

Tuve, Rosemond, *Elizabethan and Metaphysical Imagery*, Chicago, 1947, 1961.

Vautor, Thomas, *The First Set: Beeing Songs of diuers Ayres and Natures*, 1619; *EM* 34.

Walker, D. P., 'The Aims of de Baïf's Académie', *MD* i, 1946.

—— 'The Influence of *Musique Mesurée à l'Antique* on the *Air de Cour*', *MD* ii, 1948.

Walls, Peter, 'Music in the English Masque in the First Half of the Seventeenth Century', unpub. D. Phil. thesis, Oxford, 1975.

—— 'Insubstantial Pageants Preserved: the Literary and Musical Sources for the Jonsonian Masque', *Jonson and Shakespeare*, ed. Donaldson, Ian, 1983.

Ward, John, *The First Set of English Madrigals*, 1613; *EM* 19.

Ward, John, 'Music for *A Handefull of pleasant delites*', *JAMS* x, 1957.

—— 'The Lute Music of MS Royal Appendix 58', *JAMS* xiii, 1960.

—— 'Joan qd John and Other Fragments at Western Reserve University', *Aspects of Medieval and Renaissance Music*, ed. La Rue, J., 1966.

—— 'Apropos *The British Broadside Ballad and Its Music*', *JAMS* xx, 1967.

—— 'Barley's Songs Without Words', *LSJ* xii, 1970.

—— ed., *The Dublin Virginal Manuscript*, Wellesley, Mass., 2nd ed. 1964.

Warlock, Peter (Philip Heseltine), *The English Ayre*, 1926.

Watson, Thomas, *The first sett, Of Italian Madrigalls Englished*, 1590.

Weelkes, Thomas, *Madrigals*, 1597; *EM* 9.

Whythorne, Thomas, *Autobiography*, written *c*.1576, Oxford, 1961; modern spelling ed., 1962.

Willetts, Pamela J., 'Sir Nicholas Le Strange's Collection of Masque Music', *BMQ* xxix, 1965.

Wilson, Jean, *Entertainments for Elizabeth I*, Woodbridge, 1980.

Wilson, John, *Cheerfull Ayres or Ballads*, 1660.

Woodfill, Walter L., *Musicians in English Society from Elizabeth to Charles I*, Princeton, 1953.

Yates, Frances A., *The French Academies of the Sixteenth Century*, 1947.

—— 'Elizabethan Chivalry: the Romance of the Accession Day Tilts', *JCWI* 20, 1957.

—— *Shakespeare's Last Plays: A New Approach*, 1975.

Yonge, Nicholas, comp., *Mvsica Transalpina*, 1588; facs. ed. Farnborough, 1972.

—— *Mvsica Transalpina . . . The second booke*, 1597; repr. Farnborough, 1972.

Youll, Henry, *Canzonets To Three Voyces*, 1608; *EM* 28.

INDEX

Songs are indexed by first line, except for Shakespeare's: for these see individual play titles, under Shakespeare. Lyrics mentioned briefly are not indexed; all tunes are indexed.